The Crafts Business Answer Book

Also by Barbara Brabec

Creative Cash: How to Profit from Your Special Artistry, Creativity, Hand Skills, and Related Know-How

Homemade Money: Starting Smart! How to Turn Your Talents, Experience, and Know-How into a Profitable Homebased Business That's Perfect for You!

Homemade Money: Bringing in the Bucks! A Business Management and Marketing Bible for Home-Business Owners, Self-Employed Individuals, and Web Entrepreneurs Working from Home Base

Handmade for Profit! Hundreds of Secrets to Success in Selling Arts & Crafts

Make It Profitable! How to Make Your Art, Craft, Design, Writing, or Publishing Business More Efficient, More Satisfying, and More Profitable

THE
Crafts Business Answer Book

COMPLETELY REVISED AND UPDATED EDITION

*Starting, Marketing, and Managing a Homebased
Art, Crafts, or Design Business*

Barbara Brabec

M. EVANS
LANHAM • NEW YORK • BOULDER • TORONTO • OXFORD

Published by M. Evans
An imprint of The Rowman & Littlefield Publishing Group, Inc.
4501 Forbes Boulevard, Suite 200, Lanham, Maryland 20706

ISBN-13: 978-59077-108-2 (pbk.)

Manufactured in the United States of America.

All of the information in this book is presented to assist homebased businesspersons—those just getting started as well as those already in business. The author's goal is to familiarize readers with important areas of concern and enable them to ask the right questions if and when it is necessary to consult with an attorney, accountant, or other business adviser. Much of the material offered is in such "professional service" categories as legalities, taxes, and accounting. While this information has been carefully researched by the author and is accurate to the best of her knowledge as this book goes to press, it is not the business of either the author or publisher to render such professional services. Readers are therefore asked to exercise normal good judgment in determining when the services of a lawyer or another professional would be appropriate to their needs.

This book is dedicated to all the creative people who have read my articles and books through the years, sharing helpful information I could pass on to others through my writing.

Contents

A-to-Z listings in this book are grouped here in logical business categories for easy reference.

Accounting

Advertising and Marketing

See also Pricing and Selling

Banking

See also Money Management

Business Activities

Business and Office Management

See also Insurance

Employees/Labor Issues

Insurance

Laws and Regulations

See also Legal Issues

Legal Issues

See also Laws and Regulations, and Taxes

Miscellaneous Topics

Money Management

See also Accounting, and Banking

Pricing and Selling

See also Advertising and Marketing

Shipping and Mailing

Taxes

See also Employees/Labor Issues

Other Resources

Index

Alphabetical List of Articles and Sample Forms

Introduction

The first edition of this book was written in 1997, long before I had a real understanding of the Internet or the impact it would ultimately have on the average consumer or homebased business owner. With considerable reluctance, I let a friend talk me into taking up residence on her crafts business website in 1998. She felt my articles on her site would benefit her readers, and since she offered to do all the work involved in setting up and maintaining my Web pages, I figured I had nothing to lose. I quickly discovered that I loved being on the Web, so when my friend decided to sell her website a couple of years later, I hired her to help me get started on a domain of my own. Shortly thereafter, I bought *FrontPage* software and learned how to manage and redesign the site myself. To make a long story short, getting on the Web was the smartest business move I ever made, and I intend to have a presence there until I die. (What's amusing to me is that, even after I die and my website is gone, many of the promotional articles I've placed on the websites of others may remain indefinitely—a different kind of immortality, to be sure!)

A quick search of the Web for such keywords as "arts and crafts" (or any individual art or craft you can think of) will prove that millions of artists, craftspeople, designers, and other creative-thinking people have taken to the Web like cats to sunlight. Not all small business owners need a website of their own, of course, but I believe that everyone with a serious interest in building a business needs access to the Internet and the incredible wealth of information it holds. A brief discussion of how to sell on the Web is included in this book (see *Web Marketing Options*), but since its main focus is on crafts business start-up and management, you will need to look elsewhere for detailed guidelines on how to sell your art or craft on the Web. (Other books of mine do discuss this topic—check my website for more information.)

Featured in this new edition of *The Crafts Business Answer Book* are many toll-free telephone numbers and website links scattered throughout the text. When specific Web pages with helpful articles and resources were impractical to list (because Web pages are constantly being moved and long links quickly go bad), I've given you tips on what to look for on specific sites or, more commonly, special keywords to search for on Google or Yahoo! so you can turn up thousands of Web pages on any topic of interest to you.

Addressing the Problems of Business Beginners

Everyone feels a bit intimidated when they leave their comfort zone to step into unknown territory. In looking back over my lifetime of home-business experience, I remember all those times when I wanted to try something new but lacked specific information on how to do it. The big challenges, like how to begin the writing of my first book, launch a magazine, publish my own books, and get my business on the Web, took a lot of extra time and research to be sure, but it was the smaller, day-to-day problems that often caused me the most stress and worry.

For the first few years, I had many more questions than answers, and it took me a long time to work out solutions to all the little niggling problems of how to run a business at home and make a real profit from all the time and effort I was putting into my work. Although my writing and publishing work is different from your work as an artist, craftsperson, or designer, we have similar creative leanings, and we certainly share common ground when it comes to the management of our homebased business and the marketing of our products. Everyone who starts a business venture at home—no matter how small—needs to know how to stay out of legal trouble, avoid costly business pitfalls, and cut expenses to the quick to make a bigger profit. More specifically, we need to know which laws or regulations affect our particular business activity. We must learn about tax and employee issues, protect ourselves with good insurance, and solve problems related to technology. We must strive constantly to refine our sales and marketing strategies, become better money managers, and get a tighter grip on time management. And every day, it seems, we have to find the answer to yet another question or solve another small problem never encountered before.

Experience has taught me that some small business lessons are merely frustrating while others are painfully expensive in terms of lost time, money, sales, opportunities, or ego. The less experience or information we have about a particular problem or situation, the more stressful the lesson and the more we may agonize over the outcome. Having the right information at hand when we need it enables us to "keep our cool" in the face of a new problem or predicament. This eliminates unnecessary worry and automatically lowers our stress level.

I don't pretend to know everything about running a crafts business, but this book does answer the most common questions of beginning craft sellers and offers solutions to hundreds of problems likely to affect both new and long-established craft businesses at one time or another, whether they are working on or off the Web. Its encyclopedic content is based not only on my own experience but on the experiences of hundreds of professional crafters and home-business owners who have networked with me through the years. Every page offers precise and practical information to answer specific questions and help you solve small business problems as soon as they arise. You'll find tips on many topics that other books don't even touch on, with answers to questions you didn't even know you had until you read about them here.

How to Use This Book

Although this is essentially a reference book, I've tried to make it interesting to read by including personal experience stories (mine and others), special tips, and "sidebar articles" on a variety of topics. You'll also find a sprinkling of home-business humor throughout the book. An initial thumb-through of the book will reveal several topics in which you have a keen interest now. If you want to read only the articles now, look for material that has been boxed on a page or check the alphabetical list of articles after the *Contents* section. Special tips are easy to spot—all have been screened in gray.

Tip

One of the first things you should do is check "Business Activities" on the Contents pages to see if there are listings for your particular art or craft. Then check "Laws and Regulations" for references to specific laws, regulations, or warnings relative to your art or crafts activities and materials used in the production of products for sale.

Four ways to quickly find information in this book:

1. Check the *Contents* section to find a collection of information on a specific topic, such as business management, employees, taxes, or legal matters.

2. Check the text for alphabetical listings of specific words, phrases, or business terms that come to mind when a question or problem arises. Each listing either has a discussion of the topic or a reference to where it is discussed under a different alphabetical heading.

3. Check the book's *Other Resources* section for alphabetical lists of periodicals, organizations, government agencies, and suppliers that will be helpful to you.

4. Check the book's index to find page number references to individuals, businesses, periodicals, organizations, publishers, and government agencies mentioned in the text. Here you will also find page references for groupings of Web resources within the text, such as "show listing periodicals," "office suppliers," or "insurance providers."

I believe this totally revised edition of *The Crafts Business Answer Book* will empower you to learn what you need to know more quickly than ever before so you can successfully use today's technology to maximize your ability to earn an income using skills, talents, and know-how you already possess. I hope you will supplement the information in this book by visiting my website at **www.BarbaraBrabec.com**, where you'll find a growing collection of home-business/crafts marketing articles by me and other business owners. My site also includes information and resources for writers, self-publishers, computer users, nostalgia buffs, and other creative-thinking people. I welcome contact from readers by e-mail to the address on my website.

Accountant/CPA

Q: *How can I get the accounting and tax help I need without spending a lot of money?*

Business novices often hire a Certified Public Accountant (CPA) to do their annual tax return when only a Public Accountant is needed, or they may hire a tax preparer when what they really need is an accountant. Consider that:

• CPAs have more education than other accountants and are licensed by the state on completion of four years of college and one to two years of on-the-job training. Because of their extra education, CPAs not only charge more for their services but tend to specialize in corporate work. As a result, the average CPA may be totally unfamiliar with all the allowable deductions related to a homebased business. In many cases, hiring this much power for the average homebased business would be like buying a crystal goblet when all you really need is a glass.

• Public Accountants have a good understanding of tax laws and can help you understand your total financial picture. In addition to taking care of your annual tax return, an accountant can help you make business decisions that will impact your tax return, such as whether to buy or lease a vehicle, form a partnership, or incorporate your business. If you need a business loan, an accountant can prepare the financial reports your banker expects to see or stand by you in the event your tax return is audited by the IRS. (Only a CPA or IRS Enrolled Agent can *represent* you before the IRS.) If and when you decide to hire outside help or put your spouse or a child on the payroll, an accountant can take care of all those aggravating tax forms and quarterly reports that must be filed. Since accountants aren't bookkeepers, they will expect you to supply all necessary figures for your tax return, which means you have to set up a good bookkeeping system right from the beginning. (Many accountants supply their clients with handy tax organizers that make it easy to pull together all needed figures at year's end.)

• Tax preparers are best used for the preparation of personal tax returns only. History has shown that commercial tax preparers often lack an understanding of the nature of homebased businesses and the deductible expenses related to their operation. Unless a tax preparer can give you the names of other homebased businesses that are clients, it would be best to look elsewhere for the help you need with your crafts business tax return.

- Enrolled Agents (ERs) may be the best solution of all. After years of hiring high-priced accountants to do my tax return and help me with employee tax forms, I finally learned about the benefits of working with an Enrolled Agent (see *Enrolled Agents*).

See also Accounting Methods; Employees, Family; Employees, Nonfamily; Independent Contractors; *and* Legal Forms of Business.

Tip

Having your tax return prepared by an accountant, CPA, or Enrolled Agent does not mean it will be without error. When the tax season heats up and these people start putting in long hours to accommodate late-filing clients, mistakes may occur. You must take the responsibility for double-checking every figure on your tax return to make sure there are no typographical errors, misplaced figures, or deduction omissions.

Accounting Methods

Q: *Should I use the cash method of accounting or the accrual method?*

Some businesses are required by law to use the accrual accounting method, but an accountant can help you decide which of the following methods is best for you:

- **Cash Method.** All income is taxable in the year it's received, and expenses are generally deductible when paid, with some important exceptions an accountant can explain.
- **Accrual Method.** Tax is paid on earned income, whether it has been collected or not. Expenses are deducted when they are incurred, whether they have been paid or not. Some businesses are required by law to use the accrual accounting method. A recent change in IRS policy has enabled many business owners to switch

from the accrual method of accounting to the cash method, but some businesses are prohibited from using it, and you should check with an accountant to see if yours is one of them.

- **"Hybrid System."** This is a mix of the above types of accounting systems. For example, a product-oriented business might use the accrual system for inventory purchases and the cash method to record all income and expenses. (Inventory is expensed only when sold.) An accountant will help you decide which method is best for you.

See also Bookkeeping *and* Inventory.

Accounts Payable

These are the current bills your business owes for products and services already received. Money you owe others is considered a business liability and it must be listed as such on any balance sheet prepared for your business. To keep your credit record in good shape and stay on top of the record keeping needed for tax purposes, you will need to devise a good system for paying and filing bills. For tips on how to do this, see article, "Barbara's Proven System for Paying Bills and Keeping Tax Records."

See also Balance Sheet; Credit History; and Record-keeping.

Accounts Receivable

What customers and clients owe you are called *accounts receivable,* and these are business assets that should be listed on any balance sheet prepared for your business. You will need to devise some kind of tracking system to make sure your invoices are paid according to the terms you give buyers (usually thirty days). Suggestion: File copies of all invoices due in a folder and at the beginning of each month, pull any that are overdue and send statements accordingly.

See also Balance Sheet; Invoices Not Paid; Statement; *and* Terms of Sale.

Barbara's Proven System for Paying Bills and Keeping Tax Records

Here is the system I have used with success for more than thirty years. At my "bill paying desk," I keep two sets of twelve 6 x 9-inch envelopes with the months written on each. One set is for personal bills, the other for business. I pay bills every Saturday so the job is never overwhelming. Each Saturday, I open all bills that have come in and note on a calendar the particular Saturday each needs to be paid. Then I drop it either in the personal or business envelope for that month, depending on which checkbook I will use to pay it. Each Saturday I pull and pay only those bills indicated on the calendar for that date. With this system, I never have to worry about a bill being paid late.

- **Business Bills.** All paid business bills end up in one big envelope, and I never handle or look at any of these paid bills again unless I need proof a certain bill has been paid. All bills are marked with check number and date paid and filed with the latest bills to the back. As each bill is paid, all pertinent information as to what I've paid for is entered on my checkbook stub, and this information is periodically posted to my accounting system on computer.

- **Personal Bills.** Any personal bill that is fully or partly tax-deductible is filed in one of several file folders that are recycled each year. These are labeled *Car Expense*, *Donations*, *Home Maintenance*, *Interest Earned*, *Income—Miscellaneous*, *Medical Expenses*, *Telephone*, *Travel*, and *Utilities*. At year's end, the receipts and other documents in these folders will be used to figure my Home Office Deduction for Schedule C and calculate all the other figures needed for the personal tax return. When I'm through gathering figures, I store all the year's tax receipts, canceled checks, and bank statements for at least three years to meet IRS requirements.

See also Financial and Tax Records; Home Office Deduction; Petty Cash; *and article,* "Solving Cash Flow Problems."

Tip

When you hit your busy season in the fall, it's easy to get so involved producing products for sale that you let your buyers owe you money longer than they should. Remember that the people who are buying from you are just as busy as you are and may tend to overlook payment of your invoice unless you send them a timely reminder in the form of a statement. The longer you let a customer stall payment of an invoice, the harder it may be to collect payment.

Advertising

Q: *What's the most effective and least expensive kind of advertising I can do to promote my small business?*

Much depends on what you are trying to sell, how much money you have in your advertising budget, and whether you're trying to reach retail or wholesale buyers. Many beginners in business automatically think of advertising in terms of newspaper advertising or display ads in national magazines, but there are many less expensive ways to sell a line of handcrafts or build a homebased business. When your advertising budget is limited, the first thing you need to do is learn how to maximize word-of-mouth advertising from satisfied buyers. Then you need to learn how to write a news release that will bring you publicity—and business as well—locally or nationally.

• **Print Advertising to Consumers.** If you have developed a good mail piece or catalog promoting your products, consider placing classified ads in magazines read by your kind of buyers. Here you would be using the "two-step" method of advertising, explained elsewhere. Having good printed advertising materials is also essential if you plan to sell at shows and fairs, because this usually generates follow-up orders after a show is done.

When you're ready to spend several hundred dollars on an ad, consider a display ad in *Country Sampler* (**www.CountrySampler .com**), which offers display ad rates affordable to serious artists and craft sellers and a distribution of more than 400,000. Although this magazine—available on newsstands— is aimed at consumers, many advertisers report that inquiries and orders from wholesale buyers are common. This is a marketing topic I've discussed at some length in this book's marketing companion, *Handmade for Profit* (M. Evans).

- **Trade Magazine Advertising.** For starters, consider an ad in *The Crafts Report*, a magazine read by many craft shop and gallery owners. (Many helpful articles, including several of mine, are archived on this magazine's website at **www.CraftsReport.com.**) You might also check a periodicals directory at your library to turn up a variety of trade magazines that reach wholesale buyers likely to be interested in a particular product you want to wholesale in quantity. Many magazines feature new products, and sometimes you can get visibility here simply by sending a professionally written news release. At other times, you may get a bonus mention when you place your first ad.

- **Advertising on the Web.** A thorough discussion of this topic would require the space of a whole book, so let me simply emphasize here that any advertising you do on the Web should be targeted to niche audiences. The best way to do this is probably through e-mail newsletters to your own mailing list, and through exchanging links with other non-competitive website owners in your field. For more information on this topic, do a search on **www.Google.com** for "advertising on the Web" (include the quote marks to narrow your search). This will turn up several thousand Web pages listing books and articles that explain the ins and outs of online advertising.

See also Advertising Signs; Better Business Bureau; Cost of Advertising; Federal Trade Commission Rules; Independent Contractors; Libel/ Defamation of Character; Limited Editions; Mail Order Business; SASE; Telephone, Business Use of; Testimonials; Trade Shows; Two-Step Advertising; Web Marketing Options; *and* Zoning Laws.

Tip

Invest some of your advertising money into high-quality printed materials. Many craft sellers report a dramatic increase in orders when they move up to a classy catalog or start using full-color flyers that show their work at its best. (See *Printed Materials*.)

Advertising Signs

Q: *What kind of advertising signs can I put on my property?*

It depends entirely on the zoning laws in your community. While advertising signs on your vehicle or business signs in your yard will generally be prohibited in residential areas by zoning ordinances, temporary signs may be OK in your community if you want to advertise a Holiday Boutique or Open House. Call your city or county clerk to get the answer to this question.

See also Zoning Laws.

Tip

Some craft sellers wear their signs in the form of wearable art they sell at fairs, or jewelry they've made, which attracts compliments and opens the discussion on how and where to buy it. Others treat their business cards as mini-signs which can be posted to any available bulletin board.

Air Courier Services

If you ever need to ship anything by air express, both Federal Express and DHL (which merged with Airborne Express) will pick up packages at your home address and bill you later if you have established an account with them. Contact each company for complete details on their shipping and delivery policies:

- **www.Fedex.com**; 1-800-463-3339
- **www.DHL-USA.com**; 1-800-225-5345

Art/Craft Organizations

Hundreds of organizations cater to the hobby interests of creative people, and many are listed in library directories or have an online presence if you care to search the Web for them. (Go to **www.Google .com** and search for "art craft organizations" to turn up nearly 3 million Web pages on this topic.) Selected national organizations that serve the business interests of professional artists or handcraft producers are listed in *Other Resources*.

See also Craft Cooperative; Craft Emergency Relief Fund; Home-Business Organizations; *and* Trade Shows.

Attorney/Lawyer

Q: *Do I need legal assistance to start a simple homebased craft business?*

No. Hiring a lawyer to hold your hand while you start a small business at home would be comparable to hiring a limousine to drive you across the street. For what you would pay a lawyer to answer your business start-up questions, you could buy an entire library of small business reference books that will serve you for years. There may come a time in your business, however, when legal help is prudent, if not actually necessary, because the alternative could cost far more than your legal fees.

• **When You Need a Lawyer.** Unless you have a good understanding of "legalese," you would be wise to consult a lawyer any time you are asked to sign a contract, exclusive dealer or distributor agreement, licensing or franchise arrangement, or royalty contract. Legal counsel is also recommended if you decide to form a partnership, corporation, or cooperative. And never purchase property or buy a business without the guidance of a lawyer who will make sure you're not placing yourself in an uncomfortable legal or tax situation. At some point in your business, you may need the help of an attorney who specializes in patents, copyrights, or trademarks, but note that you do not need an attorney to get a simple copyright. A lawyer might charge you $100 to file the same form you can file for just $30. (See *Copyright Registration*.)

• **How to Find a Good Lawyer.** Like doctors, lawyers specialize in certain areas. Make a prospect list by first asking for recommendations from friends, business acquaintances, or your accountant. Also check the local Yellow Pages or call your city, county, or state bar association to get the names of lawyers in your area who handle cases of your type of concern. To check a lawyer's credentials, visit your library and ask for *The Martindale-Hubbell Law Directory,* a nationwide directory that details each lawyer's education, professional background, association memberships, and areas of expertise. (The international version of this directory lists Canadian lawyers.)

• **Free Legal Assistance.** Strapped for funds and can't afford a lawyer to help you with a business problem you're now facing? Artists and craftspeople who need advice, but cannot afford it, should contact Volunteer Lawyers for the Arts (**www.VLANY.org**). Headquartered in New York, this organization has branches in many states and is dedicated to providing free legal assistance to artists and arts organizations in all creative fields.

• **Initial Consultation.** Many lawyers offer free, initial consultations or may apply the fee for same toward your bill if you decide to hire them. Because lawyer's fees can vary dramatically, always ask about a lawyer's fee before you go in for a visit. Once you decide to hire a lawyer, make sure he or she puts in writing exactly what you will be paying and what you're going to get for your money.

See also Legal Resources on the Web; Prepaid Legal Services; *and* Small Claims Court.

Author/Publisher Contract

Q: *A publisher has expressed interest in a book I could write for them. Can you give me some pointers on negotiating a book publishing contract?*

Trade book publishers (those who sell to bookstores and libraries as opposed to the "floppy book" publishers who sell to craft and needlecraft shops) send all new authors a "standard contract" whose terms are naturally slanted to the publisher's financial interests. Every clause in a book publishing contract can be negotiated, but beginning writers don't have much power. If you are fortunate enough to find an agent who will represent you to publishers, you will probably get enough extra financial benefits to more than justify the commission he or she will take (generally 15 percent of royalties).

I've said earlier that it's always a good idea to have an attorney check a contract before you sign it, but it won't do you much good to hire an attorney to check an author/publisher contract unless that attorney has worked with other authors before. For example, an attorney who doesn't know the book publishing industry won't understand the significance of a clause that says royalties will be cut in half for books sold at a discount greater than 55 percent. This may not seem important until you consider that some publishers sell mostly to book clubs and library distributors that may require discounts of 60 percent or more. Suddenly, an author's total royalties could be half the amount expected.

The average attorney is also unlikely to understand the importance of clauses that stipulate how soon rights to a book will return to the author when it goes out of print. Authors who expect to take an active role in the marketing of their books should insist on a clause that gives them the right to buy books at a considerable discount, and get publishing rights back as quickly as possible when copies are no longer available for sale from the publisher. (Some contracts stipulate that rights won't be returned for two years, which is too long if you are still marketing a title at the time a publisher lets it go out of print.) And there should be a clause stipulating that a publisher cannot remainder an author's book without first giving the author the chance to buy copies at the same price (usually pennies on the dollar).

A hot issue today with writers in all fields is who controls the electronic rights to their work. Writers like me who have a presence on the Web have many reasons for wanting the electronic rights to their books, but not all publishers are willing to convey this right to an author. Some are probably concerned that a writer's use of a book's content on the Web will undermine sales of the book at the bookstore level, but if a writer at least has the right to offer book excerpts or tips from a book on the Web, that will only help promote sales of the book. An agent will be of considerable help in negotiating electronic rights. (For more insight into this topic, read the article "The All Rights/Electronic Rights Issue" on my website at **www.barbarabrabec.com/writingpublishing.htm**.)

Personal experience with six trade book publishers has given me considerable insight on the topic of author/publisher contracts. If you don't have a book agent or can't find an attorney who knows the book publishing industry, I will be happy to consult with you on the telephone and give you additional tips about things you should look for in a book contract.

For more information on the Web, visit **www.authorsguild.org** and click the "Contract Advice" button to turn up excellent articles related to both print books and ebook contracts.

See also Book Copyright *and* Royalties on Books.

Bad Check Collection Strategies

Q: *What's the best way to collect on a check that has bounced?*

Depending on why the check was returned, you will want to take different actions:

• **Nonsufficient Funds.** If a check is marked "NSF" and the bank hasn't presented it twice, you can deposit it again. (Since you can only redeposit a check one time, however, you may wish to telephone the person who wrote the check to make sure there will be sufficient funds to cover it the second time around.) Many banks automatically present checks twice before returning them, and most checks presented twice will clear the second time through. If a check comes back a second time, however, you have to decide if the size of the check is large enough to be worth the trouble it will take to collect it.

• **Account Closed.** Some people move and close an account before making certain all checks have cleared while others overdraw on their account because they have incorrectly added or subtracted. While this is a sign of carelessness, it is not evidence of fraud. In writing to a customer about this problem, begin with the assumption that the bad check was unintentional. Ask the customer to honor his or her obligation with a replacement money order. Hold the bad check as evidence of the customer's indebtedness to you, returning it upon receipt of the replacement money order.

• **Customer Refuses to Honor Obligation.** If the amount owed you is large, you can't redeposit the check, and the customer has ignored your polite letter, ask your bank to try to collect the check for you. There will be a fee for this—perhaps $30 or more—payable only if collection is completed. Your bank will instruct the bank on which the check is drawn to pay you as soon as funds have been deposited to the account. If no funds are deposited during the holding period (usually a month), you're out of luck.

See also Canadian Sales; Checks Received in the Mail; Checks Taken at Shows; COD Shipments; *and article, "When You Have Evidence of Fraud."*

Tip

To avoid bad checks in the first place, never accept checks that are undated or more than thirty days old. Checks should be written in ink and legibly signed. According to experts on this topic, checks without a printed address or with a sequence number below 300 are more likely to bounce.

Balance Sheet

A balance sheet shows what a business owns (assets) and what it owes on a specific date (liabilities). While most businesses prepare monthly balance sheets, the small homebased business whose books are done by hand and whose income and expenses have settled into a comfortable pattern may find the preparation of a quarterly Balance Sheet, Income Statement, and P&L Statement to be more than sufficient. If you use a computer software accounting package, these reports will be generated automatically as soon as you've entered all the income and expense figures for a particular month. Nearby you will find a worksheet to help you prepare a balance sheet that will be acceptable to your banker. Note that (1) Net Worth is the difference between Total Assets and Total Current Liabilities and (2) Total Assets must be the same as the figure shown for Total Net Worth and Liabilities.

• **Assets.** There are two kinds: Current and Fixed. Current assets of a typical homebased business would include cash on hand (in business checking account); Accounts Receivable; and the value of inventory (raw materials, work in progress, and finished work ready for shipping). Fixed assets would include the depreciated value of office equipment (computer system, fax, telephones, etc.); office furnishings (desks, filing cabinets, chairs, etc.); workshop furnishings (tools of your trade); your business reference library; and even your mail list if it happens to have value for rental purposes.

When You Have Evidence of Fraud

If a check is marked "account closed" or "no account," this may be evidence of fraud. If the amount in question is substantial and you believe there was intent to defraud, you may wish to notify your customer that your next step will be to take legal action. Your best legal options are to:

1. Send a copy of the returned check, along with notes about your efforts to collect the money, to your state's attorney general. (You can find this office by searching Google.com for "attorney general, [your state's name, spelled out]".)

2. Contact your sheriff or police department. Although it is not their business to act as a debt collector, it is a crime to write a bad check, and they may be willing to make a call for you. If the bad check is from an out-of-state customer in an amount of $250 or more, this makes the matter a felony instead of a misdemeanor. After making a trip to her sheriff's office, one crafter reported she had her money within ten days. The bad-check passer was told by the sheriff in his area to either pay up or be presented with a warrant for his arrest.

3. Consider trying to collect through Small Claims Court. First, learn about your state's Bad Check Law by checking this website: **www.ckfraud.org/penalties.html.** In my state of Illinois, for example, any person who writes an NSF check can be sued in small claims court for three times the amount of the check plus the face value of the check. Just being able to quote your state's law to a delinquent account would add weight to your demands for payment. The only trouble with a bad check law is that it works only if both you and check-writer live in the same state.

See also Bad Check Collection Strategies *and* Small Claims Court.

• **Liabilities.** Again, there are two kinds: Current and Fixed. Current liabilities are all the unpaid bills you have at the time you prepare a balance sheet (your Accounts Payable), any short-term loans that will be paid off within a year, plus any taxes due but not yet paid. Fixed liabilities would include any long-term business loans you may have taken.

See also Accounts Payable; Accounts Receivable; Financial Statements; *and Balance Sheet Worksheet.*

Bank Loans

Q: *What are my chances of getting a bank loan for my homebased business?*

It depends on whether you're already established in business or just getting started. Banks do not give business loans to fledgling homebased businesses, but they will always consider making a loan to a small business that has a steady income, a good credit rating, and good financial reports. It also helps to deal with a bank you've been doing business with for some time. Most people who start homebased businesses tap their own financial resources to get started, borrowing from a savings account, insurance policy, or the equity in their home. Others generate cash by selling whatever they've got and putting that money into their business. (Check your attic or basement for salable treasures for eBay (**www.ebay.com**) or a garage sale—you may have a gold mine there.)

See also Business Plan; Collateral; Credit Rating; Credit History; eBay, Selling on; Financial Statements; Financing a Business; Home Equity Loans; Line of Credit; *and* SBA Loans.

Bar Codes (UPC)

Q: *How do bar codes work, and do crafters have to use them on handmade products?*

A UPC (Universal Product Code) is a set of numbers that identifies a company and a product it sells. The first six digits (which are assigned by the Uniform Code Council [UCC]) identify the company while the next five digits (which are assigned by the manufacturer) indicate the product. A last "check digit" provides additional identity information. Once you have become a member of the UCC, you can

BALANCE SHEET WORKSHEET

_____(name of your business)_____

BALANCE SHEET

For Period Ending _____

A: CURRENT ASSETS

		D: CURRENT LIABILITIES	
Cash in Checking	$_____	Mscl. Bills	$_____
Accounts Receivable	$_____	Unpaid taxes	$_____
Inventory	$_____		
TOTAL CURRENT ASSETS	$_____	**E: TERM DEBT**	
		Loans	$_____
		TOTAL CURRENT LIABILITIES	$_____
B: FIXED ASSETS			
Tools and equipment	$_____		
Office Furnishings	$_____		
Computer System	$_____		
(Other)_____	$_____	**F: NET WORTH**	$_____
C: TOTAL ASSETS	$_____	**G: TOTAL NET WORTH AND LIABILITIES**	$_____

print your own bar code labels using off-the-shelf software. (Membership is hefty: currently $750 to join, with an annual renewal fee of $150/year.)

Fortunately, most artists and craftspeople don't have to worry about bar coding their handcrafted products because they are not yet commonly required by gift shops, craft shops, craft malls, etc. Retailers also have the capability of creating their own labels for products purchased from "specialty suppliers." Bar coding may be required, however, on products wholesaled to large retailers, chain stores, and bookstores that use a computerized inventory system. (When bar codes are scanned at the checkout counter, the retailer's inventory figures are automatically adjusted.)

You can get more information about UCC's annual membership fee and bar coding of products on the Web at **www.UC-Council .org**. A good article, "Bar Code Basics," can also be found at **http:// www.barcodehq.com/primer.html**.

Bedding and Upholstered Furniture Law

Q: *I've heard that some states require certain stuffed items to have a special label affixed to them. Can you provide details on this?*

If you sell items with a concealed filling or stuffing (dolls, teddy bears, quilts, pillows, soft picture frames, etc.) you should know about the Bedding and Upholstered Furniture Law. At one time all states had a bedding law, but only twenty-nine states have one today, says Morna McEver Golletz, editor of *The Professional Quilter* (**www.ProfessionalQuilter.com**). In researching this topic in the late nineties, she confirmed my earlier research about this being a law rarely enforced today. (If you search Google for "bedding, upholstered furniture law," [omit the quote marks], you may be able to find information on your state's law.)

One of my readers said a state official told her they only check on this if and when they receive a complaint. Like zoning laws, this particular law seems only to affect those who bring attention to it or themselves, or who are turned in by others who haven't been fortunate enough to go unnoticed. (Sometimes a complaint will be registered by a disgruntled seller who has been forced to obtain the special license and affix the labels and then reports other craft sellers in his or her state who aren't complying with the law.)

Those sellers unlucky enough to get noticed by state officials may be required to purchase a license costing anywhere between $25 and $100 (depending on which state it is), and will have to attach printed tags that bear a special registry number. A reader in Texas reported she was required to purchase 500 one-cent bedding stamps which then had to be placed on the label of each piece of merchandise offered for sale. She was directed to a source for the labels that had a blank space where information about the contents could be rubber-stamped.

Similar to state bedding laws are acts some states have on their books about the manufacture of stuffed toys. I have no idea how many states have such a law, but a note about Pennsylvania's "stuffed toys act" came to my attention while I was writing this book. Although Pennsylvania's law is thirty years old, the state has only recently begun to enforce it. "State officials are now visiting craft shows and inspecting merchandise to make sure it is both safe for children and properly labeled," a show listing publisher reported to me. "Crafters may call their items collectibles, but Pennsylvania law says it's a toy if it looks like a toy and contains any fiber, chemical, or other stuffing."

Fortunately, this law (administered by the Pennsylvania Department of Labor and Industry, Division of Bedding and Upholstery in Harrison) isn't a big problem for crafters. Everyone who sells toys in this state must submit samples of each product they intend to sell in the state, buy a license that costs $25 per year, and place an appropriately worded label on each item that bears the seller's state registration number.

See also Labels or Tags Required by Law. *If you make dolls, teddy bears or other toys, see also* Toymaking.

Tip

The only penalty that appears to be connected with a violation of either state bedding or stuffed toy laws is removal of merchandise from store shelves or a fine if a seller refuses to comply with the law after being notified of it. For that reason, most sellers ignore this law until they are challenged by authorities.

Better Business Bureau

Q: *If I join the Better Business Bureau, could I mention my membership in my advertisements or other printed materials?*

No, this is strictly prohibited. The Better Business Bureau's "BBB" symbol and name are registered trademarks owned by the Council of Better Business Bureaus, Inc. (**www.BBB.org**), and no one can legally use its name in their promotional or printed materials or even *mention* they are a member of the BBB. In my own experience with the BBB I've learned this organization is almost paranoid about anyone even mentioning its name and, if asked, they will tell you that membership or registration provides no tangible benefits. To quote the BBB, they ". . . cannot lend credibility to an individual firm as they neither recommend nor deprecate any product, service, or company."

Membership in the BBB would do nothing for a homebased business, but such businesses may *register* with the BBB if they wish. Customers who call the BBB for information about your business may think you more credible simply because you are registered, but the BBB will deny that such registration adds to your credibility. Although a consumer may get a favorable reply about you from the BBB (meaning no complaints on file), the BBB denies this is any kind of "reference" or "recommendation." However, since it costs nothing to register and may result in favorable information being passed on to customers in your area, you should consider doing this. *Just don't tell anyone you've done it.*

Bill of Lading

This shipping document gives evidence of a carrier's receipt of the shipment and serves as a contract between the carrier and shipper. (For air shipments, it may be called an air waybill.) Note that some trade shows require a bill of lading before they will move your packed merchandise from your booth to your vehicle at the close of a show.

Book Copyright

Q: *I have a book idea I'd like to offer to a publisher. Do I need to copyright the book before I send it to publishers for consideration?*

No. If your book is accepted for publication, the book publisher will take care of the copyright registration process for you. Do ask that the copyright be registered in your name, however. Your book contract will stipulate the royalties you are to receive on your book and temporarily convey to the publisher the right to publish your work. But unless you agree to it in your contract, the publisher cannot put your words on a recording or sell them to anyone else, such as a magazine. (Such rights are generally included in a book contract, with the author receiving half the amount the publisher receives from such extra sales of the work.) If and when your book is no longer offered for sale by the publisher and goes out of print, the copyright will revert back to you according to the terms established in your contract.

See also Author/Publisher Contract *and* LC Number.

Bookkeeping

Q: *What kind of books do I have to keep to meet IRS requirements?*

The IRS does not require any special kind of bookkeeping system, except that it must be one that clearly and accurately shows true income and expenses. You can do this with a business checkbook, a cash receipts journal, a cash disbursements ledger, and a petty cash fund. Many home businesses use single-entry bookkeeping systems that keep paperwork, figure work, and headaches to a minimum while still providing all the information needed to properly manage a business and prepare accurate tax returns. Very small businesses may find that all they need is a standard record-keeping book such as the *Dome Simplified Monthly,* which can be found in any office supply store. If you have a computer, there are a variety of easy-to-use accounting packages that will make your bookkeeping fun. (P.S. Did you know that "bookkeeping" is the only word in the English language that has three double letters in a row?)

See also Accounting Methods; Checking Account; Financial Statements; Petty Cash; Record-keeping; *and* Schedule C Form.

Tip

"Small business owners should keep their own books as long as possible, just to learn how to read and use the books once they've been posted," advises Bernard Kamoroff, CPA and author of *Small Time Operator—How to Start Your Own Business, Keep Your Books, Pay Your Taxes and Stay Out of Trouble* (**www.BellSprings.com**). If bookkeeping is not your strong point, this small business classic (updated annually) includes all the information, ledgers, and worksheets needed to set up a good manual bookkeeping system.

Book Publishing

Q: *I've always wanted to have a published book, and since I don't think a major trade publisher would want to publish what I've written, I've been thinking about self-publishing it. How can I get started as a self-publisher?*

Thanks to computer technology and the way the Web has enabled all of us to sell products and services, many creative people are now publishing their own art, craft, or hobby books in print or electronic form (or both). Before you think of publishing your own work, however, be sure to familiarize yourself with all aspects of the Copyright Law (discussed at length in this book) because it's easy for beginners to run into legal problems here. Also do your homework to learn how self-published books are publicized and sold. Once you've written your book, you should also hire someone to edit it so you don't end up with egg on your face due to glaring errors in grammar, punctuation, spelling, and so on. (See my website for helpful guidelines on this topic.)

A book that greatly inspired me when I was just beginning as a writer and publisher is *How to Get Happily Published* by Judith Applebaum (5th ed., Bantam). Her website at **www.HappilyPublished .com** includes a collection of articles and links to all the best resources for both would-be and published authors. The other "must read" book for all self-publishers is Dan Poynter's classic *Self-Publishing Manual—How to Write, Print and Sell Your Own Book*. Call 1-800-PARAPUB for more information or visit **www.ParaPublishing.com**

You Can Publish Your Own Book

The secret to success as a small book publisher lies in publishing for a niche market. For example, if you are a woodworker, seamstress, or teddy bear designer who has learned secrets likely to benefit others in the same field, you're a book publisher just waiting to be born.

Although the fields of Art and Crafts are big niche markets in their own right, each has many smaller niches of its own. Take woodworking for example. Within this niche market are countless individuals interested in specific types of woodworking such as woodcarving, woodturning, woodburning, and marquetry and the kinds of products that can be made from wood, such as home accessories, furniture, toys, games, or jewelry.

In an article for *SPAN Connection* (newsletter of the Small Publishers Association of North America (**www.Spannet.org**), author and self-publisher Gordon Burgett (**www.GordonBurgett.com**) emphasized how easy it is for anyone with a computer to publish books today and pointed to the market for books that are need-meeting or hope-fulfilling: "Today, anybody can produce a tightly targeted book that is page-made at home, zip it off to the printer for a short turnaround, then sell it to several hundred or many thousands of eager souls at costs that make the pages a bargain."

As a former book publisher, I can confirm the profitability of putting words into printed book form and offering them to others by mail. These days, however, as an older writer who no longer wants to handle inventories of printed books, I am far more excited by the possibilities of electronic publishing and marketing, and you can easily find thousands of Web pages on this topic by searching for "ebook publishing" on Google or Yahoo!. A search for "self-publishing" or "writing books" will turn up literally millions of other Web pages of possible interest. Remember that a study of only a few websites or the reading of a couple of books will open a world of possibilities for you.

to find hundreds of pages of information and free documents with links to many other self-publishing resources. Dan also publishes a free ezine that I find invaluable to my self-publishing interests.

This topic is beyond the scope of this book, but a search of the Web or any bookstore will turn up countless other books and articles for would-be self-publishers.

See also Drop-Shipping *and article, "You Can Publish Your Own Book."*

Tip

Never pick up information from other publications and put it in a book or directory of any kind without going directly to the source to make sure all information is still up to date. Publishing inaccurate or out-of-date information is not only a disservice to readers but a poor reflection on both the author and publisher. It could also lead to legal problems if an incorrect listing were to cause financial loss to someone listed in your directory. If you plan to quote from another published source, you must also get written permission to use that copyrighted material in your book.

Break-Even Point

This is the point at which total revenue equals total expenses. You can do break-even calculations for the profitability of your business, a direct mailing, an advertisement, or the profitability of a new product you've just introduced to the marketplace. By estimating the break-even point prior to making a mailing, placing an advertisement, or launching a new product, you gain valuable insight into whether the action you have planned will actually be profitable. Examples:

a) You know it will cost $810 to print and mail your new catalog to 1,500 names on your prospect/customer list. If you also know that your average order is $22, you can estimate that your break-even point on this particular mailing will come after you have received 37 orders ($810 ÷ by $22). However, this is only the point at which your actual cash expenditures have been recaptured. Now, to find out if you can actually make a profit on this mailing, you must take it a step further and do another break-even analysis. Let's assume that your average $22 order has a cost-of-goods expense in it that will lower your net profit per sale to just $13. Now you can see that it will take 62 orders to break even on this particular mailing ($810 ÷ by $13). The answer to the question of whether this mailing will be profitable for you lies in the percentage of response you normally receive to a catalog mailing. If you normally receive only a 3 percent order response, you are likely to receive only 45 orders (.03 × 1,500), which is not enough to break even on this mailing. A 5 percent response, however, would be 75 orders, and 75 × $13 is $975, which would cover the cost of your mailing and give you a small profit.

b) You are planning to spend $500 for a small display ad that will offer a product priced at $22.95 plus shipping. If your profit on this product is $13.95, you will break even on this ad after you have received 36 orders ($500 ÷ by $13.95). Knowing this, you can estimate the likelihood of your getting this many orders based on the magazine's circulation and the percentage of people who typically respond to a display ad. (You might think that one in a thousand will order (.001 percent), but it could as easily be one in ten thousand (.0001 percent). Multiply those percentage figures times the circulation of the magazine in question and see what you come up with. Example: 225,000 circulation × .001 % = 225 orders. Times .0001, however, the likely number of orders drops dramatically to just 22.5, suggesting that an ad might not be profitable. This is all a big guessing game, of course; you'll never know whether an ad will work until you try it. The trick is to never spend more for an ad than you can afford to lose.

c) You are planning to produce 100 pattern packages that will cost $1.75 each to print and package ($175 total cost). The pattern will be priced at $6.95, so the break-even point will come when 25 pattern packages have been sold ($175 ÷ by $6.95). As you can see, this will be a profitable product since the remaining 75 pattern packages will yield a net profit of $5.20 each, or $390.

Brochure

Q: *Do I need a brochure if I sell only at craft fairs or in malls?*

Brochures are generally distributed on a selective basis to people who request additional information about you or your products, and they

Standard Printer's Folds

1. Single fold

2. Accordion fold

3. Standard letter fold

4. Double parallel fold

5. French fold

6. Gate fold

are valuable because they give you professional credibility. For example, if you decide to expand into wholesaling, a brochure (or the use of full-color flyers) will tell buyers you are serious about selling and will be a reliable supplier for them. Not every craft seller needs a fancy brochure, but every seller needs good printed materials of one kind or another to get initial sales and follow-up orders (unless they are selling exclusively on the Web). Even then, many Web sellers have found that print catalogs mailed at regular intervals to their customer and prospect lists generate a good order response. Moreover, when brochures, flyers, price lists, or other printed materials are tucked into customers' bags at both retail and wholesale shows, they often lead to follow-up sales by mail.

A brochure can be something as simple as a one-page sheet that tells who you are and what you do. Standard brochures, however, measure 8½ × 11 inches or 8½ × 13 inches (legal-size), are printed on heavyweight paper or lightweight card stock, then folded (see illustration). Your local printer will be happy to provide samples.

See also Printed Materials *and* Price List.

Tip

Each time you do a new show, check your mailing list for buyers in that area and send them a brochure, postcard, or even a personal note inviting them to stop by to see your newest products. One seller reported that 85 percent of her show sales were from customers who had received her mailings in the past.

Budget

Theoretically, a budget is a financial plan to control spending, but I like these humorous definitions better: A budget is what you stay within if you go without, and balancing the budget is when money in the bank and the days of the month come out together.

One thing is certain: putting your homebased business on a budget will force you to think more creatively, especially when you don't have money to buy advertising. The longer you are in business, you will find, as I did, that the less money you have to promote your business, the more innovative you are likely to become in digging up new prospects and reselling buyers already on your mailing list.

Bulk Mailings

Q: *Can I save money by mailing my brochures, catalogs, or newsletters at bulk rates instead of first-class?*

I used to send thousands of pieces of mail at bulk rates every year because the rate was then about half the cost of a first-class stamp. In recent years, however, the cost of bulk mail has increased to the point where the difference between first-class and bulk mail (now called "Standard Mail") is only a few cents per piece. Thus, if you're thinking in terms of mailing only a couple hundred brochures or catalogs, the use of first-class mail will not only give you a faster turnaround on your mailing, but will let you keep your mailing list up to date since undelivered mail is automatically returned to sender at no extra cost.

If you are the exception and are thinking in terms of mailing a few thousand brochures or catalogs, talk to someone at your post office to make sure you get all the rules related to this type of mailing. For example, when the postal service introduced its reclassification program in mid-1996, it also changed all the rules on how bulk mailings were to be sorted and bundled. Now, instead of sorting addresses in pure ZIP code order (the same way they come out of our computers), business mailers must prepare "regional bundles" that include assorted ZIP codes from several states. If you don't have a software program that can rearrange your mailing list in this peculiar numerical order, it may take three times as long to sort and bundle a mailing.

Furthermore, in spite of what the postal service may tell you, it still takes up to thirty days for bulk mail to be delivered, and if you ask for address corrections on this mail, it can take weeks or months for some mail pieces to be returned. In comparing what I spent for address corrections on the last bulk mailing I did, I figured I would have been money ahead to send the whole mailing by first-class mail. Not only would I have gotten quicker delivery, but all my address corrections would have come back free of charge.

See also Indicia; Mail, Classes/Types of; Mailing Lists, Rental of; Mail, Size Regulations; *and article, "Money-Saving Postal Tips."*

Business Cards

Q: *I'm getting ready to design my business card. Are there any "rules" about this that I need to know?*

There are no formal rules, just general guidelines. The primary purpose of a business card is to help people remember who you are and how they can find you when they want you, so give careful thought to the content you put on your card. Unless you are using a post office box address for your homebased business, think twice before including your home address on a business card. Either that, or be selective in handing them out. This is particularly important if you are doing an art or craft that would be enticing to thieves. For example, jewelers who work in gold or silver would never put their address on a business card because that could set them up for a possible robbery. These days, the content on a business card can often be limited to your business name, *business* telephone number (it's illegal to put your home phone number on a business card—see *Telephone, Business Use of*), e-mail address, and your Web page, if you have one.

As for the actual size and design of a card, most business cards are rectangular and measure 3 ½ × 2 inches, but cards used by artists and craftspeople come in all sizes, shapes, and colors and may be folded as well. (See my book, *Handmade for Profit,* for illustrations of several cards, along with tips on how to design a card that will be most effective for you.)

See also Freebies; Premiums; *and* Telephone, Business Use of.

Business Expenses, Tax-Deductible

Q: *What home-business expenses can I deduct on my Schedule C form?*

Use the following checklist as a reminder of the many deductions available to you as a home-business owner. Once you have begun your business, any expense that is *ordinary, necessary, and somehow connected with the operation and potential profit of your business* is deductible. Given the unique nature of homebased businesses, you will surely think of some items not included here.

Deductions marked with an asterisk are limited to some degree, as explained in IRS's *Tax Guide for Small Business* (Publication 334), available to you from any IRS office. See also the special notes at the end of this checklist.

Accounting or bookkeeping services
Advertising expenses
Bank charges
Books and periodicals related to your business
Briefcase or samples case
Bulletin board
Business equipment

Business gifts
Child care expenses *(see note 6)*
Christmas cards for business associates
Cleaning supplies/services *(business portion of home)*
Commissions *(sales reps, agents, other sellers)*
Computer, software, and related expenses *(see note 3)*
Consulting fees
Conventions and trade show expense
Copyrights *(see note 10)*
Delivery charges
Donations
Dues and memberships, professional
Educational expense *(business seminars/workshops/classes)*
Employee benefits
Entertainment *(must be carefully documented)*
Equipment lease costs
Equipment purchases *(may be depreciated or expensed; see note 9)*
Equipment repairs
Exhibit/display expenses
Freight and shipping charges
Health insurance *(see note 7)*
Indirect expenses on use of home for business *(see note 1)*
Insurance premiums
Interest on business loans or late tax payments
Inventory purchases
IRA, Keogh, or SEP account deposits
Labor costs *(independent contractors)*
Legal and professional fees *(see note 2)*
Licenses and permits
Mail list development and maintenance
Maintenance contracts on office equipment
Membership fees in business-related organizations
Moving expenses *(related to business portion)*
Office decor *(drapes, blinds, carpeting, artwork, etc.)*
Office furnishings *(depreciated or expensed; see note 9)*
Office supplies
Postage and postal fees
Presentation packages *(sales)*

Product displays, exhibiting expenses
Professional services *(artists, designers, copywriters, etc.)*
Refunds to customers
Remodeling costs/expenses *(to business area of home)*
Rental fees *(to malls, rent-a-space shops)*
Repairs to area or room used exclusively for business
Research and development expenses *(see note 2)*
Safe deposit box *(for business-related documents or computer backups)*
Sales commissions
Show fees
Stationery and printing
Subscriptions to craft or business periodicals
Supplies and materials
Tax preparer's fee *(portion related to Schedule C)*
Telephone *(see note 4)*
Tools of your trade
Trademark expense *(see note 10)*
Travel expenses *(meals and lodging; see note 8)*
Uniforms or special costumes used only in trade or profession
Vehicle *(see note 5)*
Wages to employees *(including spouse or children)*

NOTES:

1. In addition to the *direct expenses* above—which may be itemized on your Schedule C tax form—you are entitled to deduct a portion of certain *indirect expenses* that benefit both the business and personal parts of your home. (See also *Home Office Deduction*.)

2. Previously, start-up expenses such as research and development costs, educational expenses, and legal and accounting fees incurred before a business had generated any revenue had to be amortized. Beginning in 2005, however, up to $5,000 of such expenses could be deducted. Talk to an accountant about this.

3. To deduct expenses for a computer that is also for personal use, you must calculate the percentage of time the computer is used for business to get the amount you can deduct as a business expense. Related supplies and materials are also deductible.

4. If your personal telephone is used for business, you may not deduct any part of the cost of the first line into your home, but you

may deduct business-related long distance calls and charges for extra lines, business extensions, call forwarding, etc. (See also *Telephone, Business Use of.*)

5. When you use the family vehicle for business, you may deduct expenses either for business mileage or actual operating expenses related to business use. (See also *Vehicle Used for Business.*)

6. If you pay someone to care for your child or an invalid parent or spouse so you can work, a portion of the cost may be deductible.

7. Self-employed individuals may now deduct 100 percent of the cost of health insurance on page one of their annual tax return.

8. The deduction for business-related meal and travel expenses is currently limited to 50 percent. Spousal travel deductions are allowed only when spouse is an employee of the company. (Note that the percentage of allowable deductions could change at any time.)

9. Some purchases must be depreciated while others (like inventory purchases bought for resale) are expensed only when actually sold. Expensing is a good strategy to use in years when your income takes a jump but your regular expenses remain the same. Discuss this with your accountant.

10. The costs of trademarks (as well as copyrights and patents), once deductible only when sold, can now be deducted over a fifteen-year period.

See also Personal Property Used for Business *and* Schedule C Form.

Tip

The IRS considers payment has been made on the date of a credit card transaction, not when you actually pay the bill. Thus, business expenses charged to a third-party credit card (such as Visa or Master-Card) can be deducted even though the credit card bill hasn't been paid by year's end.

Business or Trade Name Registration/Protection

Q: *I have a very small business. Do I really have to register my business name with local authorities?*

Registration of a business operated under any name other than your own is required by law because a fictitious name must be connected to the name of an individual who can be held responsible for the actions of a business. Moreover, if you like the name you've given your business, the only way to protect it is to register it locally. (See *Fictitious Name Statement*.) Otherwise, anyone can take it from you simply by registering your business name in connection with theirs.

Some states require registration even when one's real name is part of the business name, so you'll need to check this on your own. Simply call your city or county clerk (depending on whether you live within or outside city limits). Since registration of a business name is a simple and inexpensive matter, take care of it today. Don't worry about your failure to do this earlier if you've been in business for some time because the form you have to complete doesn't ask for the date your business was started. When you register, be sure to ask when you have to renew the registration of your name because you won't be notified. You should also register your business name with the state (call your state capital) to prevent its use by any corporate entity. To protect your name and business logo on a national level, consider filing a trademark.

See also Checking Account; Hobby Business; Fictitious Name Statement; Printed Materials; Supplies, Buying Wholesale; *and* Trademark.

Tip

In selecting a business name, pick one that doesn't tie you down to just one activity since it's hard to tell where your business will lead you in the future. Avoid crafty-sounding names that might give suppliers and prospective customers the impression you're just a hobbyist. (Examples: *Kitty's Krafty Kreations, Homemade Treasures,* or *Handmade by Sue.*) Since manufacturers and distributors will not sell to individual hobby sellers, you should do everything possible to remove the hobbyist image from their minds as well as from the minds of prospective customers if you want to make a real profit on the things you sell. Attaching your first name to your business may make you happy, but it can also be a signal that you're just a hobby seller. Using your personal name for a business works best if you are trying to build a reputation for yourself as an artist, crafts designer, writer, speaker, etc.

Business Plan

Q: *I just want to make crafts and sell as much as possible. What do I need a business plan for?*

The primary reason for writing a formal business plan is to impress a banker if you're asking for a business loan. Since home-business owners can't get a bank loan to launch a new business, you could logically conclude there is no reason to write a business plan for a small crafts business at home. As I see it, however, even a hobby business needs a plan of some kind. Otherwise, it's like going to the grocery store without a shopping list: you wander around trying to remember what you wanted to buy, pick up on impulse things you don't need, and end up at home without the lettuce.

Without a plan for your crafts business, you might dabble first in one craft and then another without ever developing a coordinated line of salable products. Or you might not make a point of doing market research to learn if one type of sales outlet might be better for you than another. A written business plan simply lays out a plan of action you can follow to be more efficient and productive in whatever you are doing. The more serious you are about making money from your activity, the more serious you will be about writing a plan.

To begin, refer back to the Contents pages and note how business topics are listed under general categories such as "Accounting," "Business and Office Management," "Legal Issues," and so on. Make a photocopy of this list so you'll have a worksheet. Then, with the list in hand, set up an outline for your business plan, including various listings under main category headings such as:

• **Business Statement.** Indicate how or why your business came into being. Briefly describe your business goals, products, or services (who you are and what you do).

• **Business Start-up or Development Checklist.** Glean the entire list of Contents to find topics relative to your interests or present situation, paying particular attention to topics under "Banking," "Insurance," "Laws and Regulations," and "Legal Issues." Highlight information in the text for easy reference. Suggestion: Start a four-column list of (1) things that need immediate investigation or action; (2) things you want to check on or do in a few weeks; (3) things you want to investigate or do six months to a year from now; and (4) long-term goals and plans related to or suggested by text topics.

• **Manufacturing/Production Plan.** Describe how you plan to produce goods for sale, listing any special equipment, tools, or facilities needed to make your products. Indicate where and how you will obtain necessary raw materials, what they will cost, and where you will store them. Explain how products will be made. Will you do all the work, or hire family members or outside workers to assist you? (See all listings under "Employees/Labor Issues.")

• **Office Setup or Modification.** Describe how and where you're going to set up your office or improve current working conditions, acquire needed equipment, business services, stationery, office supplies, etc. (See listings under "Business and Office Management.")

• **Financial Plan.** Indicate the amount of money needed for start-up or expansion. Estimate your expected sales and expenses for a year and do a cash flow statement. (See listings under "Accounting," "Banking," and "Money Management.")

• **Marketing Plan.** Describe your market, your customers, and your competition. List the individual products you plan to sell, including unique features or customer benefits related to each. Focus on these benefits when writing advertising copy or descriptive listings for your brochure or catalog. Indicate how and where you will advertise and what this will cost. List the market research steps you will take to learn more about new sales outlets that might be right for your products. (See all listings under "Advertising and Marketing" and "Pricing and Selling." See also this book's companion volume, *Handmade for Profit*, for insider tips on how to successfully sell through sixteen different types of retail outlets as well as on the Web.)

See also article, "A Business Planning/Goal Setting Checklist."

Tip

The greatest benefit of a written plan is that it forces you to think about your goals and the paths you must take to realize them. The biggest problem of a written plan is that it quickly goes out of date. For this reason, it's a good idea to put your plan on computer so you can regularly review and update it.

A Business-Planning/
Goal-Setting Checklist

Business planning never stops. It is something you must do at the beginning, in the middle, and even at the end of your business. By putting all your plans in writing, you will more easily achieve both your personal and financial goals. Before you begin to write your business plan, first write a mission statement that links what you stand for (your values) to what you are seeking to accomplish (your vision). Include this mission statement in your annual business plan. Here are some additional tips to keep in mind:

• Keep good records so your business plan will contain the kind of details you need to analyze various aspects of your business.

• Review your plan each year, adding annual updates as needed. Use your plan as both a guide and a goal to work toward, one step at a time.

• Put all your goals in written form since they will automatically become a plan. Keep them large enough to motivate you to go forward, yet small enough to be easily achieved.

• Although everything should be kept on the computer, information is much more usable in a notebook. For visual inspiration, set up one or more notebooks to organize your various idea lists, projects, marketing goals, sketches, and so on.

• Photocopy information that can't be saved on computer and put it in a safe deposit box or fireproof drawer to protect it against loss.

• Make "to do" lists every day to help you stay on schedule and ensure that you don't forget anything important. Throughout the year, make lists of things to research, books to read, people to contact, ideas to explore, etc.

• Critically review your daily activities in terms of their contribution to your long- and short-term goals, constantly striving to make improvements. Never lose faith in your ability to achieve success.

Business Records, Protection of

Q: *What's the best way to protect my most important business records?*

I cringe every time I hear someone say they have lost everything in a fire, flooded basement, tornado, hurricane, or earthquake because there are many things people can do to protect themselves against such disasters. It's never too early to develop such a plan. Begin by asking yourself what would happen if you suddenly lost all your customer and prospect files? All the patterns and designs used to create products for sale? All your reference material for something you're writing? All your financial, tax and insurance records? Printed materials, office forms, and correspondence? The book manuscript you're currently working on? Once you decide which information and materials are vital to the success of your business, look at different ways you might protect it. Renting a safe deposit box is an excellent solution for protecting valuable materials off-site, but if you need regular access to material, you might consider the purchase of a fireproof safe or file drawer. Here are some more specific ideas:

- **Computer Files.** If you use a computer for your business, protect not only your documents, but your original software and information on how to reinstall it, along with a file of all your passwords and phone numbers for technical support. In between trips to my safe deposit box to exchange my computer backup discs, I carry a CD of all my document files in my purse. I figure if the house burns down or is burgled while I'm gone, I'll have the bulk of my business in the palm of my hand. (At home, my purse hangs on my office door where it can be grabbed quickly day or night in case of fire.)

- **Important Papers.** Make a list of all business documents, mailing lists, correspondence, artwork, designs, patterns, etc., that you consider absolutely vital to the continuation of your business. Copy as much of this material as possible for permanent storage in a safe deposit box or fireproof file. Since printed materials are an important part of any business, it's a good idea to get in the habit of setting aside a couple of master copies of everything you have printed. If the original art is lost and you don't have the printed piece on computer, at least you'll have an image to work from and all your valuable copywriting won't have been lost.

- **Other Files.** Material that can't be protected by copying should be centrally located in your home office, workshop, or studio so you can grab it at a moment's notice when you get a tornado warning or the smoke alarm goes off. For example, at my bill-paying desk, all the files and records I use every week are stored on one shelf so they can be grabbed quickly when the tornado siren warns of impending disaster. When I'm working on any new writing project, my reference files are vital, so I keep them all together in a large filing tub I can grab in an emergency.

For a long time, I thought I was being prudent by keeping some of my valuable files on the lower level of our home. I figured if a tornado took off the roof, at least it wouldn't blow away all my files. I had never given flooding a thought because we don't live anywhere near a river. But when Naperville and surrounding cities flooded in 1996 after a "storm of the century" dropped twenty-two inches of rain in twenty-four hours, we found ourselves mopping water in the basement for fifteen hours straight. In our area alone, more than two dozen homes were hit by lightning and nearly 8,000 homes had serious flood damage. We escaped with only minor damage, but I suddenly saw the necessity of moving precious things and stored business records at least four feet off the floor. An old Arabic saying seems appropriate here: Trust in God but tie up your camel.

See also Financial and Tax Records *and* Safe Deposit Box.

Canadian Sales

Q: *What do I need to consider when soliciting orders from Canadian residents?*

Although you may be happy to send your catalog or brochure to any Canadian prospect who requests it as a result of your advertising or publicity, you may find that sending unsolicited brochures and catalogs into Canada is prohibitively expensive. In addition to having to pay higher postage rates for Canadian mail, all of it (except for postcards) must be put in an envelope. This not only adds another dime or so to the cost of a mail piece, but the extra weight is likely to throw the package over the one-ounce mark.

Canadian checks can also be a problem. Be sure to ask your bank about its policy for handling Canadian checks. Many banks in the United States are not equipped to handle foreign checks, so your deposit of Canadian checks might incur high handling charges. In addition, the service charge for handling a bad (returned) check through international channels can amount to $30 or more. For these reasons, and because the rate of exchange is constantly changing, you should ask Canadians (and buyers in other countries) to remit in U.S. funds. Before you ask all your Canadian prospects to pay with a money order, however, consider the amount of business you might lose. (NOTE: I sold my publications to Canadians for nearly thirty years and never received a bad check.)

See also Money Orders; Shipping and Handling Charges; *and* United Parcel Service.

Tip

If you can accept payment by credit card, all your Canadian order problems will be resolved. You simply write the charge slip for the amount of purchase in U.S. funds, and when your bank processes the charge slip, it credits your account with that amount and automatically calculates the rate of exchange for your Canadian customer.

Care Labels

Q: *I thought I only needed to add a care label to the garments I'm offering for sale, but someone told me that other fabric items in my line also need care labels. Please explain.*

In connection with its *Fabric Care Labeling Rule,* the Federal Trade Commission (**www.FTC.gov**) requires a permanently affixed care label on both textile wearing apparel and household furnishings. These labels must indicate if an item is to be dry cleaned or washed and, if it is to be washed, whether to use hot or cold water. You must also indicate whether bleach may or may not be used and specify at what heat the item may be ironed. You can design your own labels or order standard care labels from manufacturers such as Charm

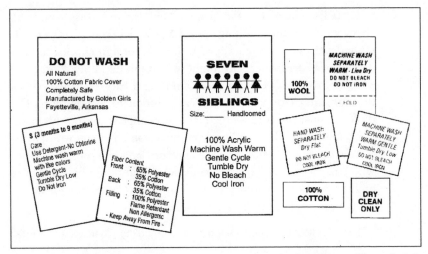

Samples from Widby Enterprises   *Samples from Charm Woven Labels*

Woven Labels (**www.CharmWoven.com**) and Widby Enterprises (**www.WidbyLabel.com**).

See also Hang Tags and Designer Labels; Labels or Tags Required by Law; *and* Textile Fiber Products Identification Act.

Cash Flow Projection

Q: *How can I begin to create a cash flow report for a new business when I have no real figures to work with?*

A cash flow report is simply a picture showing how cash is flowing in and out of a business. Realize, of course, that all you are doing here is estimating figures to the best of your ability and making wild guesses if you have no previous experience or financial records for reference. After you've been in business for a while, cash flow projections are easier to do because you can refer to earlier records of sales and expenses.

You can create cash flow projection worksheets for a period of one to six months as needed, but bankers may want to see a year's projection. Even if you never apply for a loan, you will find it helpful to

How to Create a Cash Flow Statement

Begin with a blank columnar page and list the names of the months across the top. For each month, jot down the appropriate figures.

In the sample below, one-month totals are shown to illustrate how figures are added and subtracted in a cash flow statement. These figures, of course, are literally drawn out of the air and may seem high or low depending on whether you've just started selling or have been in business for a while. In this particular "financial picture," let's assume that a fellow who has been selling handmade furniture with great success for three months has an accident late in May that will prevent him from making or selling crafts in the months of June and July. (The income in June is from an invoice for goods delivered to a shop in May.) The question to be answered by this cash flow projection is whether money in the business checking account will be sufficient to cover fixed business expenses that will continue in June and July whether there is income or not.

	MAY	JUNE	JULY
Sales Receipts *(list all expected sources of income)*			
Total Sales	**$1,800**	**$ 350**	**$ - 0 -**
Cost of Sales *(list expenses individually and subtract from Sales)*			
Total Cost of Sales	**$ 540**	**$ - 0 -**	**$ - 0 -**
Gross Profit	**$1,260**	**$ 350**	**$ - 0 -**
Total Income This Month	$1,800	$ 350	$ - 0 -
Beginning Cash Balance	$ 175	$1,375	$1,125
Cumulative Cash	**$1,975**	**$1,725**	**$1,125**
Operating Expenses *(list individually and subtract from gross Profit)*			
Total Cash Disbursements	$ 600	$ 600	$ 600
Ending Cash Balance	**$1,375**	**$1,125**	**$ 525**

(Carry forward to next month's column as "Beginning Cash Balance" figure)

As you can see, by the end of July, there will be insufficient cash to cover all operating expenses, but the amount lacking is small and these are merely estimates after all. For that reason, this business owner ought to make another cash flow projection at the end of June to see if the picture has become better or worse once exact sales and expense figures are known. The larger a business and the more important its profits are to a family's income, the more important cash flow projections like this will be.

Solving Cash Flow Problems

There is a knack to learning how to delay payment when money is tight or you're waiting for accounts to pay up. Here are some things you can do when your cash flow situation is desperate because of unanticipated or excessive expenses at a time when your income is not as high or as regular as expected.

Some bills can be delayed without hurting your credit rating while others must be paid on time to avoid late reports to the credit bureaus. Banks, finance companies, and major credit card companies generally report to credit agencies right away, so these bills always need to be paid on time. (Note: Most credit card companies now add as much as $30 to your bill if you pay it late—and they may further penalize you by replacing your lower-interest rate with their maximum rate.) Telephone and cable television companies also assess late charges. You aren't likely to ruin your credit rating, however, by stalling a doctor or dentist bill, and gas companies may not report late payments until an account is several months overdue.

If you can't make your mortgage payment on time, call the financial institution that holds your mortgage and ask how many days of grace you have. (At least once a year, you have the legal right to pay only the interest due on your monthly mortgage payment.) Car and house insurance payments also have grace periods (usually thirty days) before the insurance would be cancelled, but double-check with your agent to be sure.

If you have been doing business with a printer or other supplier for a long time and find you cannot pay a bill on time, call and explain your situation and ask if you can have a thirty-day extension if you agree to pay a month's interest on the money. Few suppliers will say no because they won't want to lose you as a customer.

See also Cash Flow Projection.

occasionally make cash flow statements for your business, particularly when you find yourself coming into a period where you're worried about whether you will have sufficient income to meet anticipated expenses. By creating a cash flow projection in advance of an anticipated situation, you can identify if and when a financial problem is likely to occur and get a handle on what you might need to do to solve it. You might find you have to do something to generate extra income or apply for a short-term loan. Sometimes a cash flow projection proves that you aren't going to have a problem at all.

See also articles, "How to Create a Cash Flow Statement" and "Solving Cash Flow Problems."

Catalog Houses, Selling to

Q: *I have a handcrafted item I can make in quantity and I'm thinking about offering it to a major mail order catalog. What are my chances for success here?*

It's hard to say, but one thing is for sure: Mass market catalogs are not a good market for anyone who makes labor-intensive handcrafts. Your product might be accepted by a catalog buyer, but the real question is how profitable this kind of selling will actually be, given all the time you will spend manufacturing it. A four-times markup (sometimes more) is standard in this industry, which means a product that would normally retail for $29.95 would have to be wholesaled to a catalog house for around $7.50. This suggests that the only handcrafts that might conceivably be sold to a catalog house at a profit would have to be priced in the neighborhood of $75 or more.

If this is something you decide to pursue, however, contact catalog companies of interest and ask to speak to the Director of Merchandise or the Catalog Merchandise Buyer. If there is interest in your product, you may be asked to send an information package and photo. Do not send a sample unless specifically requested because it won't be returned.

See also cautionary article, "Selling to Catalog Houses."

Celebrity Rights Act

Q: *I'm thinking about creating a Charlie Chaplin "Little Tramp" doll. I figure this is okay because the movie star is now deceased. Right?*

Wrong. The rights of deceased personalities are protected either by special state laws known as the *Celebrity Rights Act,* or by attorneys or agencies who handle the estates of deceased movie stars. Without a license or special permission to use a particular personality's characterization in some way, no one may produce a product, advertise a product, or provide a service that in any way utilizes the name, voice, signature, photograph, or likeness of a deceased person during a period lasting fifty years after their death. Manufacturers who violate this law are not the only ones who must be careful here since distributors and retailers caught selling unlicensed products can also be sued. To find out who handles the estate of a particular individual, contact the Screen Actors Guild or the Academy of Motion Picture Arts and Sciences in Los Angeles.

Chamber of Commerce

Q: *Is there any reason for a small homebased business to join the local chamber of commerce?*

Throughout the United States, chambers of commerce support local businesses of all sizes, and home-business owners are eligible for membership. In addition to the networking and marketing contacts you might make as a member (some chambers publish directories of licensed homebased businesses), you would also be eligible for United Chambers's low-cost group health insurance program, which many self-employed people have told me was their best option for low-cost insurance. Your local chamber will be happy to give you additional information.

See also Insurance, Medical.

Check Endorsements

When you endorse a check with only your signature, it's the same as cash to anyone who gets hold of it. When depositing checks by mail, then, always limit the endorsement by first writing "For Deposit Only." If you regularly take checks in your business, buy a rubber stamp to endorse them for deposit. Many sellers who take checks at fairs immediately rubber-stamp their checks for deposit before putting them in their cash drawer.

See also Checking Account.

Tip

To save money, don't order your check endorsement stamp through the bank because they will tack on a service charge that will make the cost of the stamp twice what you would pay if you ordered it from any other source.

Checking Account

Q: *I don't have much business right now nor many bills to pay. Do I really need a separate checking account for my business in the beginning while it's so small?*

Yes, use of a personal checking account for business is called "commingling of funds" by the IRS and it is strictly prohibited. The only way you can safely claim business deductions on your tax return is to conduct all business transactions through a separate business checking account. If an audit revealed commingling of funds, your deductions would most likely be disallowed, your taxes would be higher, and you might incur interest and penalties on taxes due.

Although a separate checking account is the only way to keep accurate records for your business, you don't need an expensive "business checking account" to satisfy the IRS. A second small checking account whose checks have the name of the business imprinted on them will suffice. Simply deposit all business revenue into this account and pay all bills from it. (See TIP below about ordering checks from a mail order check-printing company.)

To save money on service charges, compare the charges of several financial institutions in your area. Some will be much higher than others. In particular, ask:

- Is there a charge for deposits or each check deposited? (Some banks make a charge for each deposit while others charge for each out-of-state check deposited—very costly for mail order businesses.)
- Is there a charge for bounced checks? (Some banks charge up to $30.00 per check.)
- Will the checking account balance draw interest?
- Is there a minimum balance requirement?
- Does the financial institution offer small business loans or a line of credit? Merchant credit card services? Note that many banks, formerly called "savings and loan associations," offer business checking accounts but do not make business loans or offer a line of credit or merchant card services. I've always had my business checking account in this type of bank because there are no service charges of any kind (except for bad checks), and interest is paid on my checking account balance. When I wanted a line of credit not offered by my regular bank, I simply opened a second account with a local bank, where I later got merchant status as well.

See also Bad Check Collection Strategies; Check Endorsements; Checks Received in the Mail; Checks Taken at Shows; Credit History; DBA; Employee Identification Number; Partnership; *and* Stop Payment Order.

Tip

A big expense in maintaining a business checking account is the high cost of bank checks. You may already order personal checks by mail to save money, but did you know you can also order business checks and binders by mail? One check-printing company that has been in business for more than seventy years is Checks in The Mail. Currently their cost for 300 three-on-a-page business checks and binder is about one-fourth what a bank would charge for the same order. For additional information, call 1-800-733-4443 or order checks on the Web at **http://secure.checksinthemail.com**.

Checks Received in the Mail

Q: *Customers do not always write checks correctly. How do I handle "problem checks" I've received in the mail?*

Here are examples of typical problems and what to do about them:

• Check may indicate one figure on the amount line and a different one in the written description. (Example: the figure might be $10.95, but the written line reads "ten dollars and 00/100.") A bank will generally accept the amount that is written, rather than the amount shown as a figure. Knowing this will help you determine whether to return the check for correction and risk losing the order, or just let it go through as is.

• Check is unsigned. It may not be necessary to return the check. If the check is small, double-check with your bank to see if this alternative is acceptable: Write the word "over" on the signature line of the check. Then, on the back, type "lack of signature guaranteed." Include your business name, your name and title, and signature. (If the customer doesn't honor the check, this tells the bank that you will take it back as a charge against your account.) If the check is for a large amount, and you feel uncomfortable about the customer honoring the check, returning it with an SASE might be preferable.

• Check is made out to an incorrect name. This is a common problem for anyone who gets publicity mentions for a product. When I was selling my books by mail, I often received checks made out to the titles of my books instead of my personal or business name, or sometimes my name was spelled incorrectly. In such cases I simply endorsed the back of the check with the same name the check writer had used, then wrote my personal name below that and stamped the check as usual with the rubber stamp that bore all my account information.

• Check doesn't have any name or address printed on it. Is there a sequence number on the check? It's possible you have received a temporary check, which new account holders use until their supply of printed checks is received. If you feel uncomfortable about the check, either call the customer to inquire about it or hold the shipment until the check clears.

See also Bad Check Collection Strategies.

Tip

Fill your mail orders before depositing checks because people occasionally forget to include their name and address on a letter or order form, and you may have to go back to the check itself to pick it up.

Checks Taken at Shows

Q: *I plan to take checks from my craft fair customers, getting a telephone number, driver's license number, and a credit card number. Is there anything else I can do to avoid accepting a bad check?*

When asking a buyer to give you a driver's license number, always take time to look carefully at the picture to make sure it's the same person you're dealing with. It does no good to ask for a credit card number, however, since you cannot legally cover a bad check with a customer's credit card. (You might ask to *see* a card, however, as this is just one more form of identification.) When taking a stranger's check, here are four other things you should do:

1. Be cautious about accepting checks that do not have a name and address imprinted on them.
2. Phony checks are generally smooth on all four sides, so look to see if the check is perforated on at least one side.
3. Check the routing number in the lower left-hand corner. The ink on a bad check will look shiny and slightly raised, whereas the magnetic ink used on a good check will not reflect light. (Wet your finger and touch the ink if you're not sure. If it rubs off, refuse the check.)
4. Notice the check number. An expert on this topic says that more than 1.2 million bad checks are written daily in the United States, and 90 percent of them are numbered 101 to 200. This is not to say that all low-numbered checks are suspect; some may actually be new accounts. But if a low-numbered check also has no address printed on it, that's another red flag to consider.

See also Bad Check Collection Strategies *and* Scams, Home Business.

COD Shipments

Q: *What are the advantages and disadvantages of shipping merchandise COD?*

Shipping COD (collect, or cash, on delivery) to first-time buyers has become standard policy in the crafts industry. Although this can be a great solution for how to deal with customers you feel uncomfortable about invoicing, it is not without problems. While you can ship COD to an individual buyer or small shop, this is not an option when you're shipping to a hospital gift shop, department store, or catalog company. Some crafters have a policy that first orders from all new accounts must be shipped COD, but others specify "No CODs" on their order form because they don't want the hassles involved with such orders.

"Sometimes you ship COD and get the package back, which means you're out the shipping charges," explains a professional crafter who often ships COD to questionable wholesale buyers. To avoid problems, she always calls the customer before shipping an order COD. "I tell them it's ready, give them the amount they need to have on hand, and ask them if it's okay to ship today."

This is a good idea for accounts you know, but this method leaves you at risk if you're dealing with a new customer whose check might bounce, or one of the con artists who run COD scams at craft fairs. Here, the only way to protect yourself is to check the box on the COD form that says you will accept "Cash or Money Order Only." (Both UPS and the Postal Service will accept cash, but the post office won't handle any COD package valued at more than $600.) Your customer, not you, should pay the extra amount involved in sending the order COD, and some sellers add a note to this effect on their price list and order form. (Note: UPS will collect these charges for you, but if you ship by mail, the post office will collect only for the value of the goods in the box, not for postage or COD charges.)

Author and publisher Bernard Kamoroff, who has been stung by COD con artists in the past, offers this advice to others: "Be suspicious of large orders from unknown businesses, from businesses that don't have preprinted letterheads and purchase orders, and from businesses that don't list phone numbers. We always call Directory Assistance to see if a business is listed. And, like the old gambler's warning, we never ship more books than we can afford to lose. When you are dealing with hustlers, collection threats and demanding letters never work. Those people just laugh at you."

See also Bad Check Collection Strategies *and* Scams, Home Business.

Tip

If a customer asks you to send a shipment COD and it is packed in more than one carton or box, be sure to put a COD tag on each carton. A reader reported that a customer who ordered five cases of products returned the one case bearing her COD tag marked "delivery refused" but kept the other four cases and never paid for them.

Collateral

Q: *What collateral can I use to back up my business loan request?*

Collateral is security pledged for a loan, and banks are interested only in assets they may hold or assume to insure repayment of a loan. This generally includes property, stocks, bonds, savings accounts, life insurance, and current business assets. If an account owes you a considerable amount of money and you need to borrow money because their invoice hasn't been paid, the bank may consider the unpaid invoice as collateral for a loan.

Collection Agencies

Q: *How do collection agencies work, what does it cost to use one, and is this an effective way for a small business to collect accounts?*

When you decide you have done everything possible to collect unpaid invoices, you don't have much to lose by letting a collection agency try to collect for you. Understand at the beginning, however, that it may take up to a year for an agency to collect even half the unpaid accounts you send them. Be careful to select a reputable agency to begin with. A crafts manufacturer in my network told me about the problems she had with an agency: "When they solicited my business,

I gave them $7,000 worth of unpaid invoices to try to collect," she said. "But I had a hard time trying to get reports of how they were doing, and my phone calls often went unanswered. When they did talk to me, I was told accounts had been collected but it was weeks or months before I received any money from them. A year later, they had collected only half of the money I had hoped to receive, and by then some of the companies had gone out of business and other accounts were just too old to try to collect. I have since learned that not all collection agencies are reputable."

All the better agencies belong to the American Collectors Association (**www.Collector.com**), so before signing with an agency, ask if they are a member. Members of this association will collect accounts locally or nationally. (Out-of-state accounts are passed on to a member collection agency in the appropriate state.) All members of the American Collectors Association make regular ninety-day reports back to the originating agency. Agencies normally take 40 percent of a local account or 50 percent if the collection is made by a member agency.

See also Bad Check Collection Strategies; Invoices Not Paid; *and* Small Claims Court.

Tip

Some of the home-business/home office organizations listed in this book offer low-cost collection and credit reporting services to their members. If so, this service would be described in the organization's membership brochure.

Computer System, Purchase Tips

Q: *I'm ready to purchase a computer system for my business, but I feel so overwhelmed by all the choices available to me. How can I make the right buying decision?*

Computer buyers no longer have much choice in our Microsoft-Windows dominated world. One either buys an Apple/Macintosh or a standard PC clone. And when you buy a PC, you also get whatever Windows operating system Microsoft happens to be pushing at the time. Giving computer-buying advice is beyond my ability, but you'll find about four million Web pages on this topic if you just do a search for "computer buying tips" on Yahoo! or Google. Any newsstand or bookstore will also offer an assortment of magazines that give advice on how to buy a computer system and software that's right for you.

NOTE: When you buy a system "off the shelf" from your local computer store, you have to take whatever programs come with it, but you have many options when ordering a computer on the Web or from a catalog from a major company such as Dell or Gateway. Here, you can order a system made to your specifications regarding size of hard drive, backup system, type of disc drives, and monitor. Pay attention to the support you will have when you have questions or run into technical problems. Often, the support offered by computer companies and software suppliers is free for only a limited time, after which it becomes very costly to get help on the telephone. Therefore, it is prudent to find someone locally you can call for help when you need it.

See also Computer, Value to Business; Health Hazards; *and* Surge Suppressor.

Tip

Ideally, the dealer from whom you buy your machine will also be equipped to repair it in the event of problems. If you buy a computer from a discount store such as Best Buy, however, repairs could take up to two weeks due to the huge volume of repair work done on all the electronic equipment sold in these stores—an important consideration if you couldn't be without your computer for that long a period. For several helpful computer articles and a link to the affordable online computer repair service I now use, check the "Computertalk" department of my website at **www.BarbaraBrabec.com**.

Computer, Value to Business

Q: *I've gotten along for years without a computer. Besides giving me e-mail and access to the World Wide Web, what else would a computer do for my small homebased business?*

It's true that many small business owners are still struggling along without the help of a computer. Sooner or later, however, you will have to become computer literate if you hope to stay abreast of your competition or merely in control of your business. In a few words, a computer will save you time, money, and aggravation, lower your stress level (once you're past the learning stage), and add excitement to your life. Professional artists, crafters, and other home-business owners have learned to use computer technology to manage their business (correspondence, bookkeeping, inventory control, mail list development); design printed materials (stationery, flyers, brochures, catalogs, hang tags, and labels); market their work (by e-mail, through their own website or other retail sites on the Web); develop new designs (many software programs are now available—read computer magazines to learn about them); and explore self-publishing opportunities (newsletters, directories, magazines, or books).

I've stated a computer will save you time. Let me qualify that statement by saying a computer will not save the kind of time that affords you more leisure; rather, it will enable you to do more for your business. Like capital plowed back into a growing business, time saved by computer technology is similarly used. For example, you might be able to produce twice as many products for sale if you could cut in half the amount of time you currently spend on paperwork, record-keeping, accounting, and correspondence related to your business.

Even more important than increased profitability and greater efficiency in a business, perhaps, is the surprising impact a computer tends to make on one's personal life. Many of my readers have told me how using a computer has helped them to discover creative and organizational abilities they didn't realize they had. Others have explained how conquering their computer gave them new confidence in their abilities and automatically led them into exciting businesses. Individuals once hampered by the demands of a typewriter have suddenly found themselves able to write, design, and brainstorm on a computer. My research indicates that an individual's initial fear of computer technology is seldom justified. With time and patience—and the desire to do so—anyone can master a computer and learn to use it productively in both their homebased business and personal lives.

Tip

The real secret to success is wanting to do a particular thing and having a good reason for doing it. Once you get to that point, you're halfway there. Change doesn't come easy and, without a major shift in your attitude, it cannot even be accepted as a possibility. You must first embrace the idea of change, then accept with a positive attitude the stress that is likely to accompany any intense period of learning.

Consignment Agreement

Q: *A shop in my area has invited me to place work on consignment. How can I make sure I get paid for everything of mine that sells?*

First, make sure you have a written consignment agreement. If the shop doesn't have a consignment agreement, create it yourself and make sure the shop's owner signs it. In addition to a complete list of all items being left on consignment, a good agreement will include the following things, not necessarily in this order:

- the owner's name and telephone number
- the length of time items are to be displayed and any special display requirements you may have (i.e., "do not place in sunny window")
- what insurance, if any, is offered to seller
- the percentage of the retail selling price the shop or gallery will receive on each item it sells (may vary from 30–50 percent)
- a stipulation that items may not be sold for less than the retail price you have indicated; or, if they are, you will receive your share of the higher selling price (*see also gallery pricing TIP below*)
- when you will receive payments (usually monthly, with a report of which items have been sold)
- if products are being sent by mail or UPS, who pays for shipping expenses (Ideally, costs will be equally shared by shop and seller.)
- how merchandise will be returned to seller if the shop no longer wants to carry it (Some shops have a clause in their contracts stating they can dispose of unsold merchandise if it is

not claimed within thirty to sixty days after a notice has been sent to the consignor.)
- a detailed list of the individual items (and their prices) being consigned to the shop. (Ideally, each of your products will bear a product code number the shop can use when it reports the sale of that item. As each item sells, cross it off the list and update the list as replacement merchandise is taken in.)

A discussion of the pros and cons of consignment selling will be found in this book's marketing companion, *Handmade for Profit*.

See also Consignment Laws; Insurance, on Crafts Merchandise Off-Premise; Inventory; Labels or Tags Required by Law; Sales Commissions; *and* Shop Failures.

Tip

If selling through an art gallery, ask who sets the retail price and whether the gallery assumes the right to discount the price or put an item on sale. The store and the artist should also agree on whether the agreement is exclusive or nonexclusive (that is, whether other stores in the area will carry the same item or not). For more specific help in creating a mutually successful consignment arrangement, a search on Google for "consignment agreements, art galleries" or "art consignment agreement" will turn up thousands of Web pages offering advice on how to write a good agreement.

Consignment Laws

Q: *I'm interested in consigning products to some out-of-state shops, but I'm a bit concerned about doing this because I can't physically keep an eye on my merchandise. What kind of legal protection do I have for products I've sent out on consignment?*

Consigned goods normally. remain the property of the seller until they are sold to the retail customer. However, if an establishment goes bankrupt, merchandise left on consignment may be subject to the claims of creditors and be seized by them unless certain protective steps have been taken by consignors. (A standard consignment agreement is not enough to protect you in this instance.)

Several states have consignment laws designed to protect artists and craftspeople. Those known to me are Alaska, Arizona, Arkansas, California, Colorado, Connecticut, Florida, Idaho, Illinois, Iowa, Kentucky, Massachusetts, Michigan, Minnesota, Missouri, Montana, New Hampshire, New Jersey, New Mexico, New York, North Carolina, Ohio, Oregon, Pennsylvania, Tennessee, Texas, Washington, and Wisconsin.

The pitfall in state consignment laws is that some states protect only "art" and may exclude protection to items that fall outside the area of painting, sculpture, drawing, graphic arts, pottery, weaving, batik, macrame, quilting, or "other commonly recognized art forms." Each state with a law on the books has a different interpretation of "art," and other states not listed above may or may not have a consignment law at all. For those reasons, everyone interested in selling on consignment should contact their state legislature for more information. You may also be able to turn up information about your state's consignment law on the Web.

See also Consignment Agreement.

Consumer Safety Laws

Q: *I plan to make toys for children, but I'm concerned about how to make them safe. What can I do to avoid legal problems here?*

The Consumer Product Safety Commission (CPSC), established by *The Consumer Product Safety Act of 1972,* enforces mandatory safety standards for consumer products sold in the United States. You should request free information from this agency if you (1) make toys or other products for children; (2) make garments (particularly children's wear); or (3) use any kind of paint, varnish, lacquer, or shellac on your products. One of the agency's most active regulatory programs is in the area of toys and consumer goods designed for children. Of most concern to craftspeople are these CPSC regulations:

- The small-parts requirement, which prohibits small parts that could be a choking hazard in toys and articles for children under three years of age

- The sharp-edge and sharp-point requirements that describe tests for identifying hazardously sharp edges and points in toys and articles for children under eight years of age
- Requirements for rattles to ensure that the ends or handles of rattles are large enough so they cannot enter a child's mouth and throat and cause choking
- Flammability requirements for toys that state a limit on the burning rate (Toys that pass this test may still ignite and burn, but they will not burn explosively.)

The Federal Hazardous Substances Act addresses products that are toxic, corrosive, an irritant, or a strong sensitizer, but these types of hazards are rare among toys and children's articles. If your toys (or other consumer products that might fall into the hands of children) are finished with paint, varnish, lacquer, or shellac, however, see the discussion under *Paints, Varnishes, and Other Finishes* for safety precautions you can take to avoid problems.

In summary, to be legally safe, *be careful.* All toys and other products for children should be (1) too large to be swallowed; (2) not apt to break easily or leave jagged edges; (3) free of sharp edges or points (including exposed pins, wires, or nails); (4) nontoxic, nonflammable, and nonpoisonous.

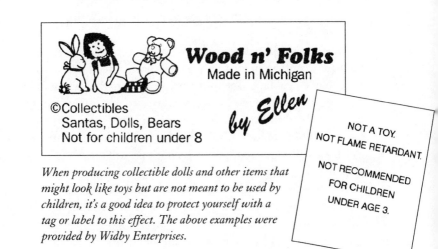

Wood n' Folks
Made in Michigan

©Collectibles
Santas, Dolls, Bears
Not for children under 8

by Ellen

NOT A TOY.
NOT FLAME RETARDANT.

NOT RECOMMENDED FOR CHILDREN UNDER AGE 3.

When producing collectible dolls and other items that might look like toys but are not meant to be used by children, it's a good idea to protect yourself with a tag or label to this effect. The above examples were provided by Widby Enterprises.

A wealth of consumer product information is available from the Consumer Product Safety Commission's toll-free Hotline, and several publications related to toys and children's products are offered. When you call 1-800-638-2772, you will get a menu of several extensions you can punch to order publications of interest or report your dissatisfaction with any product or service you've purchased. One extension will connect you with CPSC's Small Business Ombudsman department, which offers information to help small business owners comply with CPSC statues and regulations or solve problems related to them. Information is also available on the website at www.CPSC.gov.

See also Fabrics, Flammability Standards; Lead Testing; Paints, Varnishes, and Other Finishes; *and* Insurance, Product Liability.

Contracts and Legal Agreements

Q: *Must a contract be in writing to be legal?*

Technically, unless a contract is for the sale of goods over a certain amount (which varies from state to state), a verbal contract is just as legal and binding as a written one. The problem with a verbal agreement, however, is that it is difficult if not impossible to prove in court. It makes much more sense to "get it in writing," and this is very easy to do.

Whenever you make a simple verbal agreement with anyone, immediately confirm in writing what has been agreed upon. You don't have to use legal language to create a document that will stand up in court. Just state the facts clearly. Send two copies of your letter to the party involved and ask him or her to sign, date, and return one copy to you as confirmation of the facts stated. Voilà—a contract. (Enclosing a self-addressed, stamped envelope will encourage a speedy response.)

If you are entering into a more complicated legal arrangement with someone—such as a book publisher or a manufacturer who wants to mass produce one of your products—be sure to have the contract checked by an attorney familiar with the particular field involved. (An attorney friend who specializes in real estate deals may be inexpensive but unlikely to be familiar with the ins and outs of book publishing or selling designs.) Also remember that contracts aren't written in stone. If you are ever offered a "standard contract" that contains unacceptable clauses, don't blindly sign away your rights without first trying to negotiate those clauses.

See also Attorney/Lawyer; Author/Publisher Contract; Consignment Agreement; Maintenance Agreements; *and* Sales Representatives.

Tip

It's expensive to file a lawsuit out-of-state, so whenever you are negotiating a contract with an out-of-state company, make sure it contains a clause that gives you the right to litigate or file a lawsuit in your own state's courts.

Copyright Categories of Protection

Q: *What can and cannot be protected by copyright, and what's the difference between a copyright, patent, and trademark?*

Here is an example to help you remember the difference: The *artwork* on a can of cola can be copyrighted. The *name—and the way it is expressed on that can—*can be trademarked. The *formula* for the cola itself can be patented.

Ideas themselves cannot be protected by a copyright, but you may protect your *expression of an idea* by copyright if it is in tangible form, such as a design, pattern, or other written or drawn material. Some creativity and originality must be incorporated into a work for it to be copyrightable, however. For example, you cannot copyright a common form, shape, or object such as a circle, triangle, heart, rose, or butterfly, but you *can* create original designs that incorporate such common forms, shapes, and objects. You cannot stop anyone else from using the same common forms, shapes, or objects in their own designs, however. For example, six artists could paint a picture of a butterfly sitting on a rose, and each artist could copyright his or her own original picture.

To further illustrate, you can copyright the design on a craft object when that design can be identified separately from the object itself, but you cannot copyright an ordinary object such as a ring, a plate, a coffee mug, or a box. You cannot copyright anything that has fallen into public domain, but you can make and copyright your own adaptation (see *Copyrights in Public Domain*). Names, titles, and short phrases may not be copyrighted, but may qualify for trademark protection. Although inventions are protected by patents, the written description or drawing of an invention can also be protected by copyright.

Different copyright forms must be used to protect different forms of intellectual property, which falls into five main categories of interest to homebased business owners:

1. SERIALS (use Form SE). This category includes periodicals, newspapers, magazines, bulletins, newsletters, annuals, journals, and proceedings of societies.

2. TEXT (use Form TX). Included in this category are books, directories, and any other kind of text or work written in words, such as how-to instructions for a crafts project.

3. VISUAL ARTS (use Form VA). This category is used to register pictorial, graphic, or sculptural works, including fine, graphic and applied art, photographs, charts, technical drawings, diagrams, and models.

4. PERFORMING ARTS (use Form PA). Included in this category are musical works and accompanying words, dramatic works, pantomimes, choreographic works, motion pictures, and other audiovisual works.

5. SOUND RECORDINGS (use Form SR). This category includes musical, spoken, or other sounds.

See also Book Copyright; Copyright Registration; Copyrights in Public Domain; Patent; *and* Trademark.

Copyright "Fair Use" Doctrine

Q: *Who can copy my work under the "fair use" doctrine, and how much of it can they use without permission?*

Anyone can make limited use of your work without permission as long as the material is being used for research, teaching, or in connection with news reporting, criticism, or comment—but only if such use does not affect the potential market for, or value of, the copyrighted work. For example, a writer may quote briefly from a book you have copyrighted if he or she gives you credit for it. A teacher may copy a small portion of your written work or one of your patterns or designs, *provided it is used just once, for one class.* However, this copy must bear your copyright notice, and the teacher does not have the right to use your material more than once without your permission.

See also Copyright Infringement and Copyrights of Others.

Copyright-Free Designs

Q: *I have no artistic ability and can't even draw a straight line, so how can I compete in today's craft marketplace if I can't create my own designs?*

You *can* create your own designs! You may not think of yourself as an "artist," but don't ever say you are not creative or artistic. God gave all of us our own special streak of creativity or artistry—we simply need to discover it. Often, creativity is the discovery of something that's been there all along. Your special artistry may lie in such areas as your ability to arrange a bouquet of flowers, decorate a Christmas tree, or run a sewing machine.

I'm always amused by people who say they can't draw because every one of us drew pictures as children and thought they were wonderful. Some people have built businesses on childlike (sometimes called "primitive") designs, so stop berating yourself for your inability to draw a picture or design that looks like other people's art and start creating your own kind of art. If you need help, ask one of your young children or grandchildren for advice, and always remember that "art" is in the eye of the beholder.

Tip

If you can use a pair of scissors or move a pencil around, you can create original designs simply by adapting or mixing design motifs from the copyright-free design books published by Dover Publications. For more information on these books, see article, "Where to Find Copyright-Free Designs and Motifs."

Where to Find Copyright-Free Designs and Motifs

Thousands of copyright-free designs are available from Dover Publications, publisher of a series of inexpensive design books called the *Pictorial Archives* (**www.DoverPublications.com**). Each of these paperback books contains hundreds of design motifs you can use in any manner or place you wish, without further payment, permission, or acknowledgment. (If you don't have Internet access, request a free catalog from: Dover Publications, 31 East 2nd Street, Mineola, NY 11501-3852.)

Anyone who claims they "can't draw a straight line" will appreciate these books and soon discover they *can* add their own creative ideas to a design or pattern created by someone else. Throughout history, artists have studied the work of others for inspiration and ideas, often lifting or adapting the best ideas of someone else for their own use. You can, too. The *Pictorial Archive* books offer a real treasure of usable patterns, ideas, and authentic motifs from many cultures, including American Indian, Japanese, Chinese, African, Mexican, Russian and East European, North African, Egyptian, and so on. The series also includes books on American folk art, flora and fauna, geometric design and ornament, and Art Deco.

Copyright Infringement

Q: *Someone has stolen something I have copyrighted. What can I do to stop them from profiting from my creativity, and where can I go for help in doing this?*

First, a definition of "copyright infringement." This occurs whenever anyone violates the exclusive rights covered by copyright. It requires only "substantial similarity" to establish infringement, and the penalties can be high ($100,000 or more) if the infringement has affected the profits of the copyright owner. One copyright attorney says the test for infringement of copyright "is whether an ordinary observer, looking at your work and the work you claim is an infringement, would say that one work was copied from the other."

When you learn that someone has infringed one of your copyrights, the first consideration is whether you have filed a formal copyright registration of the work in question. Under present law, you cannot sue anyone who copies or infringes upon your copyright unless or until you have formally registered your copyright with the Copyright Office. Although you can file the registration after you discover the infringer, late registration will limit the kind of damages you can sue for. (This could change, however. In the past, there has been a movement in Congress to abolish the requirement that one must register a copyright in order to sue for infringement. If this ever becomes law, it will be almost impossible for anyone to investigate the copyright status of a work, and we will all have to presume everything is copyrighted.)

OPPOSITE: These illustrations are but a tiny sampling of what you will find in Dover's Pictorial Archive books. Several hundred titles are available, giving artists and craftspeople access to more than 250,000 copyright-free images (many in full color) that may be used without permission. Illustrations shown here were clipped from the following books: (a) Folk Designs from the Caucusus for Weaving and Needlework; (b) 390 Traditional Stained Glass Designs; (c) 1001 Cartoon-Style Illustrations; (d) Plants and Flowers; (e) 2,286 Traditional Stencil Designs; (f) Carousel Animals Cut & Use Stencils; (g) Designs and Patterns for Embroiderers and Craftspeople; (h) Modern Monograms: 1310 Graphic Designs; (i) Traditional Floral Designs and Motifs for Artists and Craftspeople; (j) Old-Time Silhouettes.

Coping With Copycats

"A big problem the craft world faces is that there is so much duplication of designs," a basketmaker told me. "Any new idea is quickly copied by crafters and then offered for sale at lower prices. Before long, you can see the same item at every other booth in every craft show around." What's interesting about this statement is that I first heard it thirty years ago. Nothing has changed in this department, except that people have become more bold in their copying.

Every craft seller hates them: the people who saunter up to a booth, pull out paper and pencil, and begin to copy the designs found on exhibited products, or worse, snap pictures. One crafter told me that at the last show she did, there were signs around the building stating "PLEASE: NO PHOTOS OR SKETCHES," but people ignored them, and she had two people in her booth sketching her work.

Another crafter reported in a magazine article that she has had some very rude and inconsiderate people stand in her booth and draw right in front of her. "I made them mad when I asked them to leave my booth," she said, "but at least they left."

Try this: If you see someone with a camera taking pictures of you or your booth, ask for identification. Unless that person is with a newspaper or magazine, tell him or her to stop taking pictures at once. If your craft designs are copyrighted, emphasize that you have the legal right to sue anyone who copies your designs.

The minute you put a good idea out there, the public will copy it. So the secret is to come up with new ideas every year because then you'll be ahead of the copycats. By the time they get around to copying you, you have new merchandise. Or, as one crafter puts it, "As soon as you have a new design or product, get it out there and saturate your market area, all the while dreaming up something new or a new twist on the old."

— An excerpt from *Handmade for Profit—Hundreds of Secrets to Success in Selling Arts and Crafts* by Barbara Brabec (2nd ed., M. Evans).

This is particularly true where cyberspace is concerned. If you are using the Internet, you must assume that *everything* on the Internet and World Wide Web is protected by copyright laws. This means you cannot pick up graphic designs, art illustrations, articles, and other material for posting to your website, e-mailing to others, or downloading to your printer for your own profitable use. The illegal distribution of copyrighted material over the Web or your illegal use of it off the Web could open you up to a lawsuit.

Where do you go for help when someone steals *your* creativity? Because the Copyright Office is prohibited from giving legal advice or opinions about your rights in connection with cases of alleged copyright infringement, your only options when trying to stop a copyright infringer are to (1) send a letter asking them to stop; or (2) hire a copyright attorney to do this for you and pursue the matter beyond that point, if necessary. If you are dealing with an individual who has innocently infringed your copyright, a friendly, yet strongly worded letter from you may be all it takes to resolve the matter. (It will carry more weight if it is typed on impressive stationery that at least gives the illusion you can afford to sue if necessary.) Explain that, as the legal copyright owner, you alone have the right to profit from the work in question and that you will take any legal steps necessary to protect your rights. Ask for a reply by return mail confirming that the infringement will cease at once. In many cases, this will do the trick. If you've been ripped off by a large corporation, however, skip the friendly letter and contact a copyright attorney at once. It won't cost much to have an attorney write a letter for you, but to proceed further than this will be costly.

In the end, you must ask yourself how valuable your work is to you and how much time and money you are willing to invest to protect it. I recall a very successful doll designer who quit the crafts business after years of doing battle in court with copyright infringers. They took all the joy out of her work, and legal costs took all the profits she had accumulated from several years of selling.

See also Copyright "Fair Use" Doctrine; Copyrights of Others; *and article, "Coping with Copycats."*

Tip

The best way to avoid copyright infringement problems is to follow the "Golden Rule" proposed by a United States Supreme Court justice: "Take not from others to such an extent and in such a manner that you would be resentful if they so took from you."

Copyright Notice

Q: *Does it do any good to put a copyright notice on something if I have no intention of filing a formal copyright claim?*

Copyright protection exists from the moment a work is created. Although a copyright notice is no longer required by law, it doesn't cost anything to attach a copyright notice to every original thing you create, so you should always do this. (Lack of a copyright notice only makes it easier for others to steal your creativity and claim "innocent infringement.") Even when you place a copyright notice on your original work (thereby announcing to the world your ownership of that work), you are not required by law to file a formal registration. A proper copyright notice includes three elements:

1. the word "copyright" or its abbreviation, "copr.," or the copyright symbol, ©
2. the year of first publication of the work (when it was first shown or sold to the public)
3. the name of the copyright owner. Sometimes the words "All Rights Reserved" will be added, meaning that copyright protection has been extended to include all of the Western Hemisphere. (*Example:* © 2006 by Barbara Brabec. All Rights Reserved.)

See also Copyright Categories of Protection *and* Copyright Infringement.

Tip

Place the copyright notice where it can be seen. You can stamp copyright notices, cast them, engrave them, paint them, etch them, stitch them, print them, or write notices by hand. If you create fabric crafts, you can order custom-designed fabric labels that bear your copyright notice, logo, or any other information you wish to include. (See *Hang Tags and Designer Labels.*)

Copyright Registration

Q: *How do I register a copyright claim and how much does this cost?*

Currently, it costs $30 to file a copyright claim, and this is easy to do. Application forms include instructions on how to complete the form and they may be ordered by mail by telephoning the Copyright Office in Washington, D.C. You can also get copyright forms in PDF format online at **www.copyright.gov/forms/**. (Fill-in versions may be completed online and then printed, but to save forms, you must use the full version of Adobe Acrobat, which you can quickly download from the above Web page.)

When you call the Copyright Office's recorded information system at 1-202-707-3000, you will get a menu of recorded messages you can hear, one of which will enable you to order copyright publications or forms by mail. You can also speak directly to an information specialist if you have a technical question. Note, however, that the Copyright Office cannot give you legal advice or opinions (see discussion under *Copyright Infringement*).

A copyright should be registered within three months of the "publication date," which is the date you first sell, display, give away, or otherwise distribute the copyrighted work to the public. Although it is not necessary to formally register a copyright claim, there is a "Mandatory Deposit Requirement" for all work bearing a copyright notice. There is no charge for this, and no forms to complete. You simply mail two copies of the work to the Library of Congress. For more information, request the Copyright Office's bulletin on this topic.

See also Copyright Categories of Protection *and articles,* "Copyrights: Registering a Collection of Work" *and* "The Cabbage Patch Kids® Story."

Tip

With your copyright application form, you are required to send two copies of the best edition of any printed work. When registering three-dimensional objects, you need only send photographs (preferably 8 x 10 inches) or accurate drawings of the designs or patterns you wish to protect by copyright.

Copyrights:
Registering a Collection of Work

Instead of filing separate copyright forms for each design, pattern, or other written work you wish to protect, you can save money by registering them as a collection, with one application form and fee. To do this, all work must be from one author or creator, be assembled in an orderly fashion, and bear a single title that identifies the collection as a whole.

I met designer/writer Linda Fry Kenzle many years ago at a local print shop when she was in the process of preparing her first designs for submission to the Copyright Office. She had photocopied each design, one to a page, then turned the resulting pages into a book by adding a front and back cover of a stock heavier than the paper inside. The printer drilled three holes in it so she could bind the book. Linda's illustrations below first appeared in my newsletter, but her idea is as timely today as it was when first published. (Linda now has several published listed books on Amazon.com.)

See also Copyright Registration.

Copyrights in Public Domain

Q: *How long does a copyright last, and how can I tell if something is now in public domain?*

Generally, the copyright on all works created after January 1, 1978 lasts for the life of the author or creator plus seventy years after his/

her death. For works created before 1978, there are different terms. (More detailed information can be found in these Copyright Office publications: Circular 15a [*Duration of Copyright*] and Circular 1 [*Copyright Basics*].) Material falls into public domain when the copyright has expired or has not been claimed by another, and once in public domain, material can never by copyrighted again. Examples of work in public domain include designs on ancient objects in

---

The Cabbage Patch Kids® Story

In 1980, a Georgia dollmaker named Martha Nelson Thomas entered a million-dollar suit against Xavier Roberts and his licensed Hong Kong manufacturer and distributor, Coleco Industries, Inc., for "pirating" her soft sculpture *Doll Babies*. Four years later, Martha settled out of court for an undisclosed sum. By then, Roberts' dolls, named *Cabbage Patch Kids*®, had become a $10.4 billion toy industry that gave Roberts even greater profits in the years that followed. Martha later enjoyed financial success as the designer of a plastic doll head that a manufacturer reproduced in several variations.

At the heart of this lawsuit was the fact that Xavier Roberts had filed a copyright on his doll and Martha hadn't, which brings me to the point I wish to emphasize here: *Only the person with the registered copyright has the right to profit from it, whether that person is the original creator or not.* By failing to protect her dolls with a copyright, Martha left the door open for someone else to take them, the judge pointed out.

The popularity of these dolls prompted many crafters to make "Cabbage Patch look-alikes," and at one point, Roberts was suing people right and left for selling such items. If you are selling a soft sculpture doll that has been "inspired" by a copyrighted doll on the marketplace, be forewarned: If anyone can see a resemblance between your doll and another's, there may be sufficient grounds for a lawsuit.

See also Copyright Infringement.

---

museums or fairy-tale characters and other designs found in old books. One author of a book on copyright suggests that anything showing a copyright date more than seventy-five years ago is probably in the public domain. If in doubt, however, a copyright search can be made. (Obtain Circular 22, *How to Investigate the Copyright Status of a Work*, from the Copyright Office.)

In an article for *The Crafts Report,* attorney Leonard D. DuBoff once explained that no one could be stopped from copying a Tiffany lamp design in the public domain. "If you become creative when copying the Tiffany lamp and make substantial changes in the design," he said, "then your changes are copyrightable by you. Nobody can copy your adaptation, although they can work from the original and make their own variation." (Other copyright articles by Leonard D. Duboff can be found on the Web at **www .BusinessLaw.com.**)

Quilt designs offer an interesting example. You may have noticed the same quilt designs in several books. Because the old traditional quilt patterns were created before copyright laws were a reality, these works automatically fell into public domain. This means anyone can include traditional quilt patterns in yet another book and copyright the book. In effect, however, they are not copyrighting these old patterns themselves, *but merely the book and the way the patterns have been presented to readers.* Thus a contemporary quilt designer could take a log cabin design and make unique or dramatic design changes resulting in a new work that could be protected by copyright.

I have often been asked whether it's okay to use common expressions or sayings such as those being reproduced on scores of plaques, pictures, and sweatshirts today. Most are likely to be in public domain or could not qualify for copyright given their commonality. However, the *manner* in which such sayings are affixed to an object may be protected by copyright. For example, I believe several sellers might be able to get copyright protection for their own rendition of a common expression found on a plaque or sweatshirt simply by arranging letters or words in a unique way or adding special background art.

Note that I just said "I believe," meaning I don't know for sure. Copyright law is a complex topic. Although I am an "informed layperson," you must use all my remarks on this topic only as a guideline. Check your library for books on this topic by copyright attorneys and *always* get professional advice before entering the commercial marketplace with any product that is partly based on someone else's creativity.

See also Copyright-Free Designs.

Copyrights of Others

Q: *I am concerned about violating the copyrights of others, but I'm not sure what I need to do—or not do—to avoid legal confrontations with copyright owners. Would you offer some simple guidelines?*

As you work to protect your own intellectual property, you must also be concerned about violating the rights of others. To avoid problems, here are several things you should *not* do:

• Do not copy whole sections of any book for use as a handout in one of your classes. This is a serious violation of copyright law. (See also discussion under *Copyright "Fair Use" Doctrine.*)

• Do not use in a publication or on any product the poems or poetry of others without written permission. The use of an entire poem is a flagrant violation of copyright law because it represents the use of a whole work of an individual creator who is receiving no financial benefit from such usage.

• Do not reproduce for sale any part of any picture, photograph, painting, or piece of artwork you may have purchased. You may own the original object, but the creator still owns the copyright, and only he or she has the right to copy it as prints, postcards, greeting cards, calendars, etc., or grant the right to copy to someone else in the form of a license. (See *Licensing Arrangements.*)

• Do not make any item bearing a replica of any famous person or movie star. The fact that they are long dead does not mean others can capitalize on their fame. (This topic is discussed under the listing for *Celebrity Rights Act.*)

• Do not copy the designs on other handcrafted products and commercial gift items. All manufacturers and most professional craft sellers protect their work by copyrights or design patents and stand ready to take legal action against copyright violators. (Don't think you can get around this by changing some part of the design, using a different color or material, or turning a two-dimensional design into a three-dimensional object. The Copyright Office says a work is a copy if it repeats a "substantial part" of someone else's design, and many people have gone to court to define "substantial part.")

• *Never, ever* make anything for sale that bears a famous copyrighted character such as Snoopy, the Sesame Street gang, or Walt Disney characters. The fact that you see others doing this does not mean it is legal to do. Crafters who choose to ignore this advice "because everyone else is doing it" are inviting hefty fines or lawsuits. The Disney people are particularly aggressive in defending their copyrights.

• Do not *wholesale* items made from fabric that bears a copyright notice on the selvage. (See *Fabrics (Designer), Commercial Use of* for a lengthy discussion about this.)

• Do not photocopy patterns for sale or trade because all patterns are protected by copyright, and your distribution of photocopies denies the creator the profit from copies that might have been sold. (For a lengthy discussion of the other copyright problems related to the use of patterns found in magazines or purchased in fabric stores or mail order catalogs, see *Patterns, Commercial Use of.*)

• Do not use rubber stamps to create a product or design you plan to sell until you have contacted the rubber stamp designer or manufacturer to get permission to do this. In a survey of many rubber stamp manufacturers, the editors of *Craft Supply Magazine* (now out of print) reported on their findings: "The overall feeling was that companies will allow a single artist or PC (professional crafter) to use the companies' copyrighted images for the single artist's or PC's work if the image is hand stamped." While this suggests it is okay for the individual crafter to sell products with rubber stamp designs on them if they personally stamp the products themselves (*i.e.,* don't use employees to do it), it's important to remember that the policies of one stamp company may be entirely different from another, so to be safe, you should *always* get written permission to use rubber stamps for commercial purposes. (This includes the printed *images* of rubber stamps in a stamp company's catalog.) You must also be careful about using commercial rubber stamps on your printed materials. For an example of the kind of problems that can develop here, see the article, "Designer Paranoia."

Designer Paranoia

by Janet Burgess, AmazonDrygoods.com

I was using a rubber stamp company's images all over my envelopes (very funny and Victorian). When we outgrew having time to stamp, I had a large supply of envelopes printed with the designer's images. He gave his permission to do this in return for a free ad in our catalog that invited readers to send him a dollar to receive his catalog of rubber stamps. It was a nice trade-off until our envelopes were featured in a national trade journal for the direct marketing industry.

A business has no control over publicity like this, so when it happens I'm just delighted to receive it and glad if they get my name and address right. Well, the stamp company owner saw the article and just went crazy. The problem was that his name was not mentioned in this article, so his lawyer hit me with a demand for $10,000 in royalties to be paid annually, plus past royalties and damages. This problem cost me a great deal of time and money in legal fees. I was cleared on this because I had saved all correspondence on the matter and the stamp company's owner had saved nothing. I had not acted improperly other than inadvertently wounding his ego. In the end, I was forced to stop using the envelopes when my supply ran out, but they didn't get any money from me.

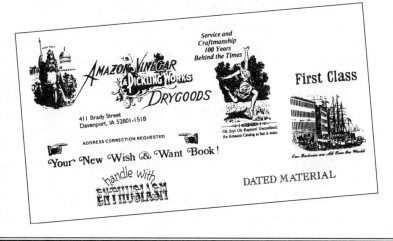

- Do not clip illustrations, artwork, or designs from any publication (especially magazines and catalogs) and use them to illustrate your own publication or printed materials. The only illustrations that are safe to use for commercial or business purposes are those being sold as commercial clip art, or designs and motifs found in the *Pictorial Archive* books published by Dover Publications (see *Copyright-Free Designs*).

I realize this is a lot of "do nots," but my goal here is to keep you out of legal trouble, and I know this is your goal, too.

See also Copyright Infringement.

Corporation

Q: *I've been advised to incorporate to gain protection for my personal assets in the event of a lawsuit. What do I need to consider where incorporation is concerned?*

A corporation is the most complicated form a business can take. If you feel incorporation of your crafts business is important, research the Web for articles on "incorporating a business" and also get professional advice from an attorney or accountant.

Corporations are of two types: "C" (general corporation) and "S" (Subchapter S). (Similar, but not the same, is an LLC [Limited Liability Company], which is discussed elsewhere.) While incorporation offers special legal advantages, it also involves extra paperwork and legal and accounting services. Unlike a partnership, a corporation is a legal entity unto itself that does not die with the retirement or death of its officers. Since it costs more to unincorporate a business than to incorporate it, you don't want to rush blindly in this direction until you have all the facts. Judith H. McQuown, author of *INC Yourself* (Bantam), says it may not be worth it to incorporate if your net business earnings are less than $25,000 or $30,000 a year.

Many small business owners mistakenly believe that incorporation of their business will give them automatic protection for their personal assets in the event of a lawsuit. For businesses with employees, incorporation does serve as a kind of door that can be shut in the event an employee does something wrong and causes a business to be sued. In that case, the owner's personal assets would be protected by the "corporation door." However, if you are the business owner and you personally commit a wrongful act that prompts a lawsuit, the "corporation door" remains open and you will be held liable for that act.

If several individuals or families are involved in a business, a C corporation or Subchapter S Corporation (see below) may be the best route to take. As a sole proprietor, however, it may be easier and less expensive simply to purchase liability insurance for your business.

Subchapter S Corporation. Many new and low-income businesses establish an S Corporation, which operates like a regular corporation except it is taxed like a partnership (at the lower personal rate). Profits or losses are reported on a shareholder's Form 1040. The owners of a party-plan business reported to me that incorporation under Subchapter S was a good solution for them. Although it didn't offer any product liability insurance, it did work to protect their personal and family properties. Given the relative safety of their inventory, their insurance agent said this type of protection should be adequate for them.

See also Insurance, Personal Liability; Limited Liability Company; Partnership; Sole Proprietorship; *and* Taxes.

Tip

A professional writer incorporated his business after nearly twenty years as a sole proprietor because he wanted to keep working after he was eligible for Social Security. By incorporating, he said, he could avoid giving his Social Security checks back to the government at the end of the year.

Cost of Advertising

To determine your advertising cost per lead, divide the dollars spent for advertising by the number of leads (buying prospects) generated. To determine cost per sale, divide the dollars you've spent to acquire leads and convert them to sales by the number of sales made. The formula looks like this:

$$ spent for advertising ÷ number of leads = cost per lead

$$ spent to acquire and convert leads ÷ number of sales = cost per sale

Cost of Goods

This figure is the total of purchase price of goods and any transportation or delivery costs involved.

See also Inventory.

Cottage Industry

Many people use this term loosely in connection with homebased businesses of all kinds, but a true cottage industry is a business that has a central marketing and management operation with production of craftwork done usually in the homes of people other than that of marketing and management.

See also Independent Contractors.

Craft Cooperative

Q: *Several of my friends and I have discussed the idea of starting a hand-craft cooperative, but we have no idea how to start such an organization. Should we pursue this idea?*

Crafters all over the country have formed craft cooperatives to gain marketing power and increase annual profits. Some simply band together as a group so they can buy craft supplies at a lower price or sell as a group at shows. Others set up formal organizations, operating as a partnership or corporation. In such cases, legal advice should be sought.

The success of a craft cooperative—or any organization, for that matter—depends on the willingness of members to contribute the time and energy necessary to get the group "up and running." Once things are rolling, new and existing members must understand the importance of sharing the workload. Many groups that I've monitored through the years have ultimately folded because a few individuals who didn't know how to say no took on too much work. This led not only to burnout for the individuals involved, but to feelings of anger toward those who weren't contributing their fair share.

I can't say whether you should start such an organization, but I've discussed the pros and cons of this topic in this book's companion marketing guide, *Handmade for Profit.* Included are examples of different types of marketing cooperatives and how they were formed and managed. Here are some co-op resources that may be helpful as well. The first two include good checklists of all the things involved in starting a cooperative, while the third includes a list of other resources on this topic:

- **Rural Cooperatives Center; www.cooperatives.ucdavis.edu**
- **The National Cooperative Business Association; www.ncba .org**
- **University of Wisconsin Center for Cooperatives; www.wisc .edu/uwcc**

See also Art/Craft Organizations *and* Organization, Formation of.

Craft Emergency Relief Fund (CERF)

Q: *I've heard that there is some financial help available to craftspeople whose businesses have been devastated by a natural disaster. How does one get this kind of help?*

CERF, a national nonprofit organization, offers direct financial and educational assistance to professional craft artists, including emergency relief assistance, business development support, and resources and referrals on topics such as health, safety, and insurance. (CERF defines "professional craft artists" as those whose primary source of income results from their personal production and sale of functional/ decorative handcrafted objects.) CERF has helped many craft professionals get back on their feet after they have suffered a devastating loss by offering no-interest loans and other services, such as booth fee waivers at craft shows and discounts on equipment and supplies. More information is available by calling 1-802-229-2306 or online at **www.craftemergency.org.**

Craft Displays, Fire Safety

If you plan to set up a display booth that involves walls, drapes, covers, and other flammable display materials, you need to be able to prove to local fire marshals that your materials have been treated to resist flames. This can be done either by showing them a certificate of compliance, or allowing them to do a field test. Depending on where you are exhibiting, the fire marshals may or may not show up, but professional sellers advise that preparation is always the best defense to insure a successful show.

Bruce Baker, an expert on booth design (**www.bbakerInc.com**), suggests always having extra material in your display that can be cut off for field testing. In an article for *The Crafts Report* (October 2004), he emphasized the importance of spraying all flammable display items with a nontoxic fire retardant, adding that "red flag" items include any booth material that hangs, as well as shredded paper and hay or straw around a booth. He also added that extension cords you've purchased at the local hardware store won't be allowed at most convention facilities.

Always discuss fire safety/flammability issues with the events coordinator of any show in which you are participating. Your local fire department can also answer other questions you may have about fire safety.

See also Fabrics, Flammability Standards.

Craft Fair Selling

This is one of most popular forms of selling for both beginning and long-established artists and crafters, and many listings in this book discuss topics related to this form of selling.

See also Brochure; Checking Account; Checks Taken at Shows; COD Shipments; Consumer Safety Laws; Custom Orders; Discounts; Home Office Deduction; Insurance, Vehicle; Inventory; Juried Shows; Labels or Tags

Required by Law; Merchant Account Providers; Patterns, Commercial Use of; Printed Materials; Sales Tax; *and* Show Listings.

Craft Mall Selling

Q: *I'm thinking about selling through craft malls, but I'm wondering if this is still a profitable way to sell high-quality handcrafts?*

Craft malls first appeared on the scene in 1988 when Rufus Coomer opened his first mall in Azle, Texas, then went on to open a chain of such stores across the country. By the end of 1995, with thirty malls in several states, Coomers had become the nation's largest retailer of American handmade crafts, gifts, and decorations for homes and offices. Through the years, however, crafters and buyers alike began to lose interest in craft malls, and many failed. Still, it came as quite a surprise to many in the crafts industry when the last six Coomers stores closed in 2005 with no explanation. No one in the crafts industry was able to get a statement directly from anyone in Coomers management, but an article in the *Houston Business Journal* (February 13, 2005) quoted one store manager in Houston as saying, "... the company's decision to close its stores came as a shock. Both craft malls were doing well and meeting their financial goals." The store manager added that it wasn't the craft mall concept that failed, but rather poor management by the malls' owners.

In discussing this with Barbara Arena, director of the National Crafts Association (**www.NCA.com**), she said the demise of Coomers wasn't likely to affect the craft mall industry one way or the other. "We've gotten some pretty good feedback from NCA members who are selling in malls and feel that they are an important part of their marketing mix. That said, those who are the most successful seem to be the ones who sell at craft malls close enough for them to monitor. This may also play a part in that they probably checked them out quite well before signing on."

In its heyday, Coomers set a high standard for the industry, and many entrepreneurs followed their lead by opening independent malls across the country. I have no idea how many of these malls still exist, but a Google search for "craft malls" yielded more than 300,000 Web pages as I was updating this book, so with some research, you can probably find several good outlets for your products. Although craft malls may remain a good outlet for many crafters, several professional craft sellers in my network report they have moved out of the malls and into other markets because they can't compete with the cheap imports and commercial gift lines being carried in most malls today.

See also Rent-a-Space Shops *and* Shop Failures.

Credit Card Sales

Q: *How much difference is it likely to make in my sales if I give customers the option of paying with a credit card?*

Most sellers have reported a 25–40 percent increase in sales once they begin to offer customers the privilege of charging purchases to a credit card. The profit from these increased sales will help to offset the fees you must pay to process credit cards, and if you get into wholesaling, these costs will increase as the dollar size of your sales increases. One wholesaler told me that, in years past, very few wholesalers paid by credit card, but today, between 50 and 75 percent of her sales are to credit cards, so be prepared when you do your first wholesale show. (She doesn't swipe cards at the show, but simply notes the customer's credit card number on the order form, and then processes the charge just prior to shipping the merchandise.)

Avoiding Bad Credit Cards. The chances for fraud are much less when you actually handle a person's credit card. Just make sure the card is signed, and if not, ask to see another form of photo identification. When taking orders on the phone or the Web from someone you don't know (especially a buyer in a foreign country), there are other things you can do to minimize fraud. First, take advantage of the Address Verification Software (AVS) that is built into most credit card processing machines. It's also part of the services offered by most merchant account providers. You should also ask for information from the back of the credit card you've been given, since someone who has stolen this card number won't have access to this information. (Specifically, ask for the three-digit code that appears on the back of every card and/or the name of the issuing bank.)

See also Internet and E-mail Scams; Merchant Account Providers; Terms of Sale; *and* Web Marketing Options.

Personal Credit Card Tips

Credit cards are one of life's greatest conveniences, but if you happen to lose them or let even one of your credit cards fall into the wrong hands, you may become a victim of identity theft—the number one scam today, according to the FTC (see *Identity Theft*). Here are some special things you should know about the use of credit cards:

• **Credit Card Insurance.** In spite of what you may be told by a smooth-talking salesperson who is selling credit card insurance, you don't need it, even when your card is lost, stolen, or illegally used by someone else. Under federal law, if you call the card issuer before unauthorized charges are made, you are automatically protected against loss. Even if you don't, you are liable for only $50 on each card (under the Fair Credit Billing Act). However, to make consumers more comfortable when shopping online, Visa, MasterCard, and American Express introduced zero-liability programs in 2001 that waived all consumer liability in case of online fraud.

Most of the credit card companies offer an inexpensive credit card and key tag/luggage registration service (about $15/year) that may be worthwhile if you have many cards that conceivably could all be lost or stolen at once. Such registration enables the service provider to immediately notify credit card companies of your loss, saving you the time it would take to do this yourself. If you haven't done the following, do it now: Make a list of every credit card you use, with complete information on whom to contact in the event of loss, and keep it up to date at all times. (Do not store this information on the computer you use to access the Web, however, as hackers could gain entry to this file.)

• **Credit Cards Used as Credit Reference.** When paying for a purchase with a check, some merchants (or craft fair sellers) may ask you to give them a credit card number for reference. This leaves you open to fraud, however, and by law you do not have to do this. Since merchants cannot legally cover bad checks with a credit card, there is no reason for them to have your credit card number. (It's okay to show a credit card as a credit reference; just don't let anyone copy the number.)

• **Telephone Solicitation.** Never give a credit card number to anyone on the phone who says they need to "verify a number for their records," or who has called you out of the blue to offer you some "special deal." In such cases, you are probably dealing with a con artist.

Credit History

If you do not have a personal credit history, this should be an immediate goal. If you're a married woman with a home business, be sure to open your business checking account in your name only. (If you add your husband's name, it becomes a joint account with credit history automatically going to his file.)

Some people are tearing up all their credit cards to avoid debt, but I believe it's a mistake not to have at least one credit card in your name you can use for business purposes. By charging business expenses to a credit card, you build not only a good paper trail of all transactions but a credit history in your name.

See also Credit Rating *and article, "Personal Credit Card Tips"*

Credit Rating

Q: *I need to check my credit rating, but I don't know how to get a copy of my credit report.*

By law, you are now able to get a free copy of your credit report once a year from each of the three credit reporting companies listed below. And be sure to get a report from all three agencies because you will find different information on each. Simply call 1-877-322-8228 or download the request form at **www.annualcreditreport.com**.

Credit bureaus used to serve local areas only, but thanks to computer technology, every credit bureau in the country now has access to everyone's credit information. There are over several hundred credit bureaus in the country but only three major credit rating firms:

Equifax: 1-800-685-1111; **www.Equifax.com**
Trans Union: 1-800-888-4213; **www.TUC.com**
Experian: 1-888-397-3742; **www.Experian.com**

Depending on how information is processed by a credit bureau, errors can sometimes slip into your personal credit history, so be sure to periodically check your credit report to make sure there are no problems. If you find any errors on these reports, you can contact each agency and request that they be corrected.

See also Credit History *and articles, "How to Check Someone's Credit" and "Solving Cash Flow Problems."*

How to Check Someone's Credit

How can you check the credit rating of a potential client, customer, or other business associate? It depends on who you are and whom you are checking on. While businesses can easily get credit information on individuals, individual business owners cannot get credit information on other businesses from credit bureaus.

• **Individual-to-Individual Business Transactions.** According to one of my credit bureau contacts, you can't get the credit rating of an individual client or customer unless you have a permissible purpose that includes a financial relationship with the individual or other party. Your best bet may be to call the Better Business Bureau to see if there have been any complaints against the party you're thinking about doing business with.

• **Business-to-Business Transactions.** If you are a small business interested in getting credit information on a specific company, check financial references such as *Dun and Bradstreet* (provided the company is large enough to be rated). If you just want to check the credit of a small shop across the country who wants you to ship and invoice, there's not much you can do to verify the shop's credit worthiness. If you know the name of the individual who owns the shop, however, you might be able to get a credit report on that individual by calling a credit bureau.

See also Credit Rating.

Credit/Trade References

In the course of doing business, you not only have to supply credit references to suppliers, but you must also get them from new accounts who ask for credit from you. What will you do the first time someone gives you a large order and asks you to ship and bill? Before agreeing to ship a large order to a new account you've never heard of before, ask that you be furnished with the following information and then check it out when you get it:

- owner or manager's name and phone number
- company's phone number, fax number, and e-mail address
- federal I.D. number
- three or more trade references with phone numbers and addresses
- a bank reference

Since you will be asking new customers for detailed credit information, it makes sense to create a standard form for the collection of all of the above. (Many buyers have already compiled this information on forms of their own which they give to suppliers at trade shows.)

A buyer's bank reference should include the bank's full address, buyer's account number, and written authorization for release of credit information. (Without such authorization, a bank won't even tell you whether a company has an account with them or not.) Be sure to check all the trade references to learn how long the buyer has had an account with each of them and whether they pay on time or not. If you have never heard of any of the trade references, call Information to verify that the telephone numbers you've been given are authentic (or, check one of the free telephone/e-mail search services on the Web). Be especially cautious if someone gives you an unusually large order and asks for shipment in a hurry. Con artists often set up phony references.

See also COD Shipments; Credit Rating; Credit Card Sales; Order Policies; Pro Forma; Scams, Home Business; *and* Internet and E-Mail Scams.

Tip

If you are unable to get satisfactory credit information on a new customer or just feel uncomfortable about shipping that first order to them, you can either ship COD or *pro forma*. Be especially careful about new business coming to you on the Web, however, as many con artists are at work here, specifically targeting small craft businesses on the Web.

Custom Orders

Q: *If someone asks me to do a custom order or commissions me to do a special art or craft project, do I ask for a deposit or bill them on completion of the job?*

Custom orders and craft commissions can be as simple as making a product in a particular size or color to decorating a nursery with creative artwork, stenciling walls, designing decorative tiles for a kitchen, or hand-carving a life-size figure. Because such work is often impossible to sell to anyone but the original buyer, you should always get a deposit to cover all material costs and insure against cancellation at the last moment

The general rule is to ask for 50 percent down before you begin the work, but there may be times when you should make an exception. As one artist told me, "Geography makes a difference. Down South, people's feelings are hurt if you ask for a deposit because they take this as a sign you don't trust them. Many of my customers would be offended if I asked them for a deposit for a custom-designed item, so I always trust my instincts here."

Some artists who accept commissions for pricey pieces may work a bit differently, taking an initial deposit until all details of the commission have been worked out, and then asking for an amount equal to one-third of the total price before supplies or materials have been ordered. To guarantee payment upon completion, finished pieces may be shipped either COD or *pro forma*.

See also COD Shipments *and* Pro Forma.

DBA

This abbreviation—sometimes written as d/b/a—means "doing business as," and it is used by banks to connect a depositor to his or her fictitious (or assumed) name. (Example: Sondra Jones, dba Glass With Class). Some banks will not open a business account for you until you have filed a Fictitious Name Statement.

See also Fictitious Name Statement.

Depreciation

See Note 9 under Business Expenses, Tax Deductible.

Design Business

Several listings in this book will be helpful to designers. In addition to the other listings referenced below, be sure to read all the various listings related to copyrights.

See also Business Records, Protection of; Contracts; Fabrics (Designer), Commercial Use of; First Rights/All Rights Sales; Patterns, Commercial Use of; *and* Patents.

Design Patent

Design patents offer legal protection for ornamental designs. They are less expensive to obtain and maintain, but give less protection than a regular patent. To qualify for protection, a design must have novel features. Examples: motifs on jewelry, furniture or fabrics, or the unique shape and design of an object such as a belt buckle or a ceramic teapot in a unique shape. For more information on this topic, contact the Patent and Trademark Office in Washington, D.C., on the Web at **www.USPTO.gov**. You can also hear a series of recorded messages by calling 1-800-786-9199.

Discounts

There are different types of discounts. For example, you may give customers a 2 percent discount off the invoice price if they pay within ten days, or offer a special 10 percent discount to preferred craft fair customers who give you follow-up orders by mail. Professional discounts are often given to business owners who are bold enough to ask for them when they are doing business with other professionals in their industry, and local retailers and mail order suppliers may give trade or quantity discounts of 10–15 percent to those who buy larger-than-usual amounts of raw materials and supplies.

See also Terms of Sale.

Tip

If you do not yet qualify to buy raw materials at wholesale prices, ask the retailers with whom you do business regularly if quantity or trade discounts are available to small business owners like you. Never do this in front of regular customers, however, and be prepared to prove you really are in business.

Discussion Lists and Web Forums

Q: *I'd like to network with other craft sellers like myself. Can you tell me how to find them on the Web?*

There are many ways to network on the Web through chat rooms, forums, bulletin boards, and so on, but because this kind of "chat" is extremely time consuming, I've done very little of it and thus have little personal advice to offer. Here are two excellent mailing lists I can recommend, however, either from past participation or from good reviews I've received about them from others:

• **The Professional Crafter's Mailing List; www.Professional Crafters.com**. This moderated discussion group has been serving the crafts community since 1997.

• **A-Craft-Biz-Connection; www.craftassoc.com/cbcelist.html**. This newsletter and discussion list is managed by the National Crafts Association. You can use it to ask questions, share contacts, resources, marketing ideas, craft show information, and much more.

The number of individuals conversing in Internet groups is absolutely mind-boggling so be prepared to spend a lot of time just looking for a couple of good groups you might join. Once you find a good group, you'll also find a great way to get answers to questions you may have while also sharing some of your helpful crafts business or marketing experiences in return. In time, you may decide to start your own group, and you'll find how-to information on each of the sites listed below:

• **www.groups.Yahoo.com**; More than 16,000 craft groups are registered here.

- **http://lists.topica.com/**; Under the "Arts" category, you'll find more than 200 craft groups.

- **www.delphiforums.com**; A forum is an interactive Web community where individuals converse, inform, debate, or ask for advice on topics related to the forum's topic. Here, everyone can participate and see what others have to say. Check the "Creative Arts" and "Hobbies & Crafts" categories for forums of possible interest to you.

Distributor/Jobber

The chain of distribution for most products is manufacturer to distributor; distributor to dealer; dealer to individual buyer. As the maker of commercial art or handcrafted goods to be sold in quantity, you may not have enough room in your pricing formula to work with distributors (wholesalers), but are more likely to sell at wholesale prices to dealers (retailers), either directly or through sales representatives, trade shows, or gift marts.

See also Trade Shows *and article, "Pricing Formulas for Handcraft Sellers."*

Drop-Shipping

Q: *Can crafters profit from drop-shipping arrangements with others?*

Drop-shipping is common in the book publishing industry and in many other product industries as well, but I don't see many craftspeople working this way. This can be a profitable way to work with others who are selling products that are similar, yet not competitive, with yours, but it works only for those who are selling through a mail order catalog (print or online). Those who supply products for sale benefit by having others who will promote and sell products for them, while those who sell products for others do not have to lay out cash for products until they have actually been sold.

For example, I used to work with several mail order book sellers who would list my books in their own catalogs, take orders for them, deposit the checks, and then write me their checks for the total amount of orders, less the agreed-upon sales commission. When

I received an order with payment and a typed address label, I drop-shipped the order directly to their customers (using the supplied address label so customers thought the book actually came from the company they had ordered from).

Drop-shipping is particularly evident today on the Web, as many catalog companies selling products of all kinds have set up affiliate programs that enable entrepreneurs with their own websites to sell non-craft related products for them through banner ads and various promotional strategies. If this is of interest, you can turn up a wealth of how-to information on this topic as well as links to companies who offer drop-ship products, by searching for "drop shipping" on Google or Yahoo!.

eBay, Selling on

See Web Marketing Options.

Employee Identification Number (EIN)

This permanent federal taxpayer identification number is needed by all employers, partnerships, corporations, and nonprofit organizations. It can be used for more than one business, and you keep this number even when you change your business name or relocate to another part of the country. Sole proprietors without employees can obtain an EIN if they want one, but most simply use their Social Security Number. Some banks, however, may not let you open a commercial account without one. To apply for an EIN, use IRS Form SS-4, available wherever tax forms are found, including the IRS website at **www.IRS.gov**.

Tip

If you apply for an EIN but don't have employees, be sure to specify on the application form that you have no employees and are getting this number for banking purposes only. Otherwise you'll begin receiving employment tax forms you don't need and will then have to explain why you're ignoring them.

E-Commerce

See Merchant Account Providers; Shopping Cart Systems; *and* Web Marketing Options.

Employees, Family

Q: *What are the tax advantages of hiring my spouse or children to work in my business?*

Spousal wages, deductible on your Schedule C tax form, will lower the amount of Self-Employment Taxes you must pay on Schedule C business profits. However, you must withhold state and federal income tax on spousal wages and file the necessary tax forms (your accountant can help you do this), and your spouse must pay Social Security taxes on his or her earnings. The main tax advantage here is being able to place Social Security deposits where they are most advantageous to the family.

The tax benefits are considerably better when you can employ your children. A child under the age of eighteen doesn't have to pay FICA taxes on earnings, nor state and federal taxes up to a certain amount. (Check with an accountant on this.) As Julian Block, a former IRS agent, explains: "Putting your youngster on your payroll can be a savvy way to take care of his or her allowance at the expense of the Internal Revenue Service. Significant tax savings can result merely by moving the money from one family pocket to another." (See the Home-Biz Advice area of **www.BarbaraBrabec.com** for "Profit From Paying Your Kids," an article by former IRS agent Julian Block. It will answer many of your questions.)

See also Employee Identification Number; Labor Laws; *and* Employees, Nonfamily.

Tip

The Tax Court has upheld deductions for children as young as seven, but if you hire young children, keep careful records of the hours they work and the kind of work they are doing for you so you can support your deduction if your return is challenged.

Employees, Nonfamily

There are three types of nonfamily workers: regular employees, statutory employees, and independent contractors. Since each state has different laws about workers who perform duties in your place of business or in their own homes, you must contact your nearest Department of Labor office for more information on this topic (**www.DOL.gov**). Your accountant or tax adviser can also explain the tax implications of hiring outside help.

If you have four or more part- or full-time employees who are *not* family members, independent contractors, or statutory employees who work for you out of their own homes, you will need Worker's Compensation Insurance. This protects business owners against lawsuits from employees who are injured on the job. Each state has its own law about when such insurance is necessary, so you should contact your state capital for more information on this topic.

> *See also* Employee Identification Number; Independent Contractors; Labor Laws; Legal Resources on the Web; OSHA Regulations; Sheltered Workshops; *and* Statutory Employees.

Endangered Species

If you use such "found objects" as feathers, bones, claws, or ivory, *do not sell any products made of these items* until you are absolutely sure none are protected by state or federal environmental protection laws.

You may know that eagles (every part of them, including feathers and claws) are protected under the *Bald and Golden Eagle Protection Act,* but you may be unaware that another law, *The Migratory Bird Treaty Act,* prohibits the sale of feathers of all North American migratory birds. Protected under other laws are certain waterfowl, marine mammals, and other endangered species. Just picking up a feather, tooth, claw, or bone of one of these endangered species and using it in a wall hanging could result in a fine of as much as $2,000. Sometimes you don't even have to sell the item to get into trouble; merely possessing it is a violation of the law.

Your state fish and game office can provide you with more information on this topic, and a complete list of threatened and endangered species (protected birds, plants, and wildlife) can be obtained from the U.S. Fish & Wildlife Service Web site at **http://endangered.fws.gov/**.

See also Found Objects *and* Nature Items.

Enrolled Agents

Q: *What's an enrolled agent, and why should I consider hiring one to prepare my annual tax return?*

Enrolled Agents (EAs) are licensed by the Treasury Department to represent taxpayers before the Internal Revenue Service. Although they have more tax training than a CPA and are qualified to answer complex tax questions and prepare annual tax returns, their fee may be lower than that of an accountant or CPA. The National Association of Enrolled Agents (NAEA) is a 9,500-member national association of EAs with a nationwide network of affiliated state organizations. (You can get a list of EAs in your area by calling 1-800-424-4339, or visit NAEA's website at **www.NAEA.org** where you can enter your zip code to find an EA in your area.) Enrolled agents also provide their expertise free of charge on the NAEA Tax Channel area of America Online.

See also Accountant/CPA.

Estimated Tax Payments

All self-employed individuals—and that includes even the smallest homebased crafts business—must file quarterly estimated tax payments if it is expected that taxes on regular and self-employment income will be $500 or more. These payments are due on the 15th of the month in April, June, September, and January. If you fail to accurately estimate your income and make the required quarterly payments, you could be socked with penalty and interest fees in April when you file your annual tax return. An accountant can help you do the estimate and give you the necessary tax forms for making quarterly payments, or you can download them on the Web at **www.IRS.gov.**

Environmental Protection

As discussed under *Licenses and Permits*, if your business causes the release of any materials into the air (such as a ceramic kiln), you may need approval from the local environmental protection agency. On **www.EPA.gov,** the website of the agency (EPA), click the "Where You Live" button to turn up a page where you can add your ZIP code. This will then give you environmental information about your community.

See also Endangered Species; Licenses and Permits; *and* Nature Items.

Exporting

Q: *I think there might be a good foreign market for a unique product I can produce in volume. How do I get started in exporting?*

Before getting involved in exporting, you need to gain a basic knowledge of the field and an understanding of such things as payment terms, shipping terminology, and methods of shipping. To avoid the paperwork hassles involved in exporting, you may want to work with agent-buyers or bona fide distributors. A successful exporter in my network reported that it was time-consuming and often nonproductive to attempt to begin an export business by contacting foreign embassies or commercial trade offices. She recommended subscribing to a periodical that specializes in providing export leads (check a periodicals directory in your library). "This usually gives me a dozen or more prospects to explore each month," she says. "I contact them initially by fax and have been able to convert about 15 percent of prospects to customers."

For more information, check your library for books about exporting and also contact the Department of Commerce for any free information booklets they may have. (Check your telephone book for local offices, or do a search on the Web at **www.DOC.gov** to find an office near you.)

Fabrics (Designer), Commercial Use of

Q: *I sell a line of fabric crafts. Are there any restrictions on the use of designer fabrics in my products?*

Yes, there are limitations on the amount of fabric you can legally use without a licensing arrangement with the fabric manufacturer or royalties payment to the fabric's designer. As you may know, all fabric designs are copyrighted to protect other manufacturers from reproducing those designs. No one goes around checking to see how regular fabric is being used, but "designer fabric" is something else. Use of designer fabrics to make items for sale at craft fairs, holiday boutiques, or craft malls is not likely to be a problem, since few crafters would exceed the limitation that most designers find acceptable. (See licensing agent's comment below.) A problem can arise, however, if you enter the wholesale marketplace with such products. Fabric designers often attend trade shows and gift marts looking for companies who are using their products and checking to see if they have a license to use their copyrighted fabrics.

The fact that you can buy designer fabrics from a fabric wholesaler or manufacturer does not mean you have unlimited commercial use of this fabric. The goal of a fabric manufacturer is to get fabrics into the marketplace. Distributors who wholesale these fabrics are supposed to notify buyers if there are any restrictions on the commercial use of them, but they are lax about doing this. The licensing agent for a well-known fabric designer explained that while most fabric manufacturers are happy to wholesale their designer fabrics, the goal of a designer's licensing agency is to make sure that *large users* pay for the privilege of making millions of dollars from the designer's fabrics. This means that someone has to keep tabs on who is using what, and how much, which explains why designers go to trade shows and marts looking for companies that are using their fabrics. (See related article, "Using Designer Fabrics—One Manufacturer's Experience.")

In a conversation with the licensing agent of a fabric designer, I learned there are no industry standards in the field of licensing. Everyone operates differently. The policy of one particular designer's licensing agency may be entirely different from the policy of

Using Designer Fabrics—
One Manufacturer's Experience

Pat, a gift manufacturer who took her line of merchandise to a gift show, was thrilled when she learned that one of the designers whose fabrics she was using had stopped by her booth to chat. But a call from this designer's licensing agency a few days later stunned her. The designer, while friendly, wasn't just being friendly. What she was doing was *policing the use of her fabrics.*

If the designer hadn't liked what she saw in Pat's booth, legally she could have demanded that all products made of her fabrics be removed from Pat's line. As it turns out, she had no objection with the way Pat was using her fabric. What did concern her was the fact that Pat had mentioned her name in her brochure ("fabrics designed by xxx"), which boiled down to Pat's illegally trading on the designer's reputation.

The designer asked her licensing agent to take care of this matter and also find out how much fabric Pat was using. Pat learned this particular designer had set a limit of 300 yards (in total) for use of her fabrics by unlicensed users like herself. Usage beyond 300 yards would require a licensing arrangement and a 5 percent royalty on sales, she was told. Needing to use more than 300 yards, and not wanting to enter into a licensing arrangement, Pat decided to stop using this designer's fabric.

another designer's agency. "The last thing we want to do is put small manufacturers out of business," the licensing agent told me. "On the other hand, we don't want to encourage the use of designer fabrics by individual crafters because we can't control the quality of the products they are putting on the market. We simply want to protect our licensees who have paid for the privilege of using our designer's fabrics for their exclusive product lines."

See also Copyrights of Others; Fabrics, Flammability Standards; *and* Sports Logos, Commercial Use of.

Tip

Before buying hundreds of yards of designer fabric for that new line of products you're planning to wholesale, ask the fabric distributor if there are any restrictions on its commercial use and whether you should contact the manufacturer for additional information on this topic. If you're still buying fabric at the retail level, always observe the warning on the selvage. When you see a copyright notice with a designer's name, do not use this fabric to make items you plan to wholesale. If there is a notice to the effect that "this fabric is for individual consumption only," don't use it to make *anything* for sale. Avoid completely the commercial use of all fabrics with high-profile designs such as copyrighted cartoon characters or NFL logos.

Fabrics, Flammability Standards

Q: *I plan to wholesale a line of garments for women and children. How can I be certain the fabric I'm buying from my wholesale supplier meets federal flammability standards?*

The Flammable Fabrics Act prohibits the introduction or movement in interstate commerce of articles of wearing apparel and fabrics that are so highly flammable as to be dangerous when worn by individuals or used for other purposes. It is difficult to tell by looking at a fabric if it is "so highly flammable as to be dangerous," explains a spokesperson for the Consumer Product Safety Commission (**www.CPSC.gov**).

"A quick test to help identify fabrics that comply with the children's sleepwear standard is to hold a match on the bottom edge of a small piece of fabric for approximately three seconds. If the fabric stops burning once the match is removed from the fabric, it is considered to be 'self-extinguishing' and will probably comply with the children's sleepwear standard (a very stringent flammability standard). If the fabric continues to burn, it will not comply with the children's sleepwear standard, but will probably comply with the flammability standard for all other fabrics intended for use in wearing apparel, doll clothing, and toys. Most fabrics comply with this latter standard, but it is difficult to make a determination of compliance by setting a match to a small piece of fabric held vertically because acceptance is based upon both the ease of ignition and the rate of burn. During the test, the fabric is held in a less stringent position (at a 45-degree angle, rather than vertical), and the flame touches the fabric in a less ignitable location (the top surface instead of the bottom edge)."

Most fabric manufacturers test their fabrics for compliance and issue a guaranty of compliance that is passed along the chain of distribution through a statement on the invoice that reads "Continuing guaranty under the Flammable Fabrics Act filed with the Consumer Product Safety Commission." If this information does not appear on the invoice you receive, ask the manufacturer, wholesaler, or distributor supplying the fabric to furnish you with a "statement of compliance" with the flammability standards. If you are purchasing fabrics at local retail outlets, you may contact the fabric manufacturer directly or call the Consumer Product Safety Commission Hotline at 1-800-638-2772 to see if the fabric manufacturer has filed a continuing guarantee under *The Flammable Fabrics Act.*

For a list of free publications, visit **www.CPSC.gov**, where you can get a list of all available free publications, including those on children's sleepwear. (To turn up articles on the site, use the search area and type "Flammable Fabrics Act" and "flammability standards.")

See also Craft Displays, Fire Safety; Garment Manufacturing; *and* Wool and Other Textiles.

Fax Machine

Q: *I can't see any reason why a small homebased business should have a fax machine. Am I missing something here?*

Many home-business owners, at first resistant to the idea of getting a fax machine, finally caved in and began to use this technology not because they thought they really needed it, but because they wanted to accommodate customers or clients who preferred this method of communication. Stand-alone fax machines are practically extinct now that we have all-in-one machines that scan, copy, print, and fax as well. In addition, businesses can also elect to send and receive faxes by e-mail. (Check **www.e-fax.com** for information, or search the Web for "fax services" or "efax" to turn up other companies that provide electronic faxing services.)

Not everyone needs fax capabilities, of course. It all depends on what you're selling and the kind of buyers you are serving. If you can't receive faxes, you may be losing sales or simply making it difficult for some of your customers to place orders. Take a look at some of the advantages of being able to both send and receive faxes:

- **Saves time and money.** If you regularly deal with wholesale buyers, you can communicate more quickly and less expensively with them by fax to confirm receipt of new orders and shipping dates, announce a new product, or send an overdue invoice reminder. Doing the same things by phone will not only take longer, but cost more. (I no longer need to fax anything, but when I was actively faxing, a study of my costs revealed that each fax transmission cost me three cents less than a first-class stamp, and I saved the cost of an envelope besides.)

- **Serves as a marketing tool.** If you are selling anything by mail, you will find that no one wants to send a credit card number by e-mail (and they shouldn't for security reasons), but they will be happy to fax an order with instructions to charge to a credit card.

- **Helps people who don't like to send e-mail.** A quilter in my network told me that half the folks she deals with don't use the computer as much as they might, and they prefer to fax orders instead of e-mailing them to her. Also, small gift shop owners who don't have easy access to the Web prefer to have wholesale information faxed to them.

- **Offers personal advantages.** It's also handy to have fax capabilities when you want your doctor to fax you a report on your latest blood test, get information to an insurance company about a claim you've filed, send an order for office supplies or other items you would normally order by mail, or just network with business pals.

See also Maintenance Agreements.

Tip

By law, fax transmissions must have a special header that shows the date, time, business name, and telephone number. (The fax instruction manual explains how to enter this information.) If you unplug your machine for any reason, you will probably lose the time and date and have to reset it. Even if you never unplug your fax, you should periodically check the accuracy of information that appears on the header line of your transmissions.

Federal Trade Commission Rules

Q: *Do FTC rules and regulations really apply to the average homebased business, or are these regulations applicable only to "big" businesses?*

Every business—no matter how small—needs to be familiar with FTC rules. Among other things, this agency is concerned with truth in advertising, mail order marketing, trade practices, product labeling, unfair or deceptive acts and practices, and unfair methods of competition. Free booklets on all these topics are available from the FTC by calling 1-877-FTC-HELP or visiting the website at **www .FTC.gov**. Specific titles of interest might be: (1) *Truth-in-Advertising Rules;* (2) *30-day Mail or Telephone Order Merchandise Rule;* (3) *The Fabric Care Labeling Rule;* (4) *The Wool Products Labeling Act of 1939;* (5) *Guide for the Jewelry Industry;* (6) *The Hand Knitting Yarn Industry;* and (7) *The Catalog Jewelry and Giftware Industry.* Here is more information about some of these rules:

- **Truth in Advertising.** The FTC says it's not what you say in actual words, but what the "average" person (not the sophisticated or skeptical person) believes after reading your ad. You aren't likely to have any problems here so long as you make no false product claims (false representation) and are truthful about what buyers can expect to receive from you.
- **Use of the Word "New."** New products can be advertised as "new" for a period of six months only. Thereafter, use of the word "new" to describe products older than this would be a violation of an FTC rule.

- **Mail or Telephone Order Merchandise Rule.** This FTC rule, usually called the "30-day rule," is strictly enforced with penalties of up to $10,000 for each violation. Unless otherwise specified in your advertising or catalog, you must ship customer orders within thirty days of receiving payment for the order or you will be in violation of this rule. (Now you know why so many advertisers include a note on their order form or other printed literature to "Allow six to eight weeks for delivery." It's not because they really think it's going to take that long for a customer's order to get shipped, but they are protecting themselves against unforeseen problems.) If you fail to indicate exactly how long it should take to receive an order, customers may legally expect to receive the product within thirty days after you get their order. (If you invoice orders after shipment, this rule does not apply to you.) If you find you cannot ship within the specified time, then you must notify the buyer of the delay, enclosing a postage-paid reply card or envelope. You must give the buyer the option to either cancel the order and get an immediate refund, or give you more time to ship the order. If the customer doesn't respond either way, the FTC rule says you may assume the customer is agreeable to the delay in shipping.

See also Guarantees and Warranties; Insurance, Product Liability; Indian Arts and Crafts; Labels or Tags Required by Law; Organization, Formation of; Prepublication Offer; Scams, Home Business; Testimonials; *and* Trade Practice Rules.

Fictitious Name Statement

This is a legal certificate that must be filed with your city or county clerk when you elect to operate a business under any name other than your own. Some states require that you publish notice of your assumed or fictitious name in a general-circulation newspaper in your county.

See also Business or Trade Name Registration/Protection.

Tip

If you're in violation of local zoning laws and don't want your neighbors to know you're running a business at home, the ad you run does not have to be placed in your hometown paper but can be run in any newspaper in the county.

Financial and Tax Records

Q: *Which records are most important to my business, and how long do I need to keep them?*

Since a tax return can be audited for up to three years after it is due or filed, you need to keep all financial records related to your tax returns for at least this long. (There is no time limit on when the IRS can begin an audit on a return they consider to be fraudulent.) Specifically, keep all records pertaining to income and expenses, including accounts payable invoices, bank deposits and statements, employee records/payroll, petty cash records, sales commission reports, and manufacturing records.

Other records that should be retained permanently include business ledgers, financial statements, check registers, all legal papers (including contracts, patents, trademarks, copyrights, etc.), depreciation schedules, inventory records, and important correspondence.

See also Business Records, Protection of.

Financial Statements

Q: *I don't anticipate ever needing a bank loan, so why should I bother to prepare financial statements for my small homebased business?*

You may think your homebased business is too small for you to take the time to create financial statements, but if you're serious about what you're doing, you should have these reports for your own information. Even if you never plan to ask a banker for a business loan, your financial statements will provide a fascinating picture of how your business is doing and enable you to monitor cost-of-goods and inventory figures, overhead costs, and net profits each year. Sometimes when you're not sure if you're just treading water or actually making gains, financial statements can offer surprising and comforting evidence that you're on the right track.

Financial statements include the Income Statement, Profit and Loss (P&L) Statement, and Balance Sheet. (See sample worksheets near listings for *Balance Sheet* and *Income Statement*.) Depending on your particular needs, you may want to prepare statements on a monthly, quarterly, semiannually, or annual basis. At the very least, you will need a set of financial statements at year's end to make preparation of your tax return easier. If you plan to apply for a loan, your banker will want to see a complete set of financial statements and may ask for your most recent annual statements as well as figures for the current month or quarter.

If you need help in bookkeeping, accounting, or the preparation of financial statements, one of the best books you will ever find is Bernard Kamoroff's *Small Time Operator—How to Start Your Own Small Business, Keep Your Books, Pay Your Taxes, and Stay Out of Trouble* (**www.BellSprings.com**). This classic guide, regularly updated, includes all the ledgers and worksheets you will need for a year.

See also Balance Sheet; Cash Flow Projection; *and* Income Statement.

Financing a Business

Q: *How do most people raise the cash they need to launch a small business at home if they can't qualify for a bank loan?*

Most people in homebased businesses today got started with some kind of personal loan, either by tapping a savings account, credit union account, life insurance policy, or the equity in their home.

If you have an insurance policy with cash value, you may be able to borrow on it at rates as low as 5 percent. If you have a Certificate of Deposit, you don't need to cash it in to get money. Instead, consider using the certificate as collateral for a temporary loan. Generally, you can borrow up to 85 percent of the amount of the certificate at an interest rate of perhaps 3 percent over what the account is earning. Since your account will continue to earn interest, that means your actual loan cost would be only 3 percent.

Although interest rates are generally very high on cash advances on a credit card (21 percent or more) many small business people take comfort in knowing that in an emergency, they have access to immediate cash up to the limit set on the card.

See also Bank Loans; Home Equity Loans; Line of Credit; *and* SBA Loans.

Tip

If you have a friend or relative who has money in a savings account, their passbook can be used as collateral for a bank loan. Although your friend or relative could not withdraw the amount outstanding on your loan, the savings account would lose no interest and, as you paid back the loan, you would free up that amount of funds in the savings account.

First Rights/All Rights Sales

Q: *I want to offer articles and how-to projects to magazines, but I'm confused about the difference between selling "first rights" and "all rights" to a publisher.*

In offering your work for publication—and this might be an article, a poem, a design, pattern, or how-to instructions for some project— you must consider whether you are going to sell only first rights or all rights to that publisher. If you elect the latter, which some beginners have to do just to get published, you will automatically lose ownership of the copyright to your material. Selling all rights means you have conveyed your copyright to the publisher, and you cannot use that material again without the publisher's written permission.

Selling first rights, on the other hand, means you have given the magazine permission to print your article once, for a specified sum of money, after which time you alone have the right to resell that article to someone else, reprint it in a publication of your own, include it in a book you are writing, incorporate it into kit instructions, and so on.

See also Book Copyright.

FOB

This means "freight, or free, on board," and this term is generally used in printed sales literature or on invoices to indicate the point to which a seller will pay freight. Since title of the goods legally changes hands at the FOB point, this notation could be important in the event a large shipment is lost or damaged in transit.

EXAMPLES: If you live in San Francisco and are buying a heavy piece of equipment from a company in Chicago, a notation of "FOB Chicago" means you have to pay the freight charges. If it reads "FOB San Francisco," it means the equipment seller is paying the freight. Thus, if you are shipping an order from San Francisco to Chicago and the customer is paying the freight, the FOB notation would read "FOB San Francisco."

Foreign Sales

See Canadian Sales and Money Orders.

Found Objects

Q: *I believe in recycling, so many of the craft items I make are made from discarded objects, nature items, and other "found objects." Are there any restrictions on selling such items?*

It's great to recycle, so long as you don't violate environmental and safety laws when you collect and use materials whose manufacturers or origins are unknown. The list of endangered species grows longer every day, and elsewhere I have discussed this topic at length, along with problems related to use of certain nature items. Many found objects are perfectly safe, and there are no restrictions on using them to create art products for sale. Given their "handicraft nature," however, they will undoubtedly have a limited market.

One thing you should never do, however, is use egg cartons or plastic meat trays to make handicraft items because there is no way to wash off the salmonella, *E. coli*, and other harmful microbes that may be lingering on them. You could become ill from using such items for craft projects, and if you sold them to someone who got sick, you could find yourself facing a lawsuit.

See also Endangered Species *and* Nature Items.

Freebies

Q: *Do you think it's a good idea to offer customers something free from time to time?*

Yes, everyone loves a freebie. Common freebies used by craft sellers include bookmarks and calendars. One artist I know uses a small yearly calendar as her business card, printing them in October so she can include one with each purchase during the Christmas sales season. I also recall a home sewer who created an interesting freebie by printing a handy fabric conversion chart on the back of her regular business card. She then laminated the card to make it a practical purse or wallet reference when shopping.

Some sellers who make toys, dolls, and other products for children often create little giveaway items from scrap materials, reasoning that if they give something to a child, they will automatically attract the parent's attention. For example, a fellow who makes custom-designed Halloween costumes prints his name and address on vinyl black half-masks, including a couple with each completed costume and telling the kids to give them to their friends.

Fur Products

If you make wearing apparel that contains any kind of fur, the *Fur Products Labeling Act* requires a very specifically worded and sized label on all such products. Request additional information on this act from the FTC. (See contact information under *Federal Trade Commission Rules*.)

Garment Manufacturing

If you sew garments for sale, there are several listings in this book you need to read to stay on safe legal ground, particularly if you are selling children's clothing or fabric toys.

See Consumer Safety Laws; Fabrics (Designer), Commercial Use of; Fabrics, Flammability Standards; Fur Products; Homework Laws; Labels or Tags Required by Law; Patterns, Commercial Use of; Textile Fiber Products Identification Act; *and* Wool and Other Textiles.

Gross Price

Gross price is the total (list) price of a product before deductions or allowances have been made. For example, your gross annual income would be the total of all income received in a year, while net income is what's left after all expenses have been deducted.

See also Net Price.

Guarantees and Warranties

Q: *What's the difference between a guarantee and a warranty, and do craftspeople have to be concerned about them?*

Neither is required by law on handmade products, but if you elect to offer any kind of guarantee, you must be careful how it is worded to comply with FTC rules. It is not enough merely to say "Satisfaction guaranteed or money back." (For examples of some guarantees used by craft sellers, see *Guaranty of Satisfaction* below.)

Warranties are of two kinds: *implied* and *express*. An implied warranty means a product will perform as similar products of its kind under normal conditions (i.e., buyer can expect that the ceramic mug they have purchased will not crack when hot coffee is poured into it). An express warranty states a specific fact about how the product will perform (i.e., "the handpainting on this ceramic coffee mug is dishwasher safe"). It is best not to make express warranties since doing so opens you to the possibility of legal obligations should the product turn out to be defective.

Guaranty of Satisfaction

Q: *Do you think it makes a difference in the number of orders a mail order seller will get if customers are offered some kind of guarantee of satisfaction? What's the best way to make sure my customers know I'll refund their money if they aren't satisfied with their purchase?*

Yes, I believe "satisfaction guarantees" are essential to good sales. All of the large mail order catalog houses allow buyers to return merchandise that is in any way unsatisfactory, so I believe most consumers expect small businesses to offer the same kind of guarantee of satisfaction. Certainly this would give them more confidence in ordering from you. If you do offer a customer guarantee, however, the FTC requires more than just a "Satisfaction Guaranteed" statement. You must also disclose the specific terms, conditions, and extent of the guarantee, plus the manner in which you will perform the guarantee. As a mail order book seller, I used a guarantee like the one below for twenty-five years, and only a couple of buyers returned books in all that time:

> SATISFACTION GUARANTEED! Book orders carry a money-back guarantee. If for any reason you are not satisfied with your purchase, simply return the undamaged book in its original mailer within ten days of receipt to receive a refund of the book's cover price.

Note that you are not expected to refund the shipping costs on any returned product. Here are a couple other examples of guarantees I have found in the literature of craft sellers:

> SATISFACTION GUARANTEED! If you are not completely satisfied with the quality of our products, return your purchase in undamaged condition within ten days to receive a refund of the retail price.

> OUR GUARANTEE: We take pride in our products. If for any reason an item does not meet your expectations, you may

return it within ten days for exchange, credit or refund (except custom made or personalized items).

See also Guarantees and Warranties; Order Form; Price List; *and* Refunds.

Hang Tags and Designer Labels

Q: *My crafts sell very well without fancy hang tags or labels, but a fellow crafter has urged me to start using them. Would this really make a difference in sales?*

Many sellers have reported an increase in sales after they began to use hang tags and designer labels. One reason may be that the average consumer has grown accustomed to seeing hang tags and labels on commercial items and thus expects to see them on handcrafted merchandise as well. They may even expect to pay more for a product that bears a striking hang tag or designer label.

Tags and labels speak volumes about your professionalism and often add personality and sales appeal to products. They can be any size, shape, or color and may be printed in your home office on lightweight card stock or printed inexpensively at any quick-copy print shop or office center that offers photocopy services. Several suppliers also offer custom-designed tags and labels. Look for their ads in

Preprinted Hang Tags from Wood Cellar Graphics (left) and E & S Creations (right).

What to Say on a Hang Tag

The size of a hang tag and the message you put on it are up to you; options are unlimited. For starters, anything that makes you or your products unique is information that can be put on a tag, such as:

- Type and source of materials used to make the product (Georgia clay, seashells from around the world, hand-dyed yarns, etc.)
- A statement about the quality of the product ("Our woodenware is designed to give you fitness for purpose, beauty of form, and a love of old-time craftsmanship.")
- Colorful information about a business ("It was our grandmother's idea to start this business . . .")
- How products are made (interesting technical information about the manufacturing process)
- Care and cleaning instructions
- Consumer safety warnings ("This is not a toy—keep out of children's hands!")
- History of an old or little-known art or craft
- A whimsical note designed to tug at a buyer's heartstrings (often the most effective way to get higher prices)

The designer who shears her sheep to make handmade felt that is turned into toys . . . the ornament maker whose wax creations are replicas of museum pieces . . . the rosemaler whose designs are completely authentic—all should use such information to their advantage on a hang tag because such stories give a product personality, and personality *sells.*

I'm reminded of a little handpainted picture on wood my husband and I once bought. It was just a sailor standing by a rowboat, and we never would have bought it except for the fact that beneath the picture was a "personality message" that made it the perfect gift for Harry's old school chum, a sailboat enthusiast: "Old sailors never die; they just get a little dinghy."

craft magazines or search Google.com for "hang tag suppliers" and "fabric labels." Here are some suppliers I am familiar with:

- GraphComm Services: 1-800-488-7436. Custom hang tags, sew-in fabric labels, and jewelry tags and labels.
- Charm Woven Labels: 1-800-843-1111; **www.CharmWoven .com**. Fabric and care labels designed to your specifications (free samples).
- Widby Enterprises: 1-888-522-2458; **www.WidbyLabel.com**. Fabric and care labels designed to your specifications (free samples).

A delightful collection of preprinted hang tags that can do double duty as price tags are available from Wood Cellar Graphics (**www.WoodCellarGraphics.com**) and E & S Creations (**www .CranberryJunction.com**).

See also Care Labels; Labels or Tags Required by Law; *and article, "What to Say on a Hang Tag."*

Health Hazards

Do you suffer from chronic fatigue, headaches, nausea, or dizziness that cannot be explained? These and other symptoms could be caused by the raw materials and substances you are using to make products for sale. If any of the following information "rings a bell" with you, be sure to discuss it with your doctor. (It may be necessary to consult with an internist, neurologist, or occupational health consultant since the average doctor may not take your complaints seriously.)

- **Harmful Materials and Substances.** Artists and crafters routinely handle materials that can be harmful if not used properly, such as paints, paint thinners, dyes, lead, plastics, photo chemicals, and dozens of other materials or substances. "100 million Americans may be using dangerous materials without knowing it," says a national clearinghouse for information on this topic. Because many materials give off dangerous hydrocarbons for months, they urge individuals to be especially cautious if they work with varnishes, lacquers, artificial leather, rubber, or plastic cement.

Toxic substances can enter the body by skin contact, through the mouth and digestive system, and through breathing. Never eat, drink, or smoke in your workshop area, and do not inhale fumes, sprays, or dusts. Improper ventilation is the major health problem in all the crafts, so take special precautions to always have adequate ventilation in your work area. (If you can smell the substance you're working with, your ventilation is inadequate and dangerous to your health.) Many materials can harm the skin directly, causing rashes, burns, and other skin problems. A good rule of thumb is to wear protective gloves when using any liquid other than water. Acute lung diseases result when strongly irritating substances burn the tissues of the air sacs in the lung, and certain fumes are injurious to the kidneys and liver with effects being cumulative. Symptoms such as weakness, fatigue, palpitations, or pale complexion may be caused by chemical substances that affect the red and white blood cells, and the entire nervous system can be affected by certain substances. Since children are more susceptible to toxic substances than adults, keep them away from your workshop *(see special TIP below)*.

• **Dust and Other Airborne Materials.** All dust is irritating to the mucous membranes in the nose, throat, eyes, and respiratory tract. Some people also have allergic skin reactions from the dust of certain woods. (Included in the list of allergenic woods are certain members of the birch, pine, dogwood, beech, mahogany, mulberry, and myrtle families.) Wear a dust mask when sawing, sculpting, grinding, or carving any materials to keep minute particles of dust from penetrating your lungs. Also wear a face shield or eye goggles. In cleaning up dust, never sweep but vacuum, wet-mop, or both.

• **Computer Hazards.** If your face gets red and itchy for no apparent reason, your doctor may tell you it's nerves, but your computer may be the culprit. According to the author of *Zap! How Your Computer Can Hurt You and What You Can Do About It* (Peachpit Press), your face may simply be reacting to the dust and particles that are being propelled toward it by the electrostatic field of the video screen. Author Don Sellers says there has been an increased incidence of facial dermatitis (reddening, itching, prickling of the face) among people who sit in front of computers all the time. His book addresses the "epidemic of modern times" that is affecting the health of millions of Americans who use computers, and covers everything from eyestrain to pregnancy issues to carpal tunnel syndrome to back problems.

For more information, visit the Art & Creative Materials Institute at **www.acminet.org** (1-781-293-4100). This website offers a wealth of information relative to what crafters, teachers, and parents need to know about the safety of art and craft materials.

See also Found Objects; Labor Laws, OSHA; Lead Testing; *and* Paints, Varnishes, and Other Finishes.

Tip

Always read the labels on the materials you or your children use to make handcrafts—particularly paints, varnishes, lacquers, sprays, and glues—and take any preventive action necessary to protect your health. By law, all art materials manufactured in the United States must be evaluated by a qualified toxicologist and labeled, if necessary, for chronic toxicity according to the chronic-hazard-labeling standard of the Federal Hazardous Substances Act. The label on such products must contain any necessary cautionary information or safe-use instructions. (For example, if a material improperly used can cause lung cancer or harm to a developing fetus, this must be noted on the label. Instructions must be provided on how to use the product properly and safely, and a warning given if the product is inappropriate for use by children.)

Hobby Business

Q: *At this time I do not foresee having enough income to allow me to deduct any business expenses. Are there advantages to being a registered business that I'm missing out on by maintaining a hobbyist status?*

There is nothing wrong with selling to support a craft hobby, but you should deduct all expenses related to your hobby income to keep your state and federal taxes on this income as low as possible. (See *Hobby Income* for information on how to do this.)

The two main disadvantages of treating your activity as a hobby instead of a business are that (1) your profit margin on finished crafts will be less because you cannot buy supplies and materials at wholesale prices; and (2) you cannot give your hobby business a business name unless you register it with local authorities.

See also Sales Tax.

Hobby Income

Q: *How does the Internal Revenue Service treat hobby income, and at what point does a "hobby business" become a "real business" in the eyes of IRS?*

Hobby income of $400 or more must be reported on Schedule C of Form 1040. You may deduct all expenses incurred to earn this income up to, but not exceeding, the amount of your hobby income. When your hobby business shows a profit, taxes will be due on this income. If you show a loss, however, it will not be deductible against other income.

A "hobby business" becomes a "real business" in the eyes of IRS at the point where you can state that you (1) are trying to make a profit, (2) are making regular business transactions, and (3) have made a profit at least three years out of five.

See also Home Office Deduction.

Tip

If you call your activity a business for tax purposes but fail to keep proper records or meet other IRS criteria, it will be ruled a "hobby" and any losses you may have deducted in the past will be disallowed.

Home-Business Organizations

Q: *What will I get from membership in a home-business or small-business organization?*

There are hundreds of small-business organizations in the United States, but only a few national organizations serve the special interests and needs of homebased business owners and other self-employed individuals. Some are primarily educational or advocacy groups, but several offer attractive membership packages that include some or all of the following benefits: discounts on business products, publications, services, online networking opportunities and forums, travel discounts and long-distance telephone savings, group insurance programs (major medical, hospital, life, disability, dental), general home-business insurance packages (including personal and product liability coverage), low-fee merchant card programs, collection services, and business loan programs. Some organizations have also arranged for their members to get special discounts from such service providers as UPS, DHL, and FedEx Kinko's copy centers.

See "Organizations" in the *Other Resources* section for selected organizations you may wish to check out. To find the names and addresses of other organizations, search Google for "art craft organizations" to turn up several million Web pages; or check such library directories as *National Trade and Professional Associations of the United States and Canada* (Columbia Books) or *Encyclopedia of Associations* (Gale Research Co.).

See also Art/Craft Organizations; Collection Agencies; Merchant Account Providers; Organization, Formation of; *and* Trade Associations/Publications.

Home Equity Loans

Q: *I need access to cash, but I can't get a traditional line of credit from my bank because my business is just getting started. Do you think it's a good idea to tap the equity in our home?*

It can be dangerous to borrow against the equity in your home unless you are a good money manager. On the other hand, if you have a lot of equity in a home and need cash right now, a home equity loan could be the perfect solution to your problem. Although it is common knowledge that homeowners can get home equity loans based on the amount of equity they have in their home, it is not as well known that home equity *lines of credit* are now available from many lenders. The interest on this kind of loan is tax-deductible, and the money can be used to finance or expand a business.

With a regular home equity loan, you would borrow a specific amount and make monthly principal/interest payments until the loan was satisfied. However, if you just want to know you have a source of money to tap in case you need it in the future, you can set up a line of credit. You would then be able to write checks to yourself or business suppliers up to the maximum amount of your credit line. Each month you would be required to pay only the interest on the amount borrowed and, depending on your bank's policy, you might have up to ten years to pay back the loan.

See also Financing a Business; Line of Credit; *and* SBA Loans.

Home Office Deduction

Q: *I've heard that if I take the Home Office Deduction, it's a red flag for the IRS that might trigger an audit. Is this true?*

The majority of today's home-business owners are not taking advantage of this important tax deduction because either they, or their accountants, believe that taking the deduction will lead to an audit. This is simply untrue. The IRS says they do not audit returns merely because this deduction is taken, and I've yet to meet anyone who has been audited even after years of taking the deduction (myself included).

If you're not cheating on your taxes and can defend all your regular tax deductions, adding legitimate home office deductions to your Schedule C report could save you thousands of dollars in the years ahead. If you qualify for this deduction, you may deduct expenses for the business use of your home, thereby lowering the amount of self-employment tax you must pay. First you must be able to show the part of your home that you use for business, then you must calculate an appropriate percentage of expenses that can be deducted. (Generally this is done by dividing the square footage of your office by the total square footage of your home.) Expenses that fall into the home office deduction area are:

- mortgage interest or rental fees
- real estate taxes paid on your home
- homeowner's insurance premiums
- utility bills (gas, electric, oil, water)

- trash collection service
- general home repairs and maintenance
- depreciation of your home *(see TIP below)*

To take a tax deduction for using a part of your home in business, that part must be used *exclusively and regularly for business*—meaning the space can't do double duty as a bedroom or den. If, however, you regularly use *part* of a room strictly for business, then you can deduct expenses for the percentage of space that is used exclusively and regularly for business. You may also take the home office deduction for expenses related to the operation of any structure that is not attached to your house or residence, such as a garage, studio, garden shed, or barn.

Note: If your business shows a loss, some or all of your home office expenses may not be deductible in that year, but may be carried to a future year. For more information on this topic, obtain IRS publication #587, "Business Use of Your Home," by calling 1-800-829-1040 or visiting **www.IRS.gov**.

See also Business Expenses, Tax-Deductible.

Tip

If you depreciate your house, there may be tax complications when you sell it. Be sure to discuss this with an accountant or tax professional, and pay particular attention to this statement from IRS Publication 587, *Business Use of Your Home*:

Basis Adjustment. You must decrease the basis of your property by the amount of depreciation you could have deducted on your tax returns under the method of depreciation you selected. If you took less depreciation that you could have under the method you selected, you must decrease the basis by the amount you could have taken under that method.

Homework Laws

Homework laws have been in existence in many states since 1937 when the legislature became aware of homework abuses and passed a federal *Industrial Homework Law.* Generally, homework laws still in effect today prohibit the manufacturing at home of such products as food and drink, wearing apparel, toys and dolls, cosmetics, and jewelry. In some cases manufacturing may be allowed if a special homeworker certificate or permit is obtained.

Some readers may recall the massive media coverage given to the case of the Vermont Knitters back in the 1980s. When these knitters united to protest government restrictions on their industry, they eventually won exemption against extreme opposition from labor unions. In 1984, thanks to their efforts, the forty-year-old nationwide ban on home knitters was lifted along with bans against at least five other home industries that had been restricted since the 1940s under the *Fair Labor Standards Act*: the manufacture of jewelry, gloves and mittens, buttons and buckles, handkerchiefs, embroideries, and knitted outerwear.

Because the problem of "sweatshops" still exists in large cities where women's and children's apparel is made, a ban still exists on hiring homeworkers to produce such goods. Knitting garments at home is also illegal in some states that have special homework laws. This means that if you are a crafter who designs and makes garments of any kind for women or children, you will not be able to expand your business by using homeworkers (independent contractors) without violating U.S. Labor Department laws. For more information on this topic, contact your state's Department of Labor office (**www.DOL.gov**).

See also Independent Contractors *and* Statutory Employees.

Identity Theft

This is the number one scam today, and you need to educate yourself on all the things you can do to avoid having your personal identity stolen. The best place to get more information on this topic is on the government's website at **www.consumer.gov/idtheft/index .html**. Following are just a few pointers on this topic:

• The majority of ID thefts involve the loss or misuse of one's credit cards, so carry only the credit or debit cards you actually need. Place passwords on all your credit card and other financial accounts, and avoid using easily available information like your mother's maiden name, your birth date, the last four digits of your Social Security Number, or your phone number. If you should ever lose your wallet or credit cards, notify not only the three primary credit bureaus (see *Credit Rating*), but the Social Security Administration's fraud line as well at 1-800-269-0271.

• Mail theft has become epidemic in some areas (particularly out in the country or where there are many mailboxes in a row), so whenever you're mailing bill payments or other documents with sensitive personal information in them, it's best to drop them in a public mailbox rather than leave them in your home mailbox for pickup.

• Don't carry your Social Security Card number, and only give it to others when absolutely necessary. If someone asks for it, ask why they need it, how it will be used, what they will do to protect it from being stolen, and whether they will accept a different kind of identifier for you.

• Unless you have excellent firewall protection, do not keep sensitive personal information on the computer you use to access the Internet. Never open files e-mailed to you by strangers, or click on hyperlinks in such messages or download programs from people you don't know. Opening attachments could expose your system to a computer virus or a program that can capture passwords and other information as you type it into your keyboard. In particular, never respond to official-looking e-mails from any company that asks you to click a link and provide sensitive personal information. This scam is called "phishing," and it's discussed in the article, "Phishing Expeditions for Your Identity" (near the listing for *Internet and E-Mail Scams*).

Income Statement

This financial report shows your income and expenses and the difference between the two. Bankers have always been impressed with my income statement, so I've included a sample of that form here as well as the profit and loss statement I have used in my home business since its beginning. (A sample balance sheet has been included near the listing for *Balance Sheet*.) Adapted from the financial statements used by a book publishing company I once worked for, they have served me well.

INCOME STATEMENT WORKSHEET

INCOME STATEMENT

_____(business name)_____

For Period Ending _____

REVENUE:

Gross Sales	$_____
Less Returns	$_____
	$_____
Other Income	$_____
Total Income	$_____

COST OF GOODS SOLD:

Inventory (type of) 1/1/____	$_____
Inventory Purchases	$_____
Other Costs (specific to your business)	$_____
Subtotal	$_____
Less Inventory as of (12/31/)	$_____
Total Cost of Goods Sold	$_____

TRADING PROFIT: $_____

SELLING EXPENSES:

Advertising	$_____
Postage	$_____
Shipping Expense	$_____
Exhibitor fees	$_____
Sales Commissions	$_____
	$_____

SELLING PROFIT: $_____

ADMINISTRATIVE EXPENSES:

Bank Charges	$_____
Postal Fees	$_____
Office Supplies	$_____
Dues/Subscriptions	$_____
Insurance	$_____
Telephone	$_____
Repairs/Maintenance	$_____
Legal/Professional Expenses	$_____
Auto Expense	$_____
Sales Tax	$_____
New Equipment (write off or depreciate)	$_____
Interest	$_____
Travel Expenses (meals & lodging)	$_____
Wages	$_____

Total Administrative Expenses $_____

NET OPERATING PROFIT BEFORE TAXES: $_____

PROFIT AND LOSS WORKSHEET

_____(name of business)_____

PROFIT AND LOSS STATEMENT
For Period Ending _____

1. SALES [1] $_____

2. COST OF GOODS SOLD [2] $_____
3. GROSS PROFIT MARGIN [3] $_____

4. ADMINISTRATIVE & GENERAL EXPENSE [4] $_____

5. NET PROFIT BEFORE TAXES [5] $_____

Explanatory Note: The figures needed for this financial statement
will be lifted from your more detailed Income Statement as follows:

     (1) Total Income figure
     (2) Total Cost of Goods Sold figure
     (3) Trading Profit figure
     (4) Total Administrative Expenses figure
     (5) Net Operating Profit Before Taxes figure

Of course, you will find many other styles of financial reports in accounting books in your library or bookstore. If you use a computer software program to do your bookkeeping, the forms will be different here, too. What's important where financial statements are concerned is not the style of form you use but whether you are giving bankers (and yourself) a true picture of your income and profit or loss from the business.

See also Balance Sheet *and* Financial Statements.

Independent Contractors

Q: *Can I hire homebased workers (independent contractors) to produce my products, give them the materials they need, and pay a per-piece price for each finished item?*

This is a now a very dangerous thing to do. For years, small business owners acted on the advice of accountants and attorneys to hire such labor on an independent contractor basis instead of an employee basis. They were told (and some may still be hearing) that this will avoid the usual tax and paperwork problems associated with the hiring of employees. The IRS has been on a campaign for some time to reclassify millions of independent contractors as employees, and if they have their way, someday there will be no independent contractors at all. Thousands of businesses that have had their workers reclassified by the IRS and Department of Labor have been fined massive amounts in back taxes and related penalties.

Small craft businesses and cottage industries are not exempt. The problem arises when you hire an individual to work for you and that individual, in truth, is not a self-employed businessperson. You may have an agreement stating that an employer/independent contractor relationship exists between you, but it won't hold water if you are questioned by the IRS or Department of Labor. If you can't prove the legitimacy of the relationship, you could be liable for back taxes and penalties on all wages paid to such workers. To quote the IRS: "If an employer-employee relationship exists, it does not matter what it is called." In other words, an employee is an employee if the IRS or the Department of Labor says so.

A note from the IRS's *Tax Guide for Small Businesses* reads: *"Penalty for treating an employee as an independent contractor. If you classify an employee as an independent contractor and you had no reasonable basis for doing so, you can be held liable to pay employment taxes for that worker. Further, if you do not withhold income, Social Security and Medicare taxes from his or her wages, you may be held personally liable for a penalty equal to such taxes if you are the person responsible for the collection and payment of withholding taxes."*

See also Homework Laws; Legal Resources on the Web; Sales Representatives; *and* Statutory Employees.

Tip

If you are presently using independent contractors to produce craft products for your business and feel you may be on unsafe legal ground, it would be wise to immediately consult with an attorney who specializes in labor law. (See article, "How One Manufacturer Solved Her Independent Contractor Problem.") Meanwhile, to avoid undue attention from legal authorities, avoid publicity or advertising of any kind that suggests you may be using outside help. Some businesses fall under scrutiny when an independent contractor is let go and then files for unemployment insurance or employee benefits under workman's compensation.

Indian Arts and Crafts

A little-known FTC truth-in-marketing law—the *Indian Arts and Crafts Act of 1990*—is designed to prohibit fraud of our country's Native American handmade crafts. It was necessitated by competition from mass-produced "Indian-styled" products being produced overseas and marketed in the United States. The *Indian Arts and Crafts Enforcement Act of 2000* updated this law. The regulations spell out when a craft can be represented as an "Indian product." Basically, such products must be entirely made and assembled by Indian hands, and work that is merely "Indian designed" but not made by Indian hands cannot be called "Indian products." For more information, visit **www.iacb.doi.gov**.

How One Manufacturer Solved Her Independent Contractor Problem

After reading my comments about the dangers of using home sewers to produce a line of goods, Jane, a homebased manufacturer in my network, began to worry about her situation. In consulting a labor attorney as I had advised, she learned that all the "good advice" she had been receiving from CPAs, accountants, and tax attorneys was dangerously incorrect.

While they said it was okay for Jane to continue using independent contractors, the labor attorney told Jane she was in a situation where her sewers had to be employees. How to "go legal" when she had been operating illegally to that point was a frightening step. By filing with the U.S. Department of Labor, Jane would actually be raising her own red flag. But she followed her attorney's advice and was told by the Labor Department that, because she had voluntarily declared herself and had always paid minimum wages or above to her workers, there would be no penalties or back taxes imposed. Thus, if you are in a similar situation—wanting to switch over to employee status but afraid to do so—start looking for an attorney *who specializes in labor law.* (Jane found hers simply by asking around.)

Indicia

An indicia is an imprint on mail that indicates postage has been prepaid on bulk mail. It includes a special permit number that has been assigned to your company. An annual fee paid to your post office will cover all mailings (both first class and standard mail or "bulk mailings") you wish to make each year.

Insurance, Computer

Q: *I've invested quite a bit in the computer system I use for my business. Does my homeowner's policy give me enough protection against loss?*

No. Personal computers used for business are not covered by a regular homeowner's or renter's policy, except possibly against loss by fire or theft. Generally, damage or destruction caused by water or power surges would not be covered. You need to speak to your insurance agent to make sure, however. The best way to insure your system against all loss is to cover it with a regular business policy or buy a separate all-risk policy such as the one offered by Safeware, The Insurance Agency, Inc. (**www.Safeware.com**; 1-800-848-3469).

See also Insurance, Home-Business Policies *and* Surge Suppressor.

Insurance, Home-Business Policies

A growing number of insurance companies now offer special home office/home-business policies that give much greater coverage than a rider or business pursuits endorsement on your homeowner's or renter's policy. One company I've investigated is RLI Insurance Company (1-800-221-7917; **www.RLICorp.com**). For as little as $150 a year with a standard $100 deductible, you can get up to $50,000 all-risk protection, $5,000 per person medical payments, theft coverage away from premises, and a million dollars in general liability insurance (both product and professional). For an independent agent near you who sells this particular policy, call the Independent Insurance Agents & Brokers of America at 1-800-221-7917; **www.iiaa.org**.

Check your Yellow Pages for the names of other insurance companies that offer homeowner's insurance, since many of these same companies have added in-home business packages to their line. Some that have come to my attention are Aetna, Liberty Mutual, and Firemen Insurance Company.

See also Insurance, on Crafts Merchandise Off-Premise.

Insurance, Homeowner's or Renter's

Q: *We have quite a bit of money invested in tools, equipment, raw materials, and finished handcrafts. Since everything is in our home, we assume our homeowner's insurance covers everything, right?*

Wrong! Homeowner's (or renter's) insurance is strictly limited to personal possessions. Anything in the home used to generate income is considered to be business-related—including "goods for sale"—and thus exempt from coverage on a personal policy. It's important to tell your insurance agent that you run a business at home because your regular homeowner's or renter's policy will not cover business equipment, supplies, inventory, nor, in all probability, any losses due to fires that may be caused by such things. You must protect them either with a special rider or Business Pursuits Endorsement to your homeowner's or renter's policy, or with an individual business insurance policy, as discussed under "Insurance, Home-Business Policies." (If you are storing more than $3,000 of inventory, you should probably obtain a separate fire, vandalism, and theft policy.)

Although a business rider on your home insurance carries no personal liability coverage for your business, a special Business Pursuits Endorsement may cover materials and products you are storing as well as provide some liability coverage for people who may come to your home for business purposes. If you have turned your garage or some outbuilding into a studio or workshop, be sure to check with your insurance agent about the need for a rider that would cover all the tools, supplies, materials, and merchandise normally stored there. Ask specific questions, such as "What would the policy pay if everything was destroyed by a fire, flood, tornado, or hurricane?" or "If a thief breaks in and steals my tools, crafts merchandise, or machines, am I fully covered against loss?"

In times of tragedy, the homebased business owner has twice as much to lose as the ordinary homeowner—both home and business. For this reason, you might want to have a chat with your insurance agent about some "special disasters" that could befall your home. Find out if you are covered and, if not, how much it would cost to add a rider or two.

Remember, too, that regular homeowner policies do not cover such things as cracks in the foundation due to earth movement, sinkholes, damage from earthquakes, sewer problems, or water damage from hurricanes and other storms. As thousands of homeowners in my community learned in 1996, you don't have to live in a flood plain to sustain serious water damage to your home. When a twenty-four-hour "storm of the century" flooded nearby streams, they overflowed into streets throughout our area, ultimately pouring tons of water into the lower levels of nearly 8,000 homes in our city alone. In talking to my insurance agent about our own problem (a crack in the foundation that was ultimately repaired), I learned that the typical homeowner's policy will cover water damage to one's furnace, water heater, washer, and drier, but not furniture, artwork and other home furnishings in lower-level (basement) family rooms. I was surprised to learn that if we had sustained water damage because of our foundation leak, our policy would not have covered the loss; however, if our basement had flooded because the power failed and the sump pump couldn't work, then we would have been covered because we have a sump pump insurance rider. Insurance is tricky, and you must ask a lot of questions to find out exactly how much coverage you've got.

Replacement-Value Insurance. Do you have this important coverage on your policy? With regular insurance, what you get in the event of loss is figured on the current value of items after depreciation is taken into consideration. When you buy replacement-value insurance, however (which costs about 15 percent more a year), the amount you receive is the amount it would take to replace items at today's prices.

If you have added a business rider to your homeowner's policy to cover equipment and materials in your workshop or studio, note that the replacement-value insurance coverage stops at your business door. That is, any loss to business materials and equipment will be figured on a depreciable basis and limited to the amounts shown on your special business rider. Since your computer system may be one of the most expensive items in your business area, it's a good idea to insure it separately with a company that specializes in this type of insurance.

See also Insurance, Computer; Insurance, Home-Business Policies; and article, "Do You Have an All-Risk Home Insurance Policy?"

Tip

If you have a special collection of art or craft objects valued at more than $1,500, consider having the collection appraised so it can be insured on a separate all-risk endorsement. (See Insurance, on Collections of Art, Crafts, or Memorabilia.)

Do You Have an All-Risk Home Insurance Policy?

When the sump pump failed one year causing our basement to flood about six inches, I faced the cleanup job secure in the knowledge that the home-business rider I had placed on our homeowner's insurance policy would cover my business loss. When I called our insurance agent to report on all the books and printed materials I had lost, however, I learned yet another small lesson about insurance.

"I lost some of my book inventory and catalogs," I said, "but that should be covered on the business rider I took out—right?"

"Wait a minute," he said. "Let me see if you have an all-risk policy."

"What do you mean—all risk?" I asked nervously. "When I bought the business rider, I asked you to sell me a policy that would protect my book inventory from damage or destruction. You didn't say anything about all-risk coverage at that time."

The agent then explained that since our regular home insurance policy was an all-risk policy, the attached business rider was automatically all-risk coverage as well. "But if you had purchased a separate policy for your business," the agent said, "you might not have collected in this instance unless the policy specifically said you had all-risk coverage."

Let this serve as a reminder to check your insurance policy to make sure your coverage is all risk because your insurance agent may not advise you about the fine print until the damage is done.

Insurance, Medical

Q: *My husband and I would like to quit our jobs to work full-time on our home business, but that would mean giving up the hospitalization/major medical insurance coverage our family now enjoys. Is there an affordable solution to this problem?*

Unless you have preexisting conditions that make it difficult to get coverage, you can probably get individual insurance through Blue Cross/Blue Shield. This is very expensive, however, and periodic premium increases are common. One solution is to join your local Chamber of Commerce so you can get into its United Chambers group health insurance program. One couple told me they were able to cut their insurance premiums in half this way. Another option is to join one of the many home-business organizations that now offer group insurance programs to their members. Most of these programs are HMO or PPO programs, but rates are more affordable than what you would pay for an individual policy. For starters, check out:

- Home Business Institute, Inc.:
  1-888-DIAL-HBI; **www.HBIweb.com**
- National Association for the Self-Employed:
  1-800-232-6273; **www.NASE.com**
- Small Business Service Bureau:
  1-800-222-5678; **www.SBSB.com**

See also Chamber of Commerce *and* Home-Business Organizations.

Insurance, on Collections of Art, Crafts, or Memorabilia

Q: *I have a large collection of art and crafts from around the world as well as memorabilia and collector's items. What's the best way to protect them against loss?*

You may have replacement-cost coverage on your homeowner's policy, but if you check the fine print, you will find certain items are excluded from such coverage. This part of our policy specifically excludes "paintings, etchings, antiques, pictures, tapestries, statuary, articles made of marble, bronze or porcelain, or any other articles which, because of their inherent nature, cannot be replaced with new articles." Further excluded are memorabilia, souvenirs, and collector's items. If you have any special collection of items valued at more than $1,500, you may want to consider having the collection appraised so it can be insured on a separate all-risk endorsement.

See also Insurance, Homeowner's or Renter's.

Insurance, on Crafts Merchandise Off-Premise

Q: *If I consign my crafts or place them in a craft mall or rent-a-space shop, will the shop or mall owner's insurance policy cover loss or damage to my products?*

Except for shops and stores in shopping malls—which are mandated to buy liability and fire insurance whether they own the merchandise in a store or not—you are unlikely to have any insurance coverage unless you buy it yourself.

Generally, craft shop and mall owners buy fire and theft insurance on their building and equipment only. If the shop burns down or your goods are otherwise damaged or stolen, you will lose all. If you ever find yourself placing a great deal of merchandise in a single location, it would be prudent to purchase a business insurance policy that includes coverage for merchandise off-premise.

Professional craft sellers who sell regularly at fairs may wish to investigate the benefits of membership in the American Craft Association, the "trade arm" of the American Craft Council (1-800-724-0859; **www.CraftCouncil.org**). In addition to offering health insurance, this organization offers a property and casualty insurance policy that lets individuals choose the types and amounts of coverage needed for such things as protection of buildings, machinery, equipment, inventory, raw materials, goods on consignment, goods at fairs and shows, and losses due to theft, burglary, or robbery. Liability insurance is also offered as part of this particular policy.

American Family Mutual Insurance has an affordable "Arts, Crafts, and Hobby Stores" business policy that offers protection against fire on merchandise consigned to stores. A policy covering goods for $20,000, with $300,000 liability and a $250 deductible for property damage, would probably cost less than $400 a year. (This particular policy would not cover items stolen or damaged in a shop, however, or loss of merchandise at a crafts fair, such as an exhibit that blows over in the wind and destroys goods.)

If you find you need liability insurance for a major show, it's possible to buy "special events liability" coverage on a per-show basis (costly, however) from John Buttine Inc. (1-212-697-1010) or online at **www.Buttine.com**.

Insurance, Personal Liability

Q: *If I start a business in my home, will the personal liability insurance I have on my homeowner's policy cover me in case one of my customers is injured while on my property?*

No. Personal liability insurance protects you against claims made by individuals who suffer bodily injury while on your property, but your homeowner's policy does not cover any *business* activities on the premises. In the event of a lawsuit, one thing that will be considered is why the injured person was on your property in the first place. For example, a person might fall in your home while attending a holiday boutique or party plan presentation, or the UPS delivery person might slip on your icy walk while delivering a business package.

You need to discuss this problem with your insurance agent. Ask if you can extend your personal liability coverage with a business rider or an "umbrella policy" of some kind. (There are both personal and business umbrella policies.) Also check out the in-home business insurance packages now available to home-business owners. They generally offer at least a million dollars' worth of product and professional liability insurance.

See also Corporation *and* Insurance, Home Business Policies.

Insurance, Product Liability

Q: *My business is small, my products are safe, and I sell only through craft malls or at fairs. Do I really need product liability insurance?*

The purchase of insurance is always an individual choice, but most craft sellers today operate without product liability insurance because they can't afford it.

What product liability insurance does is protect you against lawsuits by consumers who are injured while using one of your products. Theoretically, everyone who makes and sells a product to the public is at risk, but most handmade items are so safe that the risk of the average crafter being sued is quite small. Your need for this kind of insurance has much to do with the kind of products you make and the size of your homebased business. Your financial risk will increase in direct proportion to the volume of business you do annually and the number of individual products you put into the marketplace. The cost of product liability insurance varies greatly from state to state and is also based on annual gross (or anticipated) sales, the number of products you sell, and the possible risks associated with each of them.

Once you enter the wholesale marketplace with a line of craft products, you may find that some buyers—particularly national mail order catalog houses and buyers of children's products—won't deal with you unless you have product liability insurance. Products for children naturally fall into a higher-risk category. (For an example of weird things that can happen where children's products are concerned, we need only recall the national news stories during the 1996 Christmas season about the dolls that were "eating" children's hair.)

In discussing this topic with my American Family Insurance agent, he said product liability insurance is "an individual thing. So much depends on the size of the business, the degree of risk inherent in that particular area, and the number of such claims that have been received in the past." He then recounted the story of how coverage had been refused to a woman who was launching a needlework kit business because there was a chance children could get hold of the needles. "This is a perfect illustration of how insurance companies think," he added.

If you find you need liability insurance but cannot afford an individual product liability policy, check out the in-home business insurance packages, most of which offer a minimal amount of product liability insurance.

See also Consumer Safety Laws; Guarantees and Warranties; Insurance, Home Business Policies; *and* Lead Testing.

Tip

To lower your risk of a lawsuit due to a defective product, never make express warranties (claims) about how a product will perform. With or without insurance, it's a good idea to make your products as safe as possible. Also take a sharp look at everything you are presently selling and try to imagine the dumbest thing anyone could do to hurt themselves with your products. Create special hang tags if buyers need to be alerted in any way. (Examples: "This doll is intended for adult collectors and should be kept out of children's hands" or, "To avoid breakage, do not subject this item to extreme heat or cold.")

Insurance, Vehicle

Q: *I use my car or van part-time for business, such as delivering products to individual customers or shop outlets, driving to craft fairs, obtaining supplies, and so on. How will this occasional business use of a personal vehicle affect my car insurance?*

Your primary concern here is likely to be one of personal liability. The first thing you should do is sit down with your insurance agent and explain how you plan to use your vehicle for business and what percentage of the time you would be using it this way. (If you use it mostly for business, it may be best to get it rated for business.) Find out if your present coverage would be sufficient in the event you had an accident while "doing business," such as delivering a load of finished crafts to a shop or traveling to/from a craft show. Also, if you have an employee who uses your vehicle for any reason, inquire about your need for "non-ownership contingent liability protection" that would protect you in the event your employee had an accident while working for you.

See also Labor Laws; Insurance, Personal Liability; *and* Vehicle Used for Business.

Internet and E-Mail Scams

Q: *I'm growing more concerned every day about accidentally getting snared by a slick con artist on the Web. What can I do to make sure the businesses I connect with on the Web are ethical?*

You're smart to be concerned about this. Scheming individuals who previously used the mail and telephone to prey on unsuspecting consumers were among the first to get on the Internet. According to statistics on the **www.Fraud.org** website, each year a growing number of "Internet crooks" are using e-mail as their preferred method of contact. The U.S. Postal Inspection Service (**www.USPS .gov/postalinspectors**) works with the FTC and other federal law enforcement agencies to monitor computer online services for fraud and direct marketing scams, but the average loss to fraud victims is growing every year.

Among the top ten Internet scams are goods never delivered or misrepresented (auctions), sales of other merchandise misrepresented or not delivered, Nigerian money offers, "phishing," and fake checks. Although many con artists are ultimately closed down by the FTC or the U.S. Postal Inspection Service, others simply take on a new identify by setting up a new website or sending out millions of new, deceptive e-mail messages. Here are just a few of the scams that concern me most:

• **Business "Opportunities."** If you're looking for moneymaking opportunities on the Web, be especially cautious. With their glitzy websites and deceptive e-mail messages, con artists can make even the worst "opportunity" seem irresistible, so don't automatically equate an impressive home page with credibility or business integrity. Always remember the old adage, "If it sounds too good to be true. . . ."

• **Nigerian Scams.** I commonly receive e-mails from people in Nigeria who say they are trying to get out of the country, but they need someone to "hold" the $18.5 million they've secretly stashed away (or some variation of this "problem"), and if I help them, I'll reap a huge financial reward as soon as they're safely out of the country. What's hard to believe is that so many greedy people have fallen for this scam and lost a great deal of money in the process. Some have even lost their lives.

Another Nigerian scam began to hit craft businesses on the Web in 2004. It always begins with a website owner receiving an e-mail from someone who says they want to place a large order for products to be shipped to some location in Nigeria. What they're really trying to do, however (besides order with stolen credit cards), is get the website owner to go out and buy other merchandise for them (such as telephones, cameras, and other electronic equipment) and ship it along with the ordered website merchandise. Small craft and home businesses, as well as Christian retailers and bookstores, seem to be a major target, but anyone who sells merchandise on the Web is apt to be approached. An amazing number of people have been conned out of thousands of dollars before they saw the handwriting on the wall. Bottom line: To be safe, don't even *think* about trying to fill an order to be shipped to Nigeria. (See "Nigerian Scams on the Rise" in the Crafts Marketing Articles area of my website at **www .BarbaraBrabec.com**. It includes reports from several website owners in my network.)

- **Fake E-Mail "Alerts."** From time to time, well-meaning but poorly informed Internet users will send you e-mail alerts about such things as viruses, things that threaten to hurt you, your computer, or someone else if you don't pass on the message, etc. Paying attention to any of these messages will be a serious waste of your valuable time, and forwarding it to others will waste their time, too. If curiosity gets the best of you, however, and you want to check it out, go to **http://hoaxbusters.ciac.org**, a good site that categorizes all these Internet hoaxes, scams, and myths. Another good source to learn about computer virus myths, hoaxes, and urban legends is **www.vmyths.com.**

See also Identity Theft; Scams, Home Business; *and article, "Phishing Expeditions for Your Identity."*

Internet and World Wide Web

Dozens of books on these topics are available to anyone who wants additional information, so my discussion here will be limited to a few personal remarks. As you probably know, the Internet is a computer

Phishing Expeditions for Your Identity

"Phishing" is the term for the type of Internet scam in which users are tricked into giving up personal information, such as credit card or Social Security Numbers, pin numbers, or bank account information. (You'll find about six million Web pages on this topic if you simply Google the word "phishing.") According to **www.Clickz .com** (the Web's richest resource for trends and statistics), phishing attacks are expected to increase in number in the future and become increasingly more sophisticated in nature, so you need to understand the danger here.

Example: As a PayPal novice, I was momentarily caught off guard the first time I received an e-mail, supposedly from PayPal, saying they were "doing a routine review of all accounts," and needed some additional information from me. More specifically, the message said that my account had been placed on a restricted basis, and that I could continue to receive funds, but would now be limited in my ability to withdraw them or make PayPal purchases. But the hairs on my neck went up when I read that all I had to do was click the PayPal.com link in the e-mail and "complete their credit card verification process" because "at least one credit card is still unconfirmed."

Sure enough, these official-looking but counterfeit e-mails are all scams to get your personal identity. Legitimate companies, and financial institutions in particular, will *never* ask for this kind of information by e-mail, nor will they send you e-mail messages with attachments of any kind. All financial-oriented sites such as PayPal and eBay have security areas that explain how and where to forward suspicious "spoof" e-mails. By reporting them when you get them, you'll help stop the people who are trying to defraud you and others on the Web.

network that connects millions of computers worldwide, while the World Wide Web is simply a way of publishing and accessing information on the Internet. While the Internet is exciting technology that can be used to enrich one's life and benefit any business, it's also the worst invasion of our privacy we've ever had as well as the greatest time-waster ever to come down the pike. Many people have become addicted to spending their lives in front of a computer; in some cases, whole families have lost their ability to communicate with one another as each family member goes to his or her own personal computer terminal to work, play games alone, or chat with strangers online. As we all bend to accommodate the new technology that is literally being forced upon us day by day, we must be careful not to get so carried away with the wonder of it all that we forget it's people, not machines, that are important.

Although I was once very reluctant to accept this time-consuming, privacy-invading technology, I must admit that I now see e-mail and the Web as powerful business and marketing tools. Used wisely, both can enhance one's personal life and enable one to grow a business more quickly while also generating new streams of income. See *Web Marketing Options* for a discussion of ways which you can sell art or craft products on the Web at little cost and with a minimum expenditure of time.

See also Internet and E-Mail Scams.

Inventory

Q: *Do I really have to keep an inventory of raw materials I use to make products for sale?*

As crafters begin to sell what they make, they are not likely to concern themselves with keeping inventory records for tax purposes, but the longer one is in business and the more one sells, the more important this becomes. First, the IRS requires everyone who sells products to keep inventory records, so if you're not doing this now, it means the information on your annual Schedule C tax report is incorrect. Keeping track of what you spend each year versus what you owe is only part of the record-keeping you must do as a professional craft seller. What the IRS wants to know is how much inventory you are sitting with at the end of any given year. Only the amount of raw materials and supplies that ended up in the products you sold that year is deductible. The value of the inventory that's left must be carried forward to your next year's tax return. For tax purposes, the inventory of a craft seller includes:

- what has been spent on raw materials and supplies used to make products
- the value of the raw materials and supplies (not the retail price) in partly finished craft items
- the value of the raw materials and supplies in finished crafts still unsold at the end of the year, including orders awaiting shipment and all goods on consignment or in craft malls and rent-a-space shops.

This sounds complicated, but it really isn't. You need to keep these records anyway if you want to know whether you're making a true profit on your crafts. Following is the information the IRS will expect you to provide on your Schedule C tax return. (See also article, "How to Keep Inventory Records.")

Schedule C (Form 1040)   Page **2**

Part III   **Cost of Goods Sold** (see page C-5)

33	Method(s) used to value closing inventory: **a** ☐ Cost **b** ☐ Lower of cost or market **c** ☐ Other (attach explanation)		
34	Was there any change in determining quantities, costs, or valuations between opening and closing inventory? If "Yes," attach explanation . . . . ☐ **Yes** ☐ **No**		
35	Inventory at beginning of year. If different from last year's closing inventory, attach explanation . .	**35**	
36	Purchases less cost of items withdrawn for personal use	**36**	
37	Cost of labor. Do not include salary paid to yourself	**37**	
38	Materials and supplies	**38**	
39	Other costs	**39**	
40	Add lines 35 through 39	**40**	
41	Inventory at end of year	**41**	
42	**Cost of goods sold.** Subtract line 41 from line 40. Enter the result here and on page 1, line 4 . .	**42**	

IRS Worksheet (page 2 of Schedule C, Form 1040) for cost of goods sold.

How to Keep Inventory Records

Inventory records can be kept on computer (special programs are available) or by hand with the use of ledger sheets or a notebook. To simplify record-keeping, break down purchases of raw materials and supplies into logical categories, using a separate page for each (wood, clay, wire, screws, component parts, paint, fur, fabric, etc.). Log purchases specifically, such as "10 yards red velvet ribbon" or "500 lamp bases."

Consider creating a worksheet with headings of Date, Materials Purchased, Number Purchased, Cost Per Item, Number Used, Number Left, and Cost of Items on Hand so you can monitor all the supplies purchased and the cost of the supplies used in each item you make for sale.

At year's end when you do your physical inventory, remember that the figure IRS wants to see on your tax return is the total of unused supplies and materials on hand *plus* the amount of materials and supplies in products-in-progress, finished items on the premises not yet sold or shipped, plus unsold merchandise in consignment shops, craft malls and rent-a-space shops. To come up with these figures, you will need to refer to records you have kept (or should be keeping) of how much cost you have in materials for each of the products you sell. Whether you make one-of-a-kind creations or sell hundreds or thousands of items each year, this is information you need to record not only for yourself, but to satisfy IRS requirements.

Don't stay up nights worrying about your inventory records, but do the best estimate you can. Many crafters simply "eyeball" their inventory of raw materials and unsold craft merchandise to arrive at a good estimate for their tax return. (If you were ever audited, the IRS would have a hard time proving your estimate was incorrect.)

See also Tax Audits.

Invoice

The standard three-, four-, or five-part invoice sets available in office supply outlets will probably be sufficient for most small businesses, but you may prefer to create your own computer-generated invoices. As your business grows and you wish to make a stronger impression on your customer accounts, your local "quick printer" can print multiple-part invoices for you at a reasonable cost.

An invoice should include seller's name and address; buyer's name and address; ship-to address (if different from sold-to address); customer's purchase order number and date of order; shipping date and method of shipment; invoice number (optional); terms of payment (Net 30 days, etc.); quantity and description of items shipped with unit price and total amount indicated; and shipping charges. To protect yourself against unauthorized returns, you may also wish to include your Returns Policy on the invoice. Larger stores may request a "blind invoice copy," which is the same thing as a packing slip (a copy of the invoice that describes the merchandise but does not indicate any prices).

If you make a single shipment to an account, invoice them, and find thirty days later that payment has not been received, send a copy of the invoice with SECOND NOTICE written across the top and a note saying, "This invoice is now overdue. Please remit promptly to retain your good credit rating with us." If you have made several shipments to this account and some of the invoices have been paid while others have not (some of which are not yet overdue), a statement should be sent that lists the dates and amounts of outstanding invoices.

See also Invoices Not Paid; Returns Policy; Minimum/Maximum Order Policy; Packing List; *and* Statement.

Invoices Not Paid

Q: *What steps should I take to collect overdue invoices for merchandise shipped to shops and other buyers?*

Begin with a series of reminder letters. After one crafts wholesaler in my network let her unpaid accounts build up to $10,000 (because she was so busy producing goods she didn't take time to monitor this situation closely), she got serious about collecting the money due her.

After her statements were ignored, she sent a friendly reminder ("Has this slipped your mind?"). Thirty days later, she sent a stronger notice ("Your account is now 60 days overdue.") To this she added a personal note that brought a 20 percent response. It read: "This invoice represents (number of hours) of handwork. Please consider the time and effort we have put into manufacturing this product and sending it to you on time."

Along with the statements and reminder notices, this seller also made telephone calls. "Phone calls work better than letters when you're trying to collect," she says. "Always try to work out a payment arrangement because few people want to be hounded by a bill collector and some will finally pay just to avoid this hassle."

The final notice read: "Your account is seriously past due. If payment is not made immediately, it will be turned over for collection." In the end, this particular business owner was able to collect only about a third of her accounts. She turned the rest over to a collection agency that took more than a year to collect half of them. The balance had to be written off. "It was an expensive lesson," she adds.

See also Collection Agencies *and* Small Claims Court.

Tip

Many problems can be avoided if your customers have your payment terms in writing and you communicate with them as soon as an invoice becomes overdue. When it's time to put on your bill-collecting hat, try not to think of yourself as the person who created the products that haven't been paid for, but the practical manager of your business whose goal is to increase cash flow. If the first call doesn't bring results, be persistent and call again.

ISBN

"The ISBN is a unique machine-readable identification number, which marks any book unmistakably," states the ISBN agency on its website at **www.ISBN.org**. This number is used by publishers as an inventory code, by buyers as an order number, and for a variety of bibliographic purposes such as library catalog cards and online ordering systems. If you plan to publish a book, you need to contact the ISBN Agency (1-877-310-7333) and request a block of numbers based on the number of books you intend to publish. (Even one-book publishers should do this, as books without an ISBN won't be acceptable to bookstores and libraries.)

Juried Shows

Q: *I tried to get into a juried show but was rejected. What's wrong with my work?*

All the better art and craft shows today are juried events. That is, hopeful exhibitors must submit slides or photos of their work to show promoters or organizers to show both the quality of their work and its appropriateness for sale at a particular show. Some sellers will be juried out of a show because they are producing handcrafts not in keeping with a show's theme or type of art or craft wanted for sale. For example, a traditional craftsperson might not gain entry to a contemporary crafts show, while a hobby crafter might be excluded from a show because his or her work does not qualify as true art or craft in the opinion of the show promoter. Try not to take such rejections personally. Being juried out of a show doesn't mean your work is not good, only that it is not appropriate for sale at that particular show. Sometimes sellers are rejected because too many other sellers are offering the same type of product and a limit has been placed on the number of sellers in a particular product field that will be allowed in the show. Entering events earlier could solve this problem. Subscribe to show listing periodicals to learn about such events months in advance.

See also Show Listings.

Tip

Failure to gain entry to a juried show could lie in the way you are presenting your art or craft to a show promoter. They are as likely to be interested in the way you plan to display your work as they are in the quality of work you do. You will need good photos that show your work and sales exhibit in the best possible light.

Kitchen Laws

Q: *I'd like to sell some homemade jams, jellies, and dried foods along with my craft items. Are there any problems in offering food products for sale?*

Anyone who sells food items of any kind should investigate their state's "commercial kitchen" law and find out if any local permits or licenses are required. In many states, it is very costly, if not impossible, for anyone to set up a food-related business in their home. There are exceptions, however, and some states draw the line between commercial food businesses and small operations such as bake sales and farmers' markets. Iowa, for example, has a "home bakery provision" that allows home bakers to operate without a license if they earn less than $2,000 per year and agree not to advertise their products.

Tip

Many clever food sellers have gotten around commercial kitchen laws in their state by renting a kitchen in a commercial building such as a local pizza parlor or church. One woman who wanted to sell her jams and jellies met her state's requirement by putting the required sinks and two Coleman stoves in a storage building in her backyard.

Labels, Address

When you want to make a great impression, use printed address labels to add pizzazz to your professional image. Check office supply catalogs for two-color mailing and shipping labels that can be ordered either with your business name and address preprinted on them, or blank if you prefer to print your own labels.

In particular, check out Grayarc (1-800-243-5250; **www.Grayarc .com**), which offers a wide assortment of labels, including foil-stamped address labels and special-message information labels such as "Thank you" and "Made in the USA," etc.

See also Office Supply Catalogs.

Labels or Tags Required by Law

Q: *If I'm only selling at craft fairs or in a consignment shop or craft mall, do federal labeling laws apply to my small business?*

Yes, you become a manufacturer in the eye of the law as soon as you begin to put products on the consumer market, even if all your products are one-of-a-kind creations. Certain labels and hang tags are required by law by the Bureau of Consumer Protection and the Federal Trade Commission, so you must comply with federal labeling rules if you make any of the following products for sale:

- Textile, suede, or leather products in the form of wearing apparel or household furnishings, piece goods, yarn, rugs, or anything else made of fiber (see *Textile Fiber Products Identification Act*)
- Stuffed toys, dolls, quilts, pillows, soft sculpture, and all other items with concealed stuffing (see *Bedding and Upholstered Furniture Law*)
- Any product made of wool, or any wool or textile product that uses imported fibers (see *"Made in USA" Labels* and *Wool and Other Textiles*)
- Any product made of fur (see *Fur Products*)
- Any kind of garment (see *Care Labels*)

These federal labeling requirements may seem imposing, but it is not difficult to comply with them. You can make your own hang tags and labels or order commercial tags and labels from a number of suppliers who advertise in craft magazines and on the Web.

See also Hang Tags and Designer Labels *and* Toymaking.

Labor Laws

Q: *What labor laws are applicable to a homebased business?*

If you hire only family members to work for your business, the U.S. Department of Labor's only concern is that you are paying your family employees at least the minimum wage. If you later hire non-family members to work for your business, you need to be aware of *The Fair Labor Standards Act of 1938, as Amended.* This law establishes minimum wages, overtime pay, record-keeping, and child labor standards for employees individually engaged in or producing goods for interstate commerce, and for all employees employed in certain enterprises described in the act, unless a specific exemption applies. Direct specific questions on this topic to the Wage and Hour Division of the Department of Labor. (See "U.S. Government" in your telephone book or check the Web at **www.DOL.gov**).

See also Employees, Nonfamily; Homework Laws; Independent Contractors; OSHA Regulations; *and* Statutory Employees.

Laws and Regulations

There are many laws and regulations you must be familiar with as you enter the business world. Check the individual listings in this book for each of the local, state, and federal laws referenced below:

- **Local Laws.** *See* Advertising Signs; Business or Trade Name Registration/Protection; Fictitious Name Statement; Licenses and Permits; Taxes; Telephone, Business Use of; *and* Zoning Laws.
- **State Laws.** *See* Bedding and Upholstered Furniture Law; Business or Trade Name Registration/Protection; Celebrity Rights Act; Consignment Laws; Employees, Family; Employees, Nonfamily; Endangered Species; Homework Laws; Independent Contractors; Kitchen Laws; Labor Laws; Licenses and Permits; Limited Editions; Nature Items; *and* Taxes.
- **Federal Laws.** *See* Care Labels; Consumer Safety Laws; *all listings on* Copyrights; Endangered Species; Estimated Tax Payments; Fabrics, Flammability Standards; Fax Machine; Federal Trade Commission Rules; Fur Products; Guarantees and Warranties; Indian Arts and Crafts; Labels or Tags Required by Law; Labor Laws; Lead Testing; Nature Items; Postal Regulations; Taxes; Textile Fiber Products Identification Act; Trademark; Trade Practice Rules; *and* Wool and Other Textiles.

LC Number

If you plan to publish a book that will be sold to libraries, you must obtain an LC (Library of Congress) number and add it to the copyright page of your book. However, the Library of Congress now prohibits self-publishers and e-book publishers from requesting a listing. To get around this exclusion, you must work with a distributor that supplies libraries and ask them to get an LC number for you. One of the largest, and best, is Quality Books (1-800-323-4241; **www.QualityBooks.com**).

Lead Testing

Q: *We are careful about firing our ceramics to the temperature recommendation of the glaze manufacturer to make sure our products are free of lead and safe for food use. Do we need to take any other precautions to ensure the safety of our products?*

If you are selling ceramic items that come in contact with food or drink, you should test them for lead content before sale, *even though glazes are said to be food-safe or lead-free by the manufacturer.* I first wrote about this problem in 1972 and, unfortunately, it still exists today. For a long time, consumers were led to believe that it was only imported products that were hazardous because of improper glazing and firing. That is not the case, however. Any piece that is under-fired or incorrectly fired by an amateur potter may contain a dangerous level of lead. This is a potentially serious problem in schools where kilns are not as carefully regulated as those of professional ceramists. In other words, drinking out of that mug Junior just brought home is likely to be hazardous to your health.

The Food and Drug Administration (FDA) regularly makes random tests of pottery being shipped in interstate commerce, and they are empowered to confiscate products that fail to meet their lead release guideline of less than 0.5 parts per million. As ceramist Judith Leigh Pearson learned, being careful about regulating the temperature of her kiln and following manufacturer's firing instructions to the letter is not enough. In an article for *The Crafts Report,* she brought this problem to light while sharing her unusual experience with the FDA and her state's Department of Health. When the FDA was doing random lead testing in her area, they called Judith's studio to schedule a test of her products. So she would know what they were going to find, she immediately purchased a lead test kit (available in the paint department of most hardware stores). She was stunned to learn that many of her pieces tested positive, but not nearly as stunned, she said, as the manufacturer of the glaze she was using. According to their tests, this particular glaze was food-safe when fired to the temperature indicated on the label—the one Judith had used.

This article left several questions unanswered, but it emphasizes the importance of testing the ceramics you're putting into the commercial marketplace *if there is any chance they might be used as food containers*. No craftsperson can afford a lead poisoning lawsuit. "We as craft producers have to go the extra mile," Judith cautions, "and read beyond the labels to make sure our products are safe."

Here are some additional tips to help you avoid problems:

1. No glaze should ever be used by the hobbyist for food surfaces unless the manufacturer's label states the glaze is approved for such use when fired according to instructions—and these instructions must be followed *to the letter*.
2. Never fire by time alone—always use pyrometric cones.
3. Ceramic makers who are concerned about the safety of their products or uncertain about their ability to control their end use should design and fire decorated pieces only or make items undesirable for food and beverages by drilling holes in the sides or bottom, thus rendering them useless as containers.
4. If supervision is required in a teaching situation (such as elementary schools, hospitals, nursing homes, or other institutions), only nontoxic, lead-free hobby glazes should be used.
5. Depending on the size of the kiln and the quantity of ware being fired, the atmosphere around a kiln can constitute a very real health hazard. The kiln should be fitted with a hood exhausting to the outdoors, and should be located in an area where adults, children, or pets will not unwittingly be exposed to lead fumes.

See also Consumer Safety Laws; Environmental Protection Agency; Health Hazards; Licenses and Permits; *and* Insurance, Product Liability.

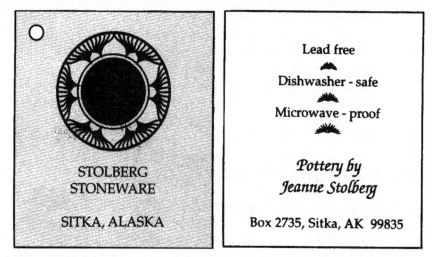

STOLBERG
STONEWARE

SITKA, ALASKA

Lead free
▲
Dishwasher - safe
▲
Microwave - proof
▲

Pottery by
Jeanne Stolberg

Box 2735, Sitka, AK 99835

When using lead-free glazes, be sure to tell your prospective buyers you have done this.
The sample tag above is a good example of how to convey this information. Note the
inclusion of two additional buyer benefits as well; products are both dishwasher-safe
and microwave-proof.

Legal Forms of Business

There are four basic legal forms a business can take, and each has
its pros and cons. Each of these topics is discussed separately in this
book.

See Corporation; Partnership; Sole Proprietorship; *and* Limited Liability
Company.

Legal Resources on the Web

Here are three helpful Web resources you can turn to the next time
you have general questions about legal matters related to the operation of your crafts or homebased business:

• **www.FreeAdvice.com.** You'll find answers to many of your
legal questions here, including information about your state's laws,
business law questions, and answers to questions about the use of
employees and independent contractors.

• **www.IvanHoffman.com.** The website of attorney Ivan Hoff-
man contains many articles related to law for writers and publishers,

entrepreneurs, website designers and owners, as well as other articles on trademarks, domain names, the Internet, and electronic rights.

- **www.LawGuru.com.** A network of more than 2,000 attorneys and law firms in more than thirty-five countries. Various attorneys answer questions online free of charge, and the website's database now includes answers to 35,000 FAQs in 45 legal categories.

See also Attorney/Lawyer.

Libel/Defamation of Character

Be careful what you say about others, since you can be held legally accountable for defamation of character if you disparage another's business reputation or character with untrue statements. In an article for *The Crafts Report,* attorney Leonard D. Duboff emphasized there is a big difference between promoting your work and reputation and undermining another's, so be careful about intentionally undermining a competitor's product or integrity when talking to strangers. "You can say your products are first-rate, but it would be risky to say that your work is better than another's unless that fact can be established," he cautions.

Licenses and Permits

Q: *What's the difference between a license and a permit, and do I need either of them to sell my crafts at local fairs and shops or by mail?*

A *license* is a certificate granted by a government agency that gives one permission to legally engage in a business, occupation, or activity. Depending on the type of business you plan to operate, you may need a license from certain municipal or county agencies. Food-related businesses, for example, are subject to special restrictions and inspections by both local and state health departments. If you work with flammable materials, you may need some kind of permit or official okay from the fire department. If your business causes the release of any materials into the air or water (even a ceramic kiln), you may need approval from the local environmental protection agency.

A *permit* is similar to a license, except it is granted by local authorities. Some communities require a permit for almost everything while others require it only for businesses that involve food, direct selling, and home shops. In years past, permits were rarely required for small craft businesses. Now, however, many communities see homebased entrepreneurs as a great source of extra revenue. So, depending on where you live, you might have to pay between $15 and $200 for a "home occupation permit" that contributes to community coffers but does absolutely nothing for you.

If a license or permit is required and you operate without it, you run the risk of discovery, which could lead to a fine or an order to cease your business. No one goes around checking to see who has a license and who doesn't, but authorities sometimes discover unlicensed businesses by checking state sales tax returns and resale licenses, or they might read about a crafter's homebased business in the local newspaper and check their records to see if the business is registered. Call your city or county clerk for more information on this topic.

See also Bedding and Upholstered Furniture Law; Business or Trade Name Registration/Protection; Environmental Protection; Kitchen Laws; *and* Zoning Laws.

Licensing Arrangements

Q: *I have been contacted by a company interested in mass producing a doll I have designed. What kind of royalties are common in such an arrangement, and what are the pitfalls in this area?*

A license grants specific rights to someone to do something that could not legally be done without the license. Creators of ideas or products may grant licenses for such things as the use of a name, a graphic image or design, a cartoon character, or an invention or unique product. In return for granting a license to a manufacturer to produce a product, a licensor is compensated with a royalty on the wholesale price that can vary from 5 to 12 percent but will more likely fall somewhere in between. An advance on royalties is common. The amount of royalties and size of advance have much to do with the industry and how marketable the product appears to be.

A licensing arrangement can be made for a period of one to five years, but most contracts are set up for two years with renewal options. If you use an agent to sell your idea or product to a manufacturer, expect to pay that person either a flat fee or a commission of between 10 and 15 percent of your total royalties. Don't sign a licensing contract until a patent or copyright attorney has checked it. (See my website at **www.BarbaraBrabec.com** for additional information on this topic and other tips for professional designers.)

Note that licensing works in reverse, too. That is, you may someday want to use someone else's designs on your products. A licensing arrangement with another creative person like yourself could be mutually profitable. For more information on this aspect of licensing, see article, "Licensing Tips for Small Manufacturers."

> *See also* Attorney/Lawyer; Copyrights of Others; Fabrics (Designer), Commercial Use of; Legal Resources on the Web; Patent; Patterns, Commercial Use of; Sports Logos, Commercial Use of; *and article, "The Cabbage Patch Kids® Story."*

Tip

To get a better handle on the market for products you might want to license to others, consider attending one of the annual licensing shows held in New York City each year, sponsored by International Licensing Merchandisers' Association. Call 1-212-244-1944 or check **www .Licensing.org**.

Limited Editions

Q: *I would like to create a limited-edition doll for collectors and offer perhaps no more than 250 for sale. Besides giving customers a certificate that states the item is a limited edition, is there anything else I should do?*

In an article for *The Crafts Report,* attorney Peter H. Karlen of La Jolla, California, explained that many states now have laws that impose strict disclosure and warranty requirements on sellers who offer limited editions of art or craftwork. These laws require the inclusion of specific information on printed materials that advertise such items by mail, and the certificate of authenticity must contain

Licensing Tips for Small Manufacturers

When working with major companies or institutions, licensing arrangements are likely to be expensive and usually involve royalties that may range from 6½ to 7½ percent of gross sales. But small business owners may be able to work with other individuals on a mutually profitable basis. For example, I recall two needlework designers who made a profitable arrangement with an artist whose work they admired. They sold him on the deal simply by stitching one of his paintings and explaining how they would market an entire line of his designs in cross stitch and needlepoint. Working with an attorney, they came to an agreement on royalties and term of contract (which included renewal options and a termination clause). Here are three tips they shared with me:

1. You or the licensor may want to branch out into other related fields, so you need a "Right of First Refusal" clause that will give you first chance at the opportunity to expand into a different area of business. If you decline, the opportunity may then be offered to others.
2. Be sure to work out what will happen in the event of death of either licensor or licensee.
3. Specify the territory in which you plan to sell . . . and don't limit yourself to a small area.

Although you may never have any intention of obtaining such a license, you may someday find yourself in a position to license others to reproduce a design you've created. Before entering into a licensing arrangement, be sure to register appropriate copyrights or trademarks, and establish quality-control standards for the manufacturer of your designs. A licensing agent or attorney can represent your interests.

a whole list of disclosures that become warranties. "If any of the disclosures are untrue," he states, "you have a breach-of-warranty problem on your hands."

In researching this topic on the Web, I learned on **www .ArtBusiness.com** that there is tremendous abuse in the "certificate of authenticity" (COA) business, particularly on eBay: "A legitimate COA must contain specific details about the art such as when and how it was produced, the names of people or companies involved in its production, the art's exact title, dimensions, and the names of reference books or similar resources that contain either specific or relevant information about the art and/or the artist. It should also state the qualifications of the individual or entity that authored the certificate, and include his or her complete and current contact information."

Given the complex legal nature of this topic, anyone thinking about offering a limited-edition item should work with an attorney who can draft the proper certificate forms.

See also Guarantees and Warranties.

Tip

There is a big difference between producing a limited number of items of a particular design (called multiples) and a "limited edition" run of that item as discussed above. If you're not into mass production of handcrafts, don't apologize for the fact that you make only multiples of your work. Instead, emphasize the uniqueness, rarity, or exclusivity of your products. Even large department stores are buying one-of-a-kind originals and craft multiples today.

Limited Liability Company

Limited Liability Companies (LLCs), first introduced in 1992, combine the best attributes of other business forms, but tax and regulatory requirements vary from state to state. "This form of business is similar to an S Corporation, with limited liability for the stockholders, and pass-through profits taxable to the owners but not to the business," explains CPA Bernard Kamoroff, author of *Small*

Time Operator. "LLCs offer more generous loss deductions than S Corporations, offer more classes of stock, and are not limited to the S Corporation's maximum of 35 individual shareholders. The IRS does not recognize LLCs for federal income tax purposes, and will tax them either as partnerships or corporations, depending on how they are legally structured."

See also Corporation.

Line of Credit

Q: *Is there any way a small business owner can get a line of credit?*

If you have a growing crafts business, you're likely to have cash flow problems. If you have been doing business with a local bank for some time, have a business checking account there plus a good credit rating, you may find it easy to get a $10,000 line of credit against which you can borrow funds as needed. Since banks love to give money to people who don't need it, the best time to apply for a line of credit is when all your bills are paid and you have some money in the bank. (If you wait until you're financially strapped and can't show how you're going to repay any loan you make, you are likely to be refused credit.)

By obtaining a line of credit before you actually need the money, you will have added peace of mind that you will be able to handle unexpected business expenses in low-cash-flow months, take advantage of special sales on supplies or equipment, or make major business purchases earlier than you might otherwise have been able to do.

The rules for borrowing on a line of credit are simple. In my experience, during a period of a year, you can borrow and repay money as often as necessary, but the bank will want to see inactivity in your account for a period of at least thirty days during the year. If you can meet this requirement, your credit line is likely to be renewed every year. Although line-of-credit loans are payable on demand, few banks call them in unless they are unduly concerned about a lender's ability to repay.

See also Bank Loans; Financing a Business; Home Equity Loans; *and* SBA Loans.

Long Distance Carriers

You have an incredible amount of choices when it comes to the long distance provider you're going to use. Some of the best rates may be available to you as a member of one of the home-business or craft organizations listed in this book. All long distance companies offer a variety of plans. What you spend per month on average, where you call, and when you make most of your calls may have much to do with the rates you can get. (Competition is so fierce in this industry that merely complaining about your phone bill and suggesting you might switch carriers could get you lower rates. I couldn't believe it when one sales rep I spoke with said, "Some people change their long distance providers every 24 hours.")

In selecting a service provider, ask how charges are determined. The two biggest moneymakers for companies that offer per-minute rates are charging for ring time (customer pays for a call even when no one answers) and charging by the minute instead of in six-second increments. (Even when you're on the phone for only half a minute, you pay for a full minute. This really adds up when you consider that every call you make is likely to have an extra minute's charge attached to it.) Many small businesses now opt for one of the special unlimited long distance plans offered by many providers.

See also Telephone, Business Use of.

"Made in USA" Labels

U.S. content must be disclosed on all textile, wool, and fur products, but there is no law that requires most other products sold in the United States to be marked or labeled "Made in USA" or have any other disclosure about their amount of U.S. content. If you choose to make claims about other products made in the USA, however, you must comply with the FTC's "Made in USA" policy, which requires that all, or virtually all, of the final product be made in the United States. A "Made in USA" claim can be express ("Made in USA") or implied ("Our products are American-made").

A textile or wool product partially manufactured in the United States and partially manufactured in another country must be labeled to show both foreign and domestic processing. To fully comply with the "Made in the USA" standard, you need to get detailed information from the FTC by phone or on its website (see listing for *Federal Trade Commission*).

See also Labels, Address; Textile Fiber Products Identification Act; *and* Wool and Other Textiles.

Mail, Classes/Types of

In mid-1996, the U.S. Postal Service improved mail standards with its "Classification Reform" program. In addition to offering special discounts for mailers who could prepare mail for automated processing, it introduced a new and very tedious system for sorting and bundling bulk mail (see *Bulk Mailings*). Now there are only four classes of mail:

1. **Express Mail:** offers guaranteed next-day delivery for anything mailable from letters to merchandise packages up to seventy pounds.
2. **First-Class Mail:** includes pieces weighing eleven ounces or less (after which point it is called Priority Mail).
3. **Periodicals** (formerly second-class mail): must meet certain requirements to qualify for the special periodicals rate. Check with your postmaster about this.
4. **Standard Mail** (formerly third- and fourth-class): is all mail not sent as First-Class Mail or entered as Periodicals. (Note: Book publishers can save money by sending book packages by "Media Mail" instead of regular parcel post. Ask your postmaster for current rates.)

For a cost over and above the cost of postage, you can get a number of special services from the post office, some of which will prove invaluable to your business. Ask your postmaster for additional information about:

- **Business Reply Mail.** This domestic mail service allows pieces bearing a specific address or label format to be mailed back to the addressee without prepayment of postage by the sender. Postage and fees are collected when the mail is delivered to the addressee who originally distributed the mail.

- **Certified Mail.** When you need legal proof that you have mailed something, send it by certified mail. The post office records the actual delivery date. For an extra fee, you can get a postcard in the mail as proof of who signed for the package and the date it was delivered. Tax advisers often recommend sending your annual tax return to the IRS by certified mail so you have evidence your return was filed on time.
- **Registered Mail.** This type of mail offers secured delivery for items of significant value, such as jewelry or stock certificates. It travels safely locked and delivery is recorded on signed receipts by postal authorities.
- **Return Receipt Mail.** When you want proof that a piece of mail has been delivered, you can get a postcard in the mail that indicates the date and time the mail was received and who signed for it.

See also Bulk Mailings; Indicia; Mail, Size Regulations; P.O. Box Address; Postage Meter; Postal Regulations; Priority Mail; Self-Mailers; *and article, "State and City Abbreviations."*

Mail Order Business

Although the Web has had a dramatic effect on mail order marketing, many art/craft sellers continue to increase sales and profits by making it easy for their customers to place orders by mail. If you decide to sell products by mail, be especially mindful of the FTC's 30-day mail order rule (discussed in the listing for Federal Trade Commission Rules). Several other listings in this book discuss topics of interest to mail order sellers, and more information will also be found in this book's companion marketing guide, *Handmade for Profit.* Also check out the benefits of membership in the National Mail Order Association (**www.NMOA.org**; 1-612-788-1673).

See also Better Business Bureau; Break-Even Point; Canadian Sales; Checking Account; COD Shipments; Guaranty of Satisfaction; Mail, Classes of; Mailing Lists, Rental of; Mail, Size Regulations; Money Orders; P.O. Box Address; Postal Regulations; Prepublication Offer; Refunds; Shipping and Handling Charges; Sole Proprietorship; Trade Practice Rules; *and* ZIP Code.

State and City Abbreviations

During the years when I operated a mail order business, thousands of people wrote to me every year requesting information about my books and reports, and every week I tossed mail without answering it for three reasons: (1) I couldn't read a person's handwriting or decipher a number in their address; (2) they had abbreviated the name of their city and I couldn't figure out what it was; or (3) they failed to include their ZIP code. The use of city abbreviations was particularly annoying. Do you know what R. S. M., CA is, or Bnvl, IN, or W. W., OK? I wasn't sure until I checked my z.c. dir. to decipher these abbreviations, which turned out to be Rancho Santa Marguerita, Boonville, and Woodward.

Not everyone will take the time to look up address information you should have provided in the first place. Therefore, to speed delivery of your mail and always get a reply to your mail, write legibly, don't abbreviate the name of your city, use the proper two-letter code for your state, and always include your ZIP code. If you don't know the two-letter abbreviations for each state, your postmaster will be happy to provide you with a list of them, or you can get them on the Web at **www.USPS.com**. A rubber stamp of your address or mini-address labels will not only save you time when ordering information or products but will speed delivery of your mail and fulfillment of your orders.

Mail, Size Regulations

Your postmaster will be happy to give you a booklet detailing all the size regulations of mail, so I'll just mention here a couple of problem areas that need emphasis:

- **Catalogs and Self-Mailers.** Before printing your new catalog or self-mailer or figuring what it will cost to mail a newsletter, ask your postmaster for a booklet that explains the various types of mail and all the rules and regulations related to each. You must be concerned not only with the size and design of mail pieces but how they are addressed. "We changed the format of our newsletter to resemble a book layout, putting the address area on the upper third of the back side," a reader reports. "When I delivered the mailing to the post office, I was told that because the address area was more than 6¼ inches from the bottom, I had to pay a penalty fee of about four cents per piece. Prior to printing our new catalog, I took a mock-up to the post office to confirm that its size and design met their regulations and qualified for the lower rates."

• **Postal Cards.** Never use 3 × 5 index cards as a substitute for postal cards because they do not meet U.S. Postal regulations. To be acceptable by the post office, a postal card may be no smaller than 3½ × 5 inches. The largest size that can use the regular postal card stamp is 4½ × 6 inches. While smaller cards may simply be rejected, the use of larger cards will result in extra postage charges.

See Postal Regulations *and article, "Money-Saving Postal Tips."*

Mail, Undeliverable

Do you know that undeliverable mail without a return address will be opened by postal employees and searched for an address or items of value? Letters that do not contain anything of value will be destroyed because of the Privacy Act, but any checks, money orders, stocks, or bonds found in such mail will be returned free of charge. Undeliverable parcels are held for ninety days, then put up for auction.

Mailing Lists, Rental of

Q: *I've developed a sizable mailing list of customers who have purchased my products by mail, and I would like to rent this list to other mail order sellers. Is there any problem with this?*

Some people do not want their names sold to others, and they have the right to privacy. In the Privacy Protection Study Commission named by former President Ford, it was recommended that list sellers give their customers (or members, subscribers, etc.) the option of having their names removed from any rental list. The following "disclosure notice" in your catalog or other mailers should suffice:

Money-Saving Postal Tips

Here is a collection of tips I compiled over more than twenty-five years of doing business by mail:

• If you're not using an accurate postal scale, you could be wasting postage on pieces that fall on the line between one ounce and another. Either double-check the weight of those pieces at the post office or get a more accurate electronic scale.

• Keep your postage costs low by designing your brochures and catalogs so they weigh an ounce or less. A change of paper weight or cover stock can make a big difference.

• If you use a business name and move, make sure you file a forwarding order for both your personal and business names. Otherwise, you may miss some of your mail.

• Although you may guarantee forwarding postage on periodicals when you move, remember that standard mail (formerly called third class) is not forwardable even when forwarding postage is guaranteed.

• If you are developing a mailing list for your business, delete any address that says "General Delivery" because such mail is forwardable for only thirty days.

• When addressing mail, always use the standard two-letter abbreviations for states with a ZIP code to enable automatic scanning and sorting. Abbreviate where you can and avoid punctuation. (AVE and ST are preferable to Avenue or Street.)

• It's a myth that you must use all caps and no punctuation for fast processing and delivery of your mail. That was true years ago when computers and optical scanners were less sophisticated at reading addresses, but no more. If you prefer to use upper and lower case letters in your computer database files, that's fine so long as you avoid the use of hard-to-read exotic typefaces.

• Always include your address on both sides of a postal card because the postmark on the front often obliterates part of an address, making it impossible to read.

> *We occasionally make our customers' names available to other reputable companies who offer quality products that might be of interest to you. If you prefer not to receive such offers, copy your name and address as it appears on the mailing label and send it to us.*

Before you advertise any mailing list for rent, make sure it's up to date. Because today's society is very mobile, a list can go out of date in a few months. After a year, 30 percent of the addresses on any mailing list could be bad. It is unethical to rent an out-of-date list, so you will need to "clean" your list by mailing to it again. Undeliverable first-class mail will automatically be returned with the new address or reason for nondelivery. For bulk mailings of larger lists, ask your post office about its "Address Service Requested" program.

See also Bulk Mailings.

Maintenance Agreements

Q: *Are maintenance agreements on office machines worth the money they cost?*

In my experience, it depends on which machine you are talking about. Because my dot matrix and laser printers worked beautifully for years without a hint of trouble, and my inkjet printer is now on its fourth year with no problems, I wouldn't encourage anyone to buy a maintenance agreement for a printer. I haven't found any reason to buy a maintenance agreement on computers, either, since they come with a guarantee that is long enough to get you past the point at which trouble is likely to occur. (If a machine is defective, problems tend to develop very early, while the guarantee is still in effect.) This is not to say that you won't need repairs on your system from time to time; only that I have found it more practical to pay for them at the time they are needed. Note there is a difference between a maintenance agreement on your computer system, and *computer insurance,* a topic discussed elsewhere.

See also Insurance, Computer *and article, "Commercial Use of Home Sewing Machines."*

Commercial Use of Home Sewing Machines

Here's an interesting story about sewing machines and Sears' maintenance contracts. When the owner of a sewing business took her machine to Sears for servicing, she made the mistake of mentioning to the clerk at the service desk that she had her own home business. Later, when her service contract came up for renewal, Sears wouldn't renew it. "I was told by Sears that their sewing machine is to be used only for home (family) sewing—never for something to be sold," she reported. "I'm sure a lot of other people don't know this."

On the warranties of many Sears appliances, there is an exclusionary clause that states, in effect, that commercial use invalidates the terms of the warranty. It's not surprising that Sears would want to protect themselves in this way. Obviously, a machine put together for light duty will not have the stamina for nearly industrial use, thus the exclusion.

Markups

This is the percentage a retail outlet adds to the wholesale price it pays for any item. In the gift and crafts industry the wholesale price is generally doubled (marked up 100 percent) to arrive at the retail price, but there are exceptions to this rule. Sometimes a crafts producer cannot wholesale an item at half the normal retail price, but buyers may want the product anyway because they know they can triple the purchase price and still sell it in their particular area. Even when you do wholesale products at half your standard retail price, buyers always have the option of using a higher markup, depending on what their traffic will bear.

Higher markups of 150 to 400 percent or more are common in other industries, so the product you make and the wholesale price you set may or may not permit selling to them.

See also Catalog Houses, Selling to *and* Pricing Guidelines.

Merchant Account Providers

Q: *My local bank won't grant me merchant status because my business is too small and too new. I need to be able to offer my customers credit card privileges but don't know how to do it.*

First, you need enough sales on a regular basis to justify the expense of offering your customers a charge card service. Don't be like the fellow who recently did some home maintenance work for me and then said I'd have to pay extra if I paid with a credit card. You cannot "bill" your customers for the privilege of using a charge card; you must simply set your prices high enough to cover this cost to begin with.

- **Merchant Accounts Offered by Organizations.** Going through your bank is going to prove costly, so first consider joining one of the crafts business organizations that offer merchant account options to their members. They have made special arrangements with banks that are favorably inclined toward homebased businesses. Two I have personally investigated and can recommend are:

  - National Craft Association:
    1-800-715-9594; **www.CraftAssoc.com**
  - TeaMac Inc./Arts and Crafts Business Solutions:
    1-800-873-1192; **www.TeaMacInc.com**

- By searching Google.com for the following keywords (be sure to put them in quotes: "National Crafts Association merchant account program" and "Arts and Crafts Business Solutions"), you will turn up many good reports about the above organizations and their merchant account programs. A good article on credit card processing will also be found in *The Crafts Report* archives at **www.craftsreport .com/april99/businessbasics.html**. It discusses the services of Arts and Crafts Business solutions, as well as a couple of other providers many craft sellers use.

- **Discover Network.** Another solution you might explore is offered by the Discover Network (**www.Discoverbiz.com**; 1-800-347-7996). It offers competitive fees (nominal transaction fees and no monthly minimums) and the processing capability to help you accept all payment options, including Visa, MasterCard, American

Express, Diners Club/Carte Blanche, and debit cards. The membership application on the Web looks simple.

- **Independent Sales Organizations (ISOs).** Avoid getting merchant status through an Independent Sales Organization, which is the most expensive and financially dangerous route you can go. In exploring my options here a few years ago, I learned that some companies in this field have questionable business ethics. At that time, in one publication or another, crafters were reporting on their experiences with ISOs, some of whom had been badly burned after paying $2,000 or more for equipment worth only $300 and getting stuck for $50 a month lease fees on a noncancellable four-year lease. Before applying to my local bank, I talked at length with one ISO that would have charged me $35 a month to lease the terminal ($1680 over a period of four years), or I could buy it for $1,000. Imagine my surprise when my local bank told me I could get the same equipment from them, including the software needed to make direct deposits to my bank account, for just $350. That gives you an idea of the high markups ISOs were then (and still may be) taking on equipment.

- **Taking Credit Cards on the Web.** If you're primarily interested in selling on the Web, your options are greater. Rather than getting stuck for the high fixed monthly charges of a regular account (and penalty fees when sales fall below a certain amount per month), many Web sellers use a merchant account provider that merely takes a percentage of each sale (see list below). Although such services are still costly, at least you know going in what your selling costs will be. Consider these for starters:

  - **www.PayPal.com**. The choice of beginners and pros alike. Fees occur only when sales are actually made. Visit the site for current rates. (I have found PayPal to be the perfect payment option for my writing, editing, and telephone consulting services, and it can also be used to sell products of any kind, with or without a shopping cart (see *Shopping Cart Systems*).

  - **www.CCnow.com**. This site offers a quick-and-easy shopping cart solution that enables sellers to accept all major credit cards. You pay a monthly fee plus 9 to 11 percent of sales over $100 a month.

NOTE: In the *Shopping Cart Systems* listing, I mention the free cart service offered by Mal's E-Commerce. On this company's website (**www.mals-e.com**), you'll also find an excellent overview article that explains payment gateways and credit card processors, with links to other reliable merchant account providers you might want to investigate.

I am reluctant to recommend other providers because there are a million and a half Web pages promoting various merchant account programs. You will have to do your homework here, and one of the best ways to find the right provider for you is to ask professional crafter friends what they use, or join one of the craft business e-mail discussion lists and see what other sellers recommend. One more thing: In spite of all the credit card "technology" available, it has been estimated that as many as two-thirds of all the craftspeople selling at shows are still using manual imprint machines, or "knucklebusters," as they are jokingly called. So don't let anyone tell you that you have to "go electronic" in order to accept credit cards at craft fairs.

See also Credit Card Sales; Discussion Lists and Web Forums; *and* Shopping Cart Systems.

Tip

For an excellent firsthand-experience article on getting merchant status, written by Betty Chypre—not only a seasoned craft seller, but publisher of one of the best show listing calendars available today—go to **www.smartfrogs.com/bankcard.html**.

Minimum/Maximum Order Policy

Q: *I'm trying to establish minimum/maximum order and reorder policies. What things do I need to consider here?*

Craft producers may have a minimum order policy of $50 to $200. More important than your minimum order policy, however, is the amount of additional merchandise you will ship to new accounts that have no credit history with you.

A crafts manufacturer explains the big ego trap many new crafters and even some old pros fall into: "Be especially cautious about invoicing large orders from new accounts. The people who are out to trick you or who have bad credit tend to order in large quantities. New crafters are so excited by large orders and rave comments that they may ship and invoice an order without question. Then, especially if it's around the holidays when shops often sell out their first shipment immediately, they may get a second order before the first order is past due. Everything looks great but before you know it, you can have three or four invoices totaling a thousand dollars or more that aren't past due yet."

The ceiling amount you set for new customers and reorders is up to you, but a good guideline would be to ask yourself how much money you could afford to lose if an account doesn't pay, and set that amount as your maximum amount. While a large crafts business might feel comfortable with a minimum of $250 to $500, the beginning crafter may not want to risk more than $100.

See also article, "Selling to Catalog Houses."

Tip

If you do not establish a high enough minimum order for dealers, you may find (especially around Christmas) that shop owners are buying your work at wholesale prices for themselves or for personal gifts. This may not bother you, but remember that very small orders can be a nuisance if you are primarily wholesaling your work.

Money Orders

Q: *When is it advisable to ask for payment by money order instead of a check?*

If someone is replacing a bad check, you should ask for repayment by money order since if one check was bad, the replacement check might be bad, too. Always give your mail order customers the option of paying by money order, but don't insist on this type of payment for

Selling to Catalog Houses

Could your business survive if you shipped $11,000 worth of merchandise and didn't get paid for it? That's what happened to Susan, a crafts designer who shared her story with me so others wouldn't get caught in a similar trap.

Susan was thrilled when a prestigious catalog company ordered 150 of her hand-decorated gourds for an invoice total of $11,000—the biggest order of her life. Uncomfortable about filling such a large order, Susan was reassured by the buyer who said not to worry—she was an investor in this reputable company.

So Susan put in hundreds of hours of around-the-clock production to meet the catalog's shipping date of August 1. Unable to do all the work herself, she hired a woman to help her, agreeing to pay her $1,000 for this work as soon as she got paid by the catalog house. Total expenses for this order—not counting Susan's time—were $4,000.

The last of the items were received by the catalog house on August 2. On August 3, the company filed for Chapter Eleven bankruptcy and Susan got caught in a terrible trap. Because her merchandise arrived before the court date, the company was not obligated to return it and could actually count it as part of their inventory, even though it was unpaid.

"While a company in Chapter Eleven can continue to operate and is protected against creditors, I learned that creditors have no rights at all," Susan told me. "The papers I received stated that, as a creditor, I (1) could *not* call to demand payment; (2) could *not* put a lien on anything owned by the company; and (3) could *not* take repossession of my property. Only the company's top twenty creditors had the legal right to file a priority claim or reclamation papers. All I was allowed to do was fill out a proof-of-claim form documenting that I was, in fact, owed $11,000 plus shipping charges. And I was given the right to seek legal counsel, which I could not afford."

(continued)

How can a company accept merchandise from a supplier one day knowing full well they are going into court the next day to declare bankruptcy? Susan never got the answer to this question. "If individuals operated like this, they'd end up in jail," she said. "This may not qualify as fraud, but it is surely immoral." Susan's advice to other crafters who are considering this kind of marketing is to *never* ship such a large first-time order to a mail order catalog house. "Such companies demand thirty-day terms but rarely pay within sixty days," she explained. "The prudent thing for a small supplier to do is sign a contract stating they will supply whatever quantity of merchandise the buyer anticipates needing for whatever period they plan to sell the item. (I had to agree to supply them for a one-year period.) Insist, however, that shipments go out in small batches, and that new shipments will not be made until outstanding invoices have been paid."

You may find this hard to believe, but a week after Susan got the bankruptcy papers, she received a new order for $3,500 worth of merchandise to be sent COD. Because she needed cash so badly, she agreed to ship this order, but insisted on a check up front and didn't ship until it cleared the bank. Although Susan tried every legal strategy she could afford, she never got her merchandise back and never got paid. This $11,000 lesson left her totally discouraged and deeply in debt. She went out of business shortly thereafter.

customers in the United States. (If you ask the average individual to pay by money order when they are used to paying by check, they will probably not order at all because it takes too much time to go out and get a money order.)

If you solicit orders from buyers in countries other than Canada (particularly when selling on the Internet), insist on payment by credit card or International Money Order. If you are selling by mail to Canadian buyers, see *Canadian Sales* for perspective on asking for payment by money order versus check.

Nature Items

Q: *Are there any laws against collecting and using natural materials in products I make for sale?*

Many crafters make products of dried nature materials such as tree bark, flowers, grapevines, pine cones, pods, dried grasses, weeds, and so on. Some also sell these dried materials to others. Legally speaking, the place from which you collect such items and the way you use them are important.

First, it's against the law to remove anything from a state park or forest preserve, including dead, dried materials. The idea here is not to disturb the balance of nature. Endangered species and their parts, from plants and wildflowers to animal bones, claws, and feathers, are also protected by state or federal environmental protection laws. In some cases merely possessing one of these protected items is a violation of the law.

If you plan to sell or are already selling nature crafts or raw materials, here are four suggestions on how to avoid problems or fines:

1. Never pick up *anything* from a state park or forest preserve.
2. Make sure you sell nothing that is protected by law.
3. Either gather all your nature items on your own property, or get written permission to collect them from other public or private areas.
4. Look in your Yellow Pages under the state government listings for the Department of Natural Resources and inquire about commercial permits that might be offered to collectors of nature materials. (Some states apparently authorize the removal of certain items at certain times, such as when greenery needs cutting back, trees need topping, or an area has to be mowed for some construction purpose.)

Finally, a note about bugs. As I was writing this, I wondered if there were any restrictions on shipping nature crafts or dried materials by mail because of tiny insects that might be clinging to such products. In checking with the post office I was amused to learn that the U.S. Postal Manual specifically says that "thoroughly dried dead insects" are mailable, so you will have no problems if your products are properly dried. (Tiny insects too small to see could be killed by freezing them overnight or zapping them in the microwave.)

See also Endangered Species *and* Found Objects.

Net Price

"Net" means free and clear. A net price is one from which deductions have been taken; net profit is what's left after all business expenses have been deducted. The opposite of net is gross.

See also Gross Price.

Newsletter/Ezine Publishing

Q: *I would like to share my enthusiasm for crafts by publishing a newsletter. This sounds easy to do, but I wonder if I'm overlooking something. Are small newsletters profitable?*

There is no market for print newsletters today, unless you're an expert on topics related to corporate business, alternative medicine, taxes, investments, etc. Almost all of the small craft and home-business newsletters that flourished in the 80s and into the 90s are now out of business, thanks to the Web. Its dramatic impact on newsletter publishing became evident in 1999 when the long-established Newsletter Publishers Association changed its name to Newsletter and Electronic Publishers Association (**www.Newsletters.org**). The industry as a whole has been hit hard by online competition, and direct mail and renewal results have been in a continuous downward spiral since 1995. In short, many people who once paid for newsletter subscriptions now get all the free information they want on the Web.

After fifteen years of newsletter publishing, I was mighty tired of the relentless publishing deadlines and regular mailings I had to do to get new readers and keep old ones, so I ceased publication of my print newsletter in 1996 to focus on writing books full-time. Although my newsletter had always turned a nice annual profit, its primary value to me was its power as an image and communications tool. Today, my website does this job for me at minuscule cost and with a lot less time and effort, and my ezine, *The Brabec Bulletin,* enables me to communicate at no cost with my growing subscriber base. (To subscribe, visit **www.BarbaraBrabec.com**.)

If you love to write and have special knowledge of interest to others, you should explore your options for publishing an Internet e-mail newsletter or "ezine." (Go to Google.com and search for "ezine publishing" to turn up more than a half-million Web pages on this topic.) If you have a book or other products or services to sell on a website, offering a free ezine in which you share expert advice related to your field can be indirectly profitable. First, having your own ezine or Web-based newsletter can position you as an authority or expert in your field, which may bring you invitations to speak, teach, or consult. Many craft sellers on the Web simply offer some kind of informative ezine because this is such a good way to stay in touch with customers and interested prospects while also promoting new products or services.

See also Book Publishing.

Office Supply Catalogs

Q: *I am miles away from an office supply store. Can you recommend companies I can order from by mail?*

Even when you live near office supply stores, it's a good idea to collect several catalogs of mail order suppliers so you can compare prices of basic supplies such as ribbons, ink cartridges, laser, inkjet and copier papers, envelopes, shipping supplies, labels, and so on. Here are some of my favorite suppliers who offer immediate shipment by UPS. Check each company's website or call to request a free catalog from:

Office Depot: **www.OfficeDepot.com**; 1-800-685-8800 (free delivery)

OfficeMax: **www.OfficeMax.com**; 1-800-788-8080 (free delivery on orders $50 or more)

Quill: **www.QuillCorp.com**; 1-800-789-1331 (free delivery on orders $50 or more)

Viking: **www.Viking.com**; 1-800-421-1222 (free delivery on orders $25 or more)

See also Preprinted Papers; Presentation Folders and Table Signs; *and* Scams, Home Business.

Online Sales

Q: *I plan to offer my products to buyers online, through my own home page as well as through other websites or malls. How should I handle sales?*

If your state has a sales tax, and you have a business in that state, you need to collect sales taxes on all taxable products or services sold online, just as you do when you sell to consumers off the Net.

See also Mail Order Business *and* Resale Tax Number.

Order Forms

Every business needs one kind of order form or another. Some craft sellers create separate order forms and price lists while others combine the two into one form. An order form should include your full business name, address, telephone, and fax number if you have one, with space for the same information about your customer. It should show the date the order was placed and the delivery date you've promised. Depending on what you sell, you may want to create an order form that allows you to write in the items that are being ordered, or one that lists all the products with their code or stock numbers listed along with the price of each. Your order form should also include your terms of payment, freight or delivery information, any special ordering instructions, and your guarantee, if one is offered (highly recommended).

See also Guaranty of Satisfaction; Price List; *and* Purchase Order.

Order Policies

See Credit/Trade References; Invoice; Invoices Not Paid; Minimum/Maximum Order Policy; Payment Methods; Price Lists; Returns Policy; Shipping and Handling Charges; *and* Terms of Sale.

Organization, Formation of

Q: *I would like to form an organization or association for creative people. What do I have to do to operate legally?*

Many people erroneously assume that all organizations and associations are run by a group of people. Actually, an organization or association of any kind may be started by one or more individuals and operated either on a profit or nonprofit basis. The thing that makes any organization "a group" is its members, not its management.

An attorney I consulted with confirmed that anyone can start an association, and there are no legal rules about the formation or registration of associations except that a nonprofit association must have some sort of organizational form. Incorporation is a matter of choice, not a legal requirement for any nonprofit or for-profit association. To obtain tax-exempt status, however, a nonprofit association must file a tax-exemption application with the IRS. If approved, the IRS then issues a "Determination Letter."

While FTC laws dictate that we cannot represent ourselves to be something other than we are, there is no law that says the owner of an association has to broadcast the fact that he or she is a one-person organization. Leading people to believe you are a nonprofit organization when you are really a for-profit business, however, would be in violation of both FTC truth-in-advertising regulations and mail order laws.

Organizations

See Art/Craft Organizations; Craft Cooperatives; Home-Business Organizations; *and* Trade Associations/Publications.

OSHA Regulations

OSHA (*Occupational Safety and Health Act of 1970*) is concerned with safe and healthful conditions in the workplace, and it covers all employers engaged in business affecting interstate commerce. Employers must comply with standards and with applicable record-keeping and reporting requirements specified in regulations issued by OSHA. If your crafts business uses paints, varnishes, and other materials that might conceivably be hazardous to your employees, check with state regulators to find out what safety requirements you must meet. If you are investigated after someone has reported you to officials, it could be very costly. I recall the story of one craft business that was put out of business by OSHA after being reported by a former employee who had been fired. When this person was denied unemployment benefits he decided to get even by claiming he had been working in an unhealthy environment due to paints and other chemicals. The crafts business owner spent thousands of dollars making modifications in his production line to meet OSHA requirements, but in the process he lost so much time and so many orders that he finally had to close up shop completely.

OSHA regulations also extend to employees' use of your vehicle. If one of them were to be hurt in an automobile accident, you could be held responsible, particularly if they were injured because they weren't wearing a seat belt. Details about OSHA regulations are available from area offices of the U.S. Department of Labor or on the Web at **www.OSHA.gov**.

See also Labor Laws.

Overhead

Q: *Most crafters I know don't figure overhead into their pricing formula. But what difference does this make when you're working at home?*

You're right in that most crafters ignore the overhead costs of a small crafts business—those "home expenses" such as the rent or mortgage payment, utility bills, telephone, and so on. Whether these costs increase as a result of your business is not the point, however. What you should consider is this: If you build your business on a no-overhead principle, what will happen if you become successful to the point where you must move to outside quarters? More than likely, you will find that you haven't set prices high enough to cover the now-unavoidable overhead costs, and you will have to do some fancy figuring to get out of this trap without losing your customers who by now have become accustomed to your low prices.

Overhead expenses are all costs not directly related to the production of your products (raw materials and labor). They include:

• **General Office Expenses:** telephone and fax; Internet Service Provider (ISP) fee; office and computer supplies; stationery and other printed materials; postage and postal fees; bank charges; legal and professional expenses; subscriptions, memberships, and conference fees.

• **Home Office Expenses:** a portion of your rent or mortgage expense, taxes, utilities, and insurance (see *Home Office Deduction*).

• **Selling costs:** show fees and display expenses; sales commissions; photography; packaging; shipping and freight charges; samples; advertising and promotional mailings; cost of merchant card service; website development/maintenance costs and hosting fee.

• **Other Expenses:** travel and auto expenses; equipment purchases, maintenance and depreciation; employee or independent contractor expense; cleaning and repairs; business interest expense; all other costs related to the overall operation of a business.

If you are serious about business, you will take overhead costs into consideration when figuring prices for your products. After totaling your annual overhead costs, divide this figure by the number of hours you worked during the year to come up with an hourly overhead rate that can be incorporated into your pricing. For example, if your hourly overhead costs are three dollars and you can produce a dozen miniature products per hour, you would add twenty-five cents overhead costs to each product. On the other hand, if you're making an item that takes three hours to complete, you would add nine dollars to the price just to cover overhead costs.

See also article, "Pricing Formulas for Handcraft Sellers."

Packing List

Each shipment to a wholesale account should include a packing list that describes the contents of each box or carton in the shipment. The information on the packing list must agree in description and number with the information shown on the invoice except that it need not include prices. Make two copies of the list, one for your files and one to be included either inside one of the cartons being shipped or, more preferably, on the outside of one of the cartons. (Any office supply store or catalog sells handy stick-on packing-slip envelopes for this purpose.) When shipping more than one box or carton, be sure to mark the cartons themselves by writing "Box 1 of 3 boxes," "Box 2 of 3 boxes" and so on.

See also Invoice *and* Packing Materials.

Packing Materials

Q: *What's the best way to pack art or craft objects for shipment?*

Crumpled newspaper is cheap, but it can be a problem when newspaper ink rubs off onto objects. A shop owner told me that shredded paper is a pain because it gets all over everything. Styrofoam peanuts and bubble-wrap are the most popular packing materials, and they can be ordered by mail from most office supply catalogs.

Shipping cartons can be a problem because box manufacturers often have minimum orders of 500–1,000 cartons. If you can't afford to buy cartons directly, contact box manufacturers for the names of distributors who can sell to you in smaller quantities. You can get started, of course, by purchasing these items at retail from one of the many office supply catalogs available today.

See also Office Supply Catalogs; Priority Mail; *and* Packing List.

Paints, Varnishes, and Other Finishes

Q: *I'd like to offer hand-painted toys and other products for children. How can I find out if paints and other finishes are lead-free, and what other things should I do to avoid problems here?*

Under the *Consumer Product Safety Act* there is a ban of paint and other surface coatings (varnish, lacquer, and shellac) that contain more than 0.06 percent lead by weight. A spokesperson for the Consumer Product Safety Commission told me the agency has no objection to the use of paint or other surface coatings on children's products so long as they comply with the lead-in-paint ban. All paints sold for household use in the United States must comply with this ban. Only paints intended for specialized uses are exempt, and such paints must bear a label that warns the paint contains lead, may be harmful if eaten or chewed, and should not be applied to toys, children's articles, or furniture.

There is one important exception: Artists' paints are exempt from the lead-in-paint ban, yet they are not required to bear a warning label regarding lead. Therefore, these paints should never be used on children's articles. Instead, use nontoxic acrylic paints.

See also Consumer Safety Laws; Health Hazards; *and* Lead Testing.

Partnership

Q: *A friend and I are thinking about forming a business partnership. What are the most important things we need to consider here?*

Partnerships between or among friends often end the friendship when disagreements over business policies occur, so serious consideration should be given to the advantages and disadvantages of such a business arrangement. There are two kinds of partnerships: General and Limited (almost never used for small businesses, so not discussed here). Two or more people may start a general partnership, with no federal requirements involved. Each partner shares the workload, contributing work, time, or money in amounts agreed to by all. Profits are divided, and earnings are personally taxed. The business ends with withdrawal of any one of the partners.

A big disadvantage of a partnership is that liability is unlimited, and the debts incurred by one partner must be assumed by all other partners. Thus, if the business fails, creditors can attach each partner's personal income and assets.

See also articles, "A Solution to the Partnership Checkbook Problem" and "Three Partnership Tips."

Patent

Q: *I've been told I should patent the unique product I've designed, but is this worth the time and money it would take?*

Many well-meaning people who suggest you "ought to patent it" are probably confused about the difference between a copyright and a patent. By all means, copyright your unique products but forget about patents because they are for big-time marketers with deep pockets. The process of getting a patent can take up to ten years and cost up to $20,000 in patent attorney fees. Then, once you've got

Three Partnership Tips

1. At the time you form a partnership, plan how you will eventually end it. Ask what you would do if either partner died, wanted out of the business, or wanted to buy out the other partner. In dissolving a partnership, it would be wise to hire an accountant to help determine the fair net worth of the business.

2. Protect yourself with partnership insurance. By law, at the death of a partner, a business is dissolved and can no longer operate until it is either liquidated or reorganized. For this reason, partners generally buy term insurance against each partner's illness, incapacity, or death so they will have a way to pay off a deceased partner's interest. They may also have an attorney prepare a Buy-Sell Agreement funded by life insurance. This establishes the price the survivor will pay for his or her share of the business and the amount the heirs will sell for, and the insurance provides the money to complete the transfer. In dissolving their partnership, two women worked out an agreement whereby one would make payments to the other over a three-year period, and the buyer covered the contract with a declining life insurance policy in case anything happened to her before her financial obligations were complete.

3. Before signing a partnership dissolution contract, make sure the tax obligations of your partners are current. The IRS (and any other creditor) can levy any partner's account for uncollected funds, even the account of the partner who did pay his or her share. One couple reported that, two years after they dissolved a partnership with another person, the IRS levied their bank account because their former partner had not paid his income taxes for two years.

A Solution to the Partnership Checkbook Problem

Having only one bank account does not limit you to working out of a single checkbook. Here is a suggestion on how to keep track of business expenses coming out of two different locations when there is just one checkbook.

Years ago when I managed the office of a direct mail advertising firm, it was my responsibility to write all the checks for routine business bills, but because the owners didn't want me knowing their salaries and other private financial transactions, they kept one checkbook (the "master checkbook" into which all deposits were made) and I kept the other. As I needed money, my boss would simply say, "Put $10,000 in your checkbook," at which time he would deduct the same amount from his checkbook. Two checkbooks—one account. It worked like a charm.

Of course this system is dependent on one partner being responsible for the master checkbook and balancing bank statements each month, and each partner must have his or her own series of check numbers. (Banks don't care if you use two sets of check numbers for a single account.) The easiest way to accomplish this is to order the second checkbook from a mail order check supplier, specifying the numbers you desire. (See *Checking Account* for the name of a supplier.)

See also Petty Cash.

your patent, you must pay high ($440 to $1,550) periodic maintenance fees to keep it from lapsing.

Actually, all a patent really does is give the inventor the right to exclude anyone else from making, using, or selling the invention. It is also possible to get a patent on something, yet not be able to use it if someone has a more encompassing, earlier patent. Thus, if you had a great idea and were successful in getting it patented, any large company with plenty of money for lawyers could easily prevent you from selling your patented product simply by proving that your patent resembled some item they had already patented. This would automatically void your patent.

The few crafters I know who have patented something just threw thousands of dollars down the drain trying to protect a product that had very little market value to begin with. As one expert told me, less than one percent of all the products on the market have a patent. "Ninety-seven percent of the U.S. patents issued never earn enough money to pay the patenting fee," he said. "They just go on a plaque on the wall or in a desk drawer to impress the grandchildren fifty years later. Except for one's ego, nothing is helped by having a patent on an unsalable idea, no matter how creative it is."

See also Copyright Categories of Protection; Design Patent; *and* Trademark.

Patterns, Commercial Use of

Q: *Is it okay to make items for sale from patterns found in magazines or commercial patterns purchased in a fabric store?*

The general rule of thumb is that you should not offer in the *wholesale marketplace* any item made from any design or pattern in a consumer crafts magazine or book, or from any pattern purchased from any other source. (With few exceptions, these patterns are intended for personal use only and, if you look closely, you may find a note on the pattern to this effect.) The fact that you can buy a pattern for a Raggedy Ann doll in your local fabric store does not give you the right to profit from the sale of Raggedy Ann dolls. Only the original creator of this doll has that right, and anyone who plans to sell such dolls commercially must enter into a licensing agreement with the copyright owner. *This is not to say you cannot sell anything you have made from a pattern.* It depends entirely on whose pattern you are using and/or where you plan to sell items made from it.

People often ask me about using garment patterns (such as *Simplicity* or *McCall's)* they have purchased in a fabric store. Although countless crafters do use such patterns to make items for sale at craft fairs, holiday boutiques, or craft malls, readers should remember that these patterns, like others mentioned above, are designed for individual use by consumers. They were never intended for commercial use. In my opinion, however, commercial use of such patterns is not as likely to create legal copyright problems as the use of designs and patterns in magazines because the pattern companies aren't going around looking for violators the way individual designers are doing. In addition, many people who sew modify commercial patterns to a considerable degree, making them virtually unrecognizable from the original pattern. Thus, if you are using commercial patterns for generic items of clothing such as vests, aprons, shirts, etc., and sell them only in limited quantity at the retail level, I don't think there is much cause for alarm. However, *the only way to be sure about this is to write to the individual pattern companies and ask them if it's okay to make a limited number of items for sale from one of their patterns.*

Individual "designer patterns" that might be sold through fabric shops and catalogs are something else entirely. Janet Burgess, owner of Amazon Drygoods (**www.AmazonDrygoods.com**), sells historic reproductions of clothing and household items as well as copyrighted patterns for Victorian and other period costumes. She says only a couple of the more than fifty pattern companies she represents include a notation on their patterns that "Reproduction for commercial purposes is expressly forbidden." From lengthy conversations with her two largest pattern suppliers, Janet has learned that one company is not much concerned about reproductions being sold on a small scale, but they really go after anyone who uses any of their charming drawings and graphics on business cards and other printed materials. "The other company is very firm in regard to any use at all of their patterns and graphics for any reason other than personal use," she reports. "If asked for permission to reproduce their patterns as ready-made garments for commercial sale, they will always say no, even if full credit and royalties are offered. Their main concern is that someone will manufacture some of their designs offshore and bring them into the United States for large-scale sale. Pirating is common today because it's difficult to catch companies before they get their merchandise through Customs."

Janet adds that other pattern companies aren't likely to be concerned about the seamstress who sews a few of their skirts each year and sells them on consignment to a small boutique. She emphasizes, however, that "one must be exceedingly careful not to use the illustrations or the name of the garment as named by the pattern company."

See also Copyrights of Others; First Rights/All Rights Sales; Licensing Arrangements; *and article,* "Products Made from How-to Projects in Magazines."

Products Made from How-to Projects in Magazines

Generally, it is okay to make products for sale from patterns and designs found in craft and needlework magazines, *provided such publications own the copyrights to those designs and authorize readers to use them for profit.* Most craft magazines have a policy of allowing their readers to make projects for resale, but the general rule is *you must make the entire project yourself and be the only one who profits from it.* That means you may not set up an assembly line, have someone else do part of the work, or sell your finished items through any outlet that takes a commission on sales.

The big question is whether the magazine or the designer owns the copyright. Some designers sell their how-to projects on an all-rights basis, while others sell only "first rights" (meaning they have retained the exclusive right to sell finished products or kits made from their own patterns or designs). If you learn that a copyright is owned by a designer, you could write to him or her in care of the magazine, requesting permission to make and sell the item (or search the Web to see if that designer has a website and e-mail address). Some designers may give permission to make a limited number of items for sale at the retail level, and most would be receptive to the idea of being paid a royalty on a product that might reach a large wholesale market.

—An excerpt from *Handmade for Profit—Hundreds of Secrets to Success in Selling Arts and Crafts* by Barbara Brabec (2nd ed., M. Evans).

Tip

Old quilt patterns are not protected by copyrights, so they can be freely used for commercial purposes. Be careful, however, not to use the copyrighted patterns of contemporary quilt designers.

Personal Property Used for Business

When you start a business that utilizes personal property already paid for (such as a typewriter, computer, desk, or other office furnishings), you can gain a tax deduction by transferring this property over to your business. Estimate the value of each item being transferred (the IRS seldom questions any reasonable amount) and make up a bill of sale. Then write a check on your business account to you or your spouse. (Yes, you can write a check to yourself, endorse it, and deposit it in another account.) Once the property has been purchased by your business, it can be depreciated or expensed like any other purchase of equipment or furnishings.

See also Business Expenses, Tax Deductible.

Petty Cash

Q: *What's the easiest way to keep track of miscellaneous cash purchases made each month for my business?*

You can either keep a petty cash box (which I think is a pain in the neck), or you can simply spindle all your receipts for things you've paid cash for. Tally them at the end of each month and reimburse your personal outlay of cash with a check written to you on your business account. Either cash this check or deposit it to your personal account. (All you're doing is moving money from one pocket to another, but this is necessary if you wish to deduct these cash expenditures on your income tax return.)

P.O. Box Address

Q: *I plan to offer products for sale by mail. Should I do business from my home address or rent a post office box? Are people as likely to order from a P.O. Box number as a street address?*

I used a P.O. Box address for nearly thirty years and never saw any indication of concern from buyers. Although the U.S. Postal Service will deliver business mail to a home address, there are some advantages to using a post office box address.

First, it enables you to keep a low profile in the community if you don't want your neighbors to know what you're doing. Second, it deters your customers from dropping by to see your workshop or studio. More important, if local zoning laws prohibit or limit the activities of a homebased business, doing business out of a post office box can be a good way to get around this problem. One of my readers reported his local license bureau told him to obtain a post office box number for his business address because the post office was in a commercial zone and that would eliminate the need for any special-use permit that zoning officials might ordinarily require.

NOTE: Some states require the inclusion of a street address along with a post office box address on business stationery and other printed materials, so check to see if this applies to you.

See also Sole Proprietorship *and* Zoning Laws.

Tip

To find the owner of a company operating out of a post office box address, request a copy of the company's registration form from the secretary of state in the state capital where the organization does business.

Postage Meter

If you plan to send a lot of mail, you might want to get information from Pitney Bowes about its postage meters. They offer a variety of systems, some of which have been designed for small mailers, such as the Mailstation™ digital postage meter (about $20 a month on a lease basis). For more information about other meters and postal solutions, call Pitney Bowes at 1-800-672-6937; **www.PitneyWorks .com**. (From this site, under the "customer support" tab, you can also download the current postal rate chart.)

Also consider "electronic postage" options. Visit **www.stamps .com** (an approved licensed vendor for the U. S. Postal Service) to learn how to print official postage right from your home office computer, or print postage for any mail class directly on envelopes, labels, or plain paper. Cost is about $16 a month, which is cheaper than leasing a postage machine, and you're not tied to any long-term commitment. (Other companies also approved by the U.S. Postal Service offer different programs and rates.)

Postal Regulations

Q: *What postal rules and regulations might affect my homebased business?*

If you use the mail to sell products or services, be aware the U.S. Postal Service is the watchdog of the mail order industry. They work in close conjunction with the FTC, which is especially concerned about truth in advertising and false representation of products. You aren't likely to have any problems here if you are always careful to accurately represent yourself and your products to your mail order customers.

Other areas of concern to the Postal Service are chain letters and small business scams. Postal authorities are constantly pursuing promoters of chain letters and pyramid schemes as well as anyone else who runs a scam that involves the mail. Don't get involved with any of these people because doing so could put your name on a list being investigated by the U.S. Postal Inspection Service.

See also Nature Items *and* Scams, Home-Business.

PPD

When you see this abbreviation after a price—and it's always written in lower case immediately following a price—it means that shipping and handling costs have been included in the price. Example: $16.95 ppd.

See also Shipping and Handling Charges.

Premiums

Q: *Are promotional premiums something the average crafts marketer should use?*

If you're talking about commercial premium items, I would say no. If you're talking about inexpensive premiums you can create yourself, yes. A promotional premium is something you give away to build customer good will, draw attention to your products, or encourage prospects to order from you. They are generally used by service providers who print their name and address on some item in hopes that customers and prospects won't forget them. You probably have several premiums in your home, from business cards to emery boards, pens, and yardsticks to refrigerator magnets, key chains, and calendars. While such commercial items aren't likely to work for a craft seller, you might experiment with some "freebie" items that express your creativity.

See also Freebies *and* Premium Sales.

Premium Sales

Premiums are items used by some companies to entice buyers into purchasing some product or service, and such sales are often made when a bright entrepreneur sees a product on the market that can be tied to one of his or her own products.

As you know, banks often use premiums to entice people to open savings accounts, and manufacturers use premiums to lure consumers into their dealer outlets to look at the newest model being offered. Publishers may use books as premiums to entice new subscribers or get expired subscribers back again. Although few craft sellers can deliver the thousands of units a premium buyer is likely to want, small publishers in this field should definitely explore their marketing opportunities here.

Prepaid Legal Services

Q: *What's the least expensive way for me to get legal help for my business on a regular basis?*

If you've ever wished you had a lawyer "on tap" you could call occasionally for quick questions and small legal jobs, it would pay to join an organization that offers its members affordable prepaid legal services. As a member of a prepaid legal plan, you are likely to get (1) unlimited calls to an attorney about either personal or business matters; (2) one letter or phone call per topic discussed; (3) review of legal documents; (4) preparation of a will; (5) representation against moving traffic violations or traffic tickets; and so on.

If you only have occasional need of legal advice, you can find a ton of it on the Web, for free. I've listed some of good legal sites under *Legal Resources on the Web*.

See also Attorney/Lawyer.

Preprinted Papers

If you have a computer and printer, you can create full-color business cards, stationery, brochures, flyers, and other printed materials by using colorful preprinted papers available from suppliers such as Paper Direct (1-800-A-PAPERS; **www.PaperDirect.com**) and Great Papers (1-800-287-8163; **www.PaperShowcase.com**). These papers are expensive (generally about $20 for a box of 100 sheets), but when you really want to make an impression on a few prospective buyers or customers, they do the job beautifully.

See also Presentation Folders and Table Signs *and* Office Supply Catalogs.

Prepublication Offer

This is a special money-saving offer made to a selected list of customers. A few weeks before a new product is scheduled for release, the seller offers it at a money-saving prepublication price (usually 20 percent off retail price). Book publishers often use this strategy to get a surge of orders to cover up-front printing costs of a new title, but other product makers have also used it successfully. You must be careful to explain to customers exactly when you will ship the new product and not make the prepublication offer until you are absolutely sure shipment will be made on the date you indicate. Otherwise, you may be in violation of the FTC's Mail or Telephone Order Merchandise Rule.

See also Federal Trade Commission Rules.

Presentation Folders and Table Signs

If you want to create an artistic presentation of your work—something that might include a cover letter, business card, photos, brochure, and price list—consider using the beautiful presentation folders and binders available from Paper Direct (see Preprinted Papers). These come in different patterns with precut slots for business cards. This company also offers attractive acrylic holders into which you can insert your printed signs or sales messages at a crafts fair or other exhibit of your work.

Price List

Q: *What information should be included on my price lists for individual buyers and wholesale accounts?*

You should have separate retail and wholesale price lists that can be adjusted and reprinted as necessary for insertion into your brochures or catalogs. (Don't include prices with the description of catalog items unless you expect those prices to remain good until your next catalog reprinting.) Your price list should include all the regular information, such as business name and logo (if you have one), address, telephone, fax number, and lines for all the information you need from customers who order.

Retail price lists (for consumers) should include information on how much sales tax and shipping charges must be added. If you don't expect to ship within thirty days, include a note about how long delivery will take so you don't violate the FTC's mail order rule. Example: "Most items are shipped within a few days, but please allow three to six weeks in case of back order."

Wholesale price lists should include any special ordering instructions you may have about minimum order/reorder requirements, terms of payment, how and when orders will be shipped, shipping charge information, your cancellation or returns policy, any special ordering instructions or information about colors and sizes, plus your guarantee, if one is offered. Here is an example of how one wholesaler presents ordering instructions on the back of its Wholesale Price List/Order Form:

- Item minimums as shown ($5 service charge for under minimum orders); $50 opening order minimum; $50 reorder minimum.
- Payment required with order, or order will ship COD. No credit cards accepted on wholesale orders. Net 15 day terms may be established with references. There will be a 1 percent penalty charge assessed on accounts over 30 days. Returned checks subject to $15 charge.
- In-stock items usually ship UPS next day. We ship UPS unless otherwise specified.
- Cancellations/Returns: Cancellations must be made 14 days in advance of ship date. Refused or returned orders subject to all freight charges.

See also Federal Trade Commission Rules; Guaranty of Satisfaction; Order Policies; *and* Wholesaling.

Pricing Guidelines

Q: *Pricing is my biggest problem. How can I tell if my prices are right for the special wholesale markets I'm trying to reach?*

A thorough discussion of how to price art and handcrafted products is beyond the scope of this book, but this book's companion volume, *Handmade for Profit*, includes a lengthy chapter on pricing. For our purposes here, I will provide only a few general pricing guidelines.

Pricing Formulas for Handcraft Sellers

Without identifying the object we are making, let's assume that our materials cost is going to be $1.50, we can make three units an hour, and we want $10/hour for our labor. (Labor cost per unit, then, will be $3.33.) In the last formula, we also will add $.20 for overhead and a 20 percent profit based on the wholesale price.

A. Materials x 3 + Labor = Wholesale price x 2 = Retail price
$1.50 x 3 = $4.50 + $3.33 = $7.83 x 2 = $15.66

B. Materials + Labor x 3 = Wholesale price x 2 = Retail price
($1.50 + $3.33) x 3 = $14.49 x 2 = $28.98

C. Materials + Labor + Overhead + Profit =
Wholesale Price x 2 = Retail Price
$1.50 + $3.33 + $.20 + $1.01 = $6.04 x 2 = $12.08
($1.50 + $3.33 + $.20 = $5.03 x 20% = $1.01)

Interesting, isn't it? Now if the item we were making happened to be a piece of jewelry, all three items would be realistic, since jewelry runs the gamut in both price and style. However, if the item happened to be a Christmas ornament or a ceramic coffee mug, all prices would be high, although certain mugs and ornaments might sell for $12 to $16 in exclusive shops. The point I'm trying to make is that formulas are fun, but they often are impractical, and the retail price still has to be adjusted to whatever consumer market one is trying to reach.

—An excerpt from *Homemade Money: Starting Smart* by Barbara Brabec (M. Evans)

If you're selling directly to consumers at retail, anything goes where pricing is concerned. Strive always to get the highest price the market will bear. The general rule of thumb is that a good price is one low enough for the product to sell and high enough to yield a satisfactory profit to its maker.

The picture changes when one moves into wholesaling, however. Now industry markups must be taken into consideration. Unless both a product and its pricing structure are just right, it will be impossible to crack certain wholesale distribution channels. Whenever you have a product you think would sell in a special market (floral or garden shop, hardware store, fabric shop, chain store, etc.), you'll have to read trade journals or visit trade shows to learn what the standard markups are for each industry of interest. Unlike craft and gift shops that normally double a seller's wholesale price to get the retail price, other buyers, such as mail order catalog houses, may triple or quadruple a seller's wholesale price, resulting in a retail price that's too high to sell.

> *See also* Break-Even Point; Catalog Houses, Selling to; Discounts; Markups; Overhead; Price List; Shipping and Handling Charges; Supplies, Buying Wholesale; Trade Shows; *and article, "Pricing Formulas for Handcraft Sellers."*

Tip

High prices force buyers to weigh their desire for your work against the money they have to spend. Some will mentally compare your beautiful creations to the price of machine-made imitations and walk away feeling your prices are unrealistic. On the other hand, if your prices are too low for the high-quality work you are offering, some people may feel you do not place a high enough value on your work, so they do not care to own it. Try to find a happy medium.

Printed Materials

Q: *Which printed materials are most important to artists and craft sellers?*

It depends on what and to whom you are trying to sell. If you sell primarily at art or craft fairs, a business card, brochure, and price list stuck in the buyer's package may be all you really need to stimulate follow-up mail order sales after a show. If you are interested in actively promoting to your craft fair buyers after a show, however, you will increase sales by sending promotional postcards to announce your next craft fair appearance and then following up with a mailing of your brochure or catalog. (You can't assume that the buyer kept these materials once they got home.)

If you are trying to wholesale products to shops and stores, you may not get the response you are seeking without good stationery and a full-color presentation of your products. I cannot give you detailed guidelines here on how to design professional-looking printed materials and use them to increase sales, but you will find this information in *Handmade for Profit*, along with several illustrations of letterheads, business cards, brochures, postcards, catalogs, hang tags, and labels used by professional artists and craft sellers.

See also Brochure; Hang Tags and Designer Labels; Mail, Size Regulations; Office Supply Catalogs; Preprinted Papers; Presentation Folders; Printing Terms; Self-Mailers; *and article, "How to Cut Printing Costs."*

Tip

Before you order stationery or brochures imprinted with your name and address, register your business name locally to make sure no one else is using the name you've selected. (See also *Business or Trade Name Registration/Protection.*)

Printing Terms

When ordering stationery, business forms, brochures, and other printing, communication with the printer will be easier if you are familiar with the following printing terms:

- Bleed: when the printed image or a color screen extends to the trim edge of the page.
- Color Proof: something you should get before authorizing a large print run of a brochure or catalog. (This costs a little extra, but it gives you a chance to spot any errors before the job is printed.)
- Color Separation: the process of separating full-color illustrations into the primary printing colors in negative or positive form.
- Matte Finish: dull paper finish without a gloss, often used on photographs.

How to Cut Printing Costs

Many small business owners are now printing their own materials with a laser or inkjet printer. This is fine when you need only a small quantity of items, but when you start needing printed materials in quantity, you'll need to find a good offset printer. Look for a printer who will listen to your needs and work within the budget you have. You may find it necessary to develop relationships with two or more printers, since each may specialize in a particular type of printing such as book printing, envelopes, catalogs, booklets, or periodicals.

Once you've found a good printer or two, give them your loyalty. The more work you have printed, the more attention your jobs will receive. As a valuable customer for the printer, you may find yourself receiving special customer discounts or Net 30-day terms instead of payment up front.

Prior to printing any job, get paper samples and cost estimates so there won't be surprises later. Always ask for recommendations on how you might cut costs without lowering quality. Color is expensive, but by substituting duotones or screens, you can create different shades of the same color and dramatically cut printing costs.

- Mechanical: a term for artwork that is all pasted up and camera-ready. (All type, photos, line art, etc., are positioned on one piece of artboard.)
- Ream: 500 sheets of paper. (Stationery is often ordered by the ream.)

See also Preprinted Papers *and article, "How to Cut Printing Costs."*

Priority Mail

Q: *Is there any advantage to using Priority Mail for small shipments of art or handcrafts instead of Insured Fourth-Class Mail or United Parcel Service?*

Yes. If you regularly ship small packages weighing more than thirteen ounces, the use of Priority Mail (which receives first-class handling) not only speeds delivery but saves you money. In many cases, Priority Mail costs only a few cents more than parcel post, and it gets preferential treatment with delivery anywhere in the country usually within two or three days. Get a rate chart from the post office to calculate postage over the standard two-pound package. (The maximum weight for Priority Mail is seventy pounds.)

You can eliminate some of your shipping costs by using the free Priority Mail envelopes and boxes offered by the post office, but to get them in quantity you may need to sign a form stating that you understand these materials are the property of the U.S. Postal System and any misuse may violate federal law. (In other words, you are prohibited by law from using these free cartons and mailers for any purpose other than sending mail at Priority rates.)

The one big advantage UPS has over Priority Mail is that each shipment is automatically covered for $100 worth of insurance, and UPS has the ability to track shipments while the postal service does not offer tracking on Priority Mail (only Express mail).

See also United Parcel Service.

Profit and Loss (P&L) Statement

See Income Statement.

Pro Forma

Shipping *pro forma* means you will send your customer an invoice for the merchandise they have ordered and ship it as soon as payment has been received. (If they send a check, wait until it clears the bank.) This is a very common method used by craftspeople, but *pro forma* shipments aren't without problems. As one crafter told me, "Half the time we pack the shipment, send the invoice and then we wait and wait, and sometimes they cancel the order and we have to restock all the merchandise."

See also COD Shipments.

Publishing

See Book Publishing *and* Newsletter/Ezine Publishing.

Purchase Order

In the typical homebased business, purchase orders generally come in, rather than go out. However, you might consider using a purchase order each time you order office supplies or raw materials of any kind. This will not only give you a handy record of whom you're doing business with, but will serve as a reminder of incoming supplies and invoices that need to be paid.

Tip

Your use of a purchase order may change the way you are perceived by manufacturers, distributors, or wholesalers who are often reluctant to give wholesale prices to craftspeople. Since only businesses generally use such forms, your use of them might make the difference in whether a supplier will sell to you at wholesale or not.

Record-keeping

Memory fails, but records endure. The longer you are in business, the more records you will find yourself needing or simply wanting to keep for curiosity's sake. Since there are no rules for keeping records, you can have fun creating those you want or need. Doing them manually or on computer will be your choice.

See also Business Records, Protection of; Financial and Tax Records, Inventory; *and* Sales Records.

Refunds

If a customer returns a product or publication in undamaged condition because you have guaranteed satisfaction, you must send a refund promptly. If the price the customer paid included shipping charges, you should keep the shipping charges and refund only the actual cost of the product unless the product was defective to begin with. (This is standard procedure with all mail order catalog houses.)

When you receive a check from a customer who has accidentally overpaid on an order (generally because of an error in addition) or one who has sent money for two products when only one is currently available, it is prudent to wait until the check clears (usually within ten days) before sending the refund. If you refund immediately and the check happens to bounce, you would lose twice. If the amount is only a couple of dollars, you might prefer to send your customer a credit memo that can be applied to any future order for any item in your catalog, or returned for cash refund.

Rent-a-Space Shops

Q: *What's the difference between craft malls and rent-a-space shops?*

Rent-a-space shops are similar to craft malls in that they both rent space to individual sellers, but they are generally smaller than craft malls. Some are laid out like a mall with one display area after another while others are set up like a gift or craft shop with display controlled by the shop owner or manager. Some shops simply rent shelf space, wall space, or a corner nook while also taking handcrafts on consignment or selling a line of commercial goods. In some shops, crafters must either work in the shop for a little while each week or pay a higher commission on sales.

See also Craft Mall Selling.

Resale Tax Number

All sellers of goods must obtain a resale tax number (also called a "sales tax number," "tax registration number," "seller's permit," and other similar names) from their state's Sales Tax Bureau, Department of Taxation and Finance. (Hobby sellers are not exempt from this law, regardless of how few sales they make.) Your reseller's permit (or "tax exemption certificate") will bear the special number that identifies you as one who is qualified to buy goods in the wholesale market without paying sales tax. Always take your tax certificate with you when you exhibit and sell in any show since a tax agent may ask to see it. (If you sell at shows in more than one state, you will need a separate tax exemption certificate for each of those states, and there will be a fee for this.)

Your resale (or sales) tax number doesn't entitle you to avoid sales tax on small purchases of supplies at the local hardware store or craft shop, but it does enable you to avoid paying sales tax on wholesale purchases of supplies that will be used to make products for sale. When considering whether to sell to you or not, your resale tax number is the first thing a wholesaler will want from you.

See also Supplies, Buying Wholesale *and* Sales Tax.

Returns Policy

Q: *How do I deal with the problem of customers wanting to return merchandise they have ordered?*

To avoid unauthorized returns from customers, you must establish a returns policy and include on your price list, order form, and invoice the terms under which returned merchandise will be accepted. Here, you must first decide whether to charge a restocking fee or not. If you allow returns, realize that a certain amount of returned merchandise will be returned in unsalable condition because it has been improperly packed for shipment or has been excessively handled prior to return. Also, many sellers have told me that merchandise is often returned without the hang tags they went out with, or they come back with price stickers you can't get off. What the restocking fee does, then, is help you salvage some of your loss. Below are some examples of returns notations I've found on craft sellers' printed literature:

- Notify within 5 days of damage or shortage. 10% restocking fee on all returned merchandise. No returns accepted after 30 days.
- All returns must be made within 30 days. Merchandise must be in the same condition as when it left our shop. Returned merchandise subject to shipping fee and 15% restocking fee.

- Cancellations must be made 14 days in advance of ship date. Refused or returned orders subject to all freight charges.

I like the personal touch one seller used: "I take a great deal of pride in my work, and if you're unhappy, I'll probably take it personally, but that's alright. Please just repack the doll carefully, include the packing slip or enclose a note with your comments and the adjustment you would like. Ship prepaid and insured. The exception is personalized items, which are nonreturnable."

See also Invoice; Invoices Not Paid; Minimum/Maximum Order Policy; Price List; *and* Refunds.

Royalties on Books

Q: *What kind of royalties are offered by book publishers, and do I need an attorney's help with the contract?*

Book royalties vary considerably, depending on current industry standards and what individual publishers can afford or are willing to pay. If you are working with a literary agent, he or she will protect your interests here. If you don't have an agent, be sure to hire an attorney that routinely works with author/publisher contracts. (See cautionary notes under *Author/Publisher Contract.*)

- **Trade Books.** Trade book publishers are those who sell primarily to bookstores, libraries, schools, etc. They work only on a royalty basis and royalties generally start at 5 percent on paperback editions and 10 percent on hardcover editions (on either retail or net price). Royalties higher than a publisher's "norm" must be negotiated. If a publisher insists on a low royalty, however, try to get an escalation clause stipulating that royalties will increase after a certain number of books have been sold (10,000, 25,000, 50,000, etc.) This may not be difficult to get since the average trade book today may never sell in such large quantities. (Aggressive marketing on an author's part will make a big difference in book sales and total royalties.)

Since publishers often wholesale books at discounts greater than 50 percent, royalty arrangements based on net receipts are not particularly desirable, especially when a contract has a clause that stipulates royalties will diminish (or be halved) on books sold at discounts greater than this. In this case, you might be envisioning royalties much greater than what you'll actually receive. Although professional writers with a track record may be able to demand and get more contract considerations from a publisher than a novice writer, beginners may get better royalties if they can find a book agent who will represent them. (To find book agents, see the *Literary Market Place* directory in your library.)

• **Art/Craft "Floppy Books" and Pattern Leaflets.** Within the crafts and needlecrafts industries are publishers who produce "floppy books." I'm sure you've seen examples of these full-color books (twelve to twenty-four pages) in craft and needlework shops. According to reports my readers have sent through the years, payments for books of this kind vary considerably. Some publishers work on a royalty basis while others buy material outright. Here are a few examples:

- 5 percent royalty on a book that sold only 5,000 copies
- $375 for material in the book, plus four cents per book after the first 10,000 copies had been printed, with a stipulation that royalties would terminate after $19,600 had been paid to the author
- 6 percent royalty on the wholesale price of a booklet retailing for $2.25 in shops
- 3 percent cash advance on an initial printing of 50,000 copies of a needlework leaflet. Her royalty (not disclosed) was based on the net (wholesale) price.
- $1,750 for all rights to several patterns and designs for stuffed animals and pillows from a publisher that often buys material outright. This same publisher had paid as little as $500 to other designers. (The difference has much to do with a designer's reputation, how many other books of a similar nature a publisher already has in its line, and how sales of such books are faring.)

See also Licensing Arrangements *and* Royalty Arrangements, Other.

Tip

In negotiating a publisher contract, one author who has worked with publishers on both an outright sale and royalty basis says you need to consider (1) how many books will be printed and (2) how long most of the publisher's books are kept in print. Another points out that designers who do not do their own artwork or written instructions are likely to receive lower royalties than those who are skilled in this area. Developing these skills now could translate to extra dollars in the future.

Royalty Arrangements, Other

In addition to the discussions given to royalties in other parts of this book, here are a few "royalty tidbits" that might be helpful to some readers:

- **Clothing Designs.** "Royalties vary from company to company," reports a manufacturer of ski-ware. "A flat fee plus a percentage is common practice. An example might be a flat fee of $1,500–$2,000, plus 6 percent for the first year, 5 percent the second year, 4 percent the third and so on. Some clothing manufacturers just pay a flat fee of from $100–$300."

- **Greeting Cards.** Generally, outright payments of between $125 and $300 per card are made until one has an established reputation and some experience with a particular company. Royalties are usually paid only to artists with substantial reputations and talents.

- **Embroidery Kits.** When one of my readers wrote to the one company in the United States that makes Bunka embroidery kits (all others come from Japan), she was told that a kit that retailed for about $30 would pay only a 25-cent royalty to the designer, and after three years the design would become theirs. Don't ever sell your creativity for so little money. You could make and sell your own needlework kits or designs for much greater profit.

See also Fabrics (Designer), Commercial Use of; Licensing Arrangements; Patent; Patterns, Commercial Use of; *and* Royalties on Books.

Safe Deposit Box

One of the best ways to protect a homebased business is to rent a safe deposit box to hold irreplaceable records, papers, and computer backup discs or tapes. Do consider, however, that while a safe deposit box may be water- and fire-resistant, it is neither waterproof nor fireproof. This could make a big difference if you happen to live in an area that is prone to floods or earthquakes.

Sales Commissions

Q: *I know I have to pay a sales commission to anyone who helps me sell my work, but what percentage is standard?*

Commissions are a percentage of sales you pay to someone for selling your work, and they run the gamut from 10 to 50 percent depending on whom you are working with. For example, you might:

- consign your work to an art gallery or consignment shop where the commission could range between 30 and 50 percent of the retail price
- consign your work to a local holiday boutique where the sales commission may vary from 25 to 40 percent
- occupy space in a rent-a-space shop that charges a monthly fee and may also take a sales commission of 16–20 percent of the retail price
- make an arrangement with the local beauty shop or some merchant to display and sell some of your products, for which you might offer a 25 percent sales commission and increase it if that isn't acceptable
- work with a literary agent whose commission will generally be 15 percent of your royalties
- hire a sales representative or agency that will typically take 15–20 percent of net sales

See also Author/Publisher Contract; Consignment Agreement; Rent-a-Space Shops; Sales Representatives; *and* Toy and Game Brokers.

Sales Representatives

Q: *I need help in reaching new wholesale outlets. How can I find a good sales rep, and what will this cost?*

Many sales rep organizations have teams of individual reps who cover specific regions or the whole country. Because artists and craft sellers cannot produce in sufficient quantity to interest most sales rep organizations, most will do better if they work with only one or two individual reps.

A crafts manufacturer who used to work with individual reps shared the following insight on her individual rep arrangements: "One rep displayed my work in a permanent showroom and received a 20 percent commission on sales (wholesale price). My contract with him did not specify particular territories, but I agreed not to sign up other reps who would be representing me at certain trade shows. I also had a couple of 'road reps' who showed my products to various shops and stores. These reps received a 15 percent commission because their overhead costs were lower than that of the showroom rep. The sales reps received their commissions as soon as I received payment for invoices. At year's end, I sent each rep a 1099 form showing their total earnings."

Some rep contracts stipulate that the sales commission must be sent as soon as they have made a sale, but this is not standard practice in the industry and you should never agree to do this. The primary concern of a sales rep is to make a sale; they are not concerned about your getting paid. If they sell to a questionable account who doesn't pay your invoice, you lose the value of your merchandise, but if the rep doesn't get paid, he or she has lost only the time it took to make that one call.

Professional sales representatives will have their own contract, probably filled with fine print you need to read very carefully. But if you should decide to hire a friend or some other entrepreneurial individual to rep for you, you may have to draft your own sales rep agreement.

Sales reps can be found by reading trade magazines, visiting trade shows or gift showrooms, or networking with other craft sellers. You

MEMORANDUM OF AGREEMENT

Made ____ *(date)* ____ between ____ *(name of sales representative or organization)* ____
(hereinafter referred to as the Associates), of ____ *(address of sales representative or organization)* ____
_____ and ____ *(your business name and address)* ____
_____ .

    This agreement shall be in force for the period of one year and shall continue thereafter for one-year periods unless either party gives notice to the other in writing six months in advance of the renewal date or on that date for a date six months hence.

    The Associates shall be our exclusive representative to the ____ *(specify trade area or industry)* ____ , both retail and jobber, in the following states or parts thereof:

(list states or territory here)

    We expect the Associates to give this territory diligent and intensive coverage for which a commission of _____ % will be paid on all invoices of sales made by the Associates. Commission payments will be sent to you on the 15th of each month, accompanied by copies of invoices for all the billing to trade accounts in your territory that have been collected to that date. All expenses of travel and maintenance will be paid by the Associates. You will call on major accounts ____ *specify how often, based on discussion with rep)* ____ .

    We grant the right of access at all times to our files of copies of all invoices to enable you to ascertain the correctness of our commission payments to you.

    We agree that your services to this company are not exclusive (meaning that the Associates will continue to represent other companies).

    Please indicate your acceptance to this agreement by signing and returning the attached copy of this agreement.

Sincerely,

____ *(your signature)* ____
for *(your business name)*

Accepted:

____ *signature of sales rep)* ____ Date: _____ *(date signed)* ____

Important Sales Rep Contract Clauses

In addition to the basic points covered in the "Sample Sales Rep Agreement," craft sellers should include contract clauses about:

1. **Product Samples.** Display room samples are generally provided free of charge while road samples may be charged to the rep's account at half the wholesale price. Make sure there is a provision for getting back your showroom samples if the agreement is cancelled.

2. **Printed Materials.** Clarify what printed materials are required by the rep and the quantities that will be needed of each.

3. **House Accounts.** Try to retain your six best accounts (the ones that reorder automatically) as "house accounts" and stipulate in your contract that the rep is not to call on these accounts nor will any sales commission be paid on orders received from them.

4. **Mail Order Promotions.** If you normally make mail order promotions to all your accounts, orders that result from accounts in the sales rep's territory would earn a commission for the rep even though you have generated the order by mail. Just make sure the rep understands you will be making such promotions. Otherwise it may look as though you're trying to compete for sales and deny the rep's commission. This is a touchy area that needs to be clarified in your agreement.

5. **Terms of Exclusivity.** Specify the territory to be covered by the rep and the trade shows or showrooms in which your products will be displayed. This will leave you free to hire reps in other areas or exhibit in other showrooms or trade shows. A crafter who makes one-of-a-kind art creations puts it this way: "Stay clear of any representative who wants you to sign a contract that makes your product his sole property, hemming you in so you cannot take advantage of any other offers."

6. **Extra Fees.** Sales reps normally pay all their own expenses, but if your products are to be displayed in a showroom or at a trade show, you will probably be asked either for extra money to pay exhibiting costs or a higher sales commission on these sales. Just make sure you understand what those fees will be and try to set a maximum on how much you will be asked to pay in any given year.

See also Trade Shows *and Sample Sales Rep Agreement.*

can also turn up more than a million Web pages that will link you to sales reps in every industry imaginable simply by searching Google for "sales representatives directory."

See also Trade Shows *and articles, "Important Sales Rep Contract Clauses" and "Sample Sales Rep Agreement."*

Tip

If an individual sales rep works for you and only you, that person cannot legally be called an independent contractor but could be considered a statutory employee for tax purposes. Individuals who work for you and other companies as well, however, can qualify as independent contractors. Both types of workers need to receive 1099 tax forms at year's end. (For more information on this topic, see *Statutory Employees*.)

Sales Tax

Q: *I'm just starting to sell my handmade products for extra income. Since this is more of a hobby than a business, do I have to collect sales tax on my sales?*

Yes. Unless you live in a state that does not have a sales tax, you must collect and remit sales taxes if you sell merchandise direct to consumers. All sellers—even hobby businesses—are required by law to register with the Department of Revenue (Sales Tax Division) in their state. If you are a seller of merchandise, then you're subject to tax, even if you sell only a couple of times a year. Most retailers file monthly sales tax reports, but if your income is low, you may only have to file quarterly or annually. Here are some special sales tax situations you may be wondering about:

• **Craft Fairs.** Craft sellers must always collect sales tax at a fair, but how and when it's paid can vary. Sometimes a show promoter will get an umbrella sales tax certificate for their event, and sellers will either report their sales to management at the show's end or actually give management a check for sales tax that will be picked up by a state sales tax agent. In most cases, however, individual sellers are required to get a temporary sales tax certificate for the run of the show, and the information on how to do this is always provided by show promoters. Each state has its own rules about when sales tax must be paid, but when you're selling in a state other than your own, you will generally have to pay the sales tax within thirty days after a show.

Many beginning sellers ignore the sales tax law completely and sell their wares at small fairs without collecting sales tax. Don't try this at a large show, however, because lawbreakers could be subject to severe financial penalties. In my state, anyone caught violating the sales tax law would be subject to a penalty of 20 percent over and above any normal tax obligation, and could receive for each offense (each return not filed) from one to six months in prison and a fine of up to $5,000. Don't mess around here because it's easy to get caught. Tax people generally attend craft fairs with tax forms in hand, and they also turn up at small business conferences whenever merchandise is being sold. On more than one occasion while selling my books at a home-business conference, I've had a tax man standing by to pick up my sales tax check at the end of the day. One show listing publisher told me that more and more shows are being visited by state income tax people to make sure that crafters have tax resale numbers. "For many of the larger shows, six to eight tax inspectors arrive at a show together so they can sweep through quickly and move on to the next one. We have even gotten reports of displays being confiscated," he said.

• **Holiday Boutiques.** If you participate in an annual holiday boutique with several other craft sellers, the cashier may collect the sales tax on all purchases, but each individual seller is responsible for collecting and reporting his or her own taxable sales. When the profits are doled out at the end of the sale, each craft seller should get back all sales tax collected on his or her sales so it can be reported and forwarded to the state when the next sales tax return is due.

• **Charitable Events.** Someone once asked me who was responsible for collecting the tax if merchandise has been consigned to a charitable organization on a 70/30 percentage basis. The answer is, the organization. Always remember the rule is *the party who makes the sale to the consumer is the one who must collect and pay sales tax to the state in question.*

- **Sales Through Other Shops and Stores.** The only time you don't need to collect sales tax is when you consign or wholesale your products or when you sell them through craft malls or rent-a-space shops. In this case, the individual shops, stores, and malls are responsible for collecting sales tax. You must keep track of all these sales, however, since such income is exempt from state sales taxes and must be itemized and deducted accordingly on your tax return.

See also Online Sales *and* Resale Tax Number.

Tip

Even when you don't have to collect sales tax, a tax exemption certificate may still be required by your state for other reasons. You will need it, too, in order to buy raw materials without paying sales tax. When selling to buyers at wholesale, you also need to get their resale tax number as proof that your sales to them are tax exempt.

Samples

Q: *In trying to sell to wholesale buyers, should I send sample products for evaluation?*

This is something you will have to decide on your own, but here are three tips:

1. Don't send a sample product to a shop or store buyer until you are asked to do so, or at least until you know you have the buyer's attention. For example, if you send a promotional mailing to a prospective buyer and get any kind of interest, you could follow up with a telephone call to ask for the order, and if there is any resistance, then ask if a small sample would help in making a buying decision. As one crafts producer told me, "I don't send a sample until I know I'm dealing with a large shop with buying volume. In that case I might send one item that costs me less than fifteen dollars, or a couple of smaller items. It depends on the size of the shop. Most small shops don't even ask for samples."

2. If you are trying to sell a product to a catalog company, a sample may be required. But call the company to get the name of the

buyer who should receive the sales literature and product sample, or it may be a waste of your time and money.

3. Don't expect sample products to be returned by anyone.

See also Sales Representatives.

Tip

Instead of offering dealer samples, consider offering first-time buyers a special "get acquainted" sampling of products at a lower-than-usual-price—something you could afford to do if this was a standard order that could be prepacked in advance. Depending on what you sell, the suggested price of a get-acquainted sampler might be in the range of $50–$100.

SASE

Q: *In my classified ads, is it a good idea to ask people to send money for my catalog or at least an SASE (self-addressed stamped envelope)?*

Advertisers use the SASE abbreviation (sometimes with periods between the letters) when they are offering free information in a classified ad or news release but don't want to stand the expense of the postage and envelope to mail it. This is common practice in the home business and crafts community as well as in the publishing industry, where book and magazine publishers expect all writers to send an SASE if they want Writer Guidelines or a response to a query letter.

Before you ask people to send fifty cents or an SASE to receive your advertising material, however, consider that this may decrease by 25–35 percent the total number of responses you will receive. By asking for money or an SASE, you are making it more difficult for people to respond. Not everyone will take the time to tape coins to a card or dig up the right size envelope. Given the number of people I see standing in line at the post office with unstamped letters in their hands, I conclude that many homes don't keep a supply of stamps on hand. Also, the average individual may not know what you mean if you ask for an LSASE (large SASE). You may want a #10 business envelope, but people reading the ad might think they have to send a 9 × 12 inch envelope. (Asking for a "business size SASE" might make it clearer to some.)

Finally, when you ask for an SASE, expect that about 5 percent of the total who respond will forget to include the envelope. Of course you must also respond to these people because they are as likely to order from you as the ones who send the SASE.

SBA Loans

Q: *My husband and I would like to expand our business, but we need more capital than we can raise on our own. Is it difficult to get a small business loan from the U.S. Small Business Administration?*

Recent cuts in funding to the SBA have resulted in fewer and smaller loans with increased borrower and lender fees. Currently, the SBA's MicroLoan Program provides very small loans to start-up, newly established, or growing small business concerns. Under this program, SBA makes funds available to nonprofit community-based lenders (intermediaries), which, in turn, make loans to eligible borrowers in amounts up to a maximum of $35,000. The average loan size is about $10,500. Applications are submitted to the local intermediary and all credit decisions are made on the local level. The maximum term allowed for a microloan is six years. Interest rates vary, depending upon the intermediary lender and costs to the intermediary from the U.S. Treasury.

One couple told me they found the SBA easy to work with when they wanted a loan to set up a crafts shop in their home. "We learned the SBA will offer up to $10,000, basically unsecured, except that they will not loan money for intellectual property, nor will they underwrite a computer programming business," they reported. "There is a monthly judging process where the plans are reviewed by a committee of ten or so who decide who's worthy of a loan. The interest rate is comparable to what banks would give, and we were offered a repayment schedule from one to six years. We paid a loan closing fee of $300."

To get an SBA loan, you will need a good credit rating and will have to provide a business/financial plan with figures for the past year and projections for the coming year. For current SBA loan information, visit **www.SBA.gov**. More information about SBA loans can also be obtained from an SBA or SCORE office near you (find one at **www.SCORE.org**), or call this toll-free number: 1-800-827-5722.

See also Business Plan; Cash Flow Projection; and SCORE.

Scams, Home-Business

Q: *Is it my imagination, or are there more con artists at work today than ever before?*

It's not your imagination—con artists are running rampant today, and this problem will only get worse as the Internet continues to grow (see *Internet and E-Mail Scams*). A growing number of home-business owners are now being targeted as victims, so it's more important than ever to not let your ego get in the way of clear thinking when something comes along that seems too good to be true. These days, it probably is. Here are some scams currently being targeted to homebased business owners:

• **COD Shipments.** A con artist places a large order for several thousand dollars' worth of merchandise and is most agreeable when you say you will have to ship COD. However, they will pay with a company check and send a letter a couple days later to say they made an error and the check may bounce. Just redeposit it, they advise, knowing full well it will bounce again. Since you can run a check through only twice, your only option then will be to notify the police or district attorney's office. The best way to avoid this scam is to insist on a certified check or money order as payment of the COD delivery. Don't be surprised if the con artist says he or she can't do business that way.

• **Simplified Payment Methods.** Be wary of companies that sell you something and then urge you to authorize a monthly automatic withdrawal from your checking account. They will say all you have to do is give your bank's name and address as well as your checking account number. The fraud occurs when counterfeit checks or phony "demand drafts" are used to make unauthorized cash withdrawals from your account.

- **Shops with Multiple Outlets.** A buyer may place a large wholesale order with terms of Net 30 days, saying they will be placing merchandise in several shops in other cities. As soon as the order is received, the buyer disappears with the merchandise.

- **Office Supply Scams.** Con artists in this field are bilking small business owners out of millions of dollars annually. They gain entrance to your business via the telephone, and they may try to sell you everything from inferior office supplies at reduced prices to cheap laser toner cartridges that could ruin your printer. Any time you are approached on the telephone with an offer that sounds too good to be true, ask that information be sent to you in the mail. If you are told this can't be done, it's probably a scam. Because fraudulent sales pitches made by mail run the risk of investigation by the U.S. Postal Service, many con artists limit their promotions to the telephone or the Internet. Although you can call the Better Business Bureau for a report on a company, by law this agency cannot release information on how long a customer has had phone service. This, of course, gives con artists a perfect shield. Be especially wary of anyone who says you've got to buy right now to get the savings, and *never* give a credit card number to someone who has called you out of the blue and suggests you put the charge on a credit card.

- **Phone-Card Scams.** This is now an international problem. Be careful when you use your long distance calling card in any public place, particularly when other people are standing nearby. Any one of them could be a con artist who is trying to see the numbers on your card, or monitor the numbers you punch when you make calls. Thieves are even using binoculars in airports to get such information. Once they have your number, of course, it will be sold and you could end up with hundreds of calls on your bill.

- **Invention Hucksters.** The Federal Trade Commission reports that thousands of amateur inventors regularly pay millions of dollars a year to invention promotion firms who just take money from unsuspecting people (fees of up to $5,000 or more) and provide no worthwhile services for it. Although such firms may be able to offer evidence of their success in marketing an invention by giving you the names of one or two clients, FTC investigations of such firms have often shown that a company may have only a handful of success stories out of thousands of clients registered with them. (See also *Patent.*)

- **Homework Scams.** Avoid classified advertisements for home sewing and craft assembly work that promise good money for making simple products like aprons, baby bibs, or jewelry. Promoters promise to buy all the products you make, but they never do, and their reason will be that your work doesn't "meet their standards" even when it's perfectly made. That's because they are interested only in selling their product kits to unsuspecting consumers.

- **Other Consumer Scams.** The U.S. Postal Service says two of the five biggest lies regularly fed to consumers are "This chain letter is perfectly legal," and "You can stuff envelopes at home and earn BIG $$$." Chain letters are not only one of life's biggest losers, they say, but any chain letter asking for money is a type of lottery that is illegal when sent through the U.S. Mail. As for stuffing envelopes, these ads are simply lures to try to get you to set up your own business to conduct the same scheme as the advertiser's. When you continue a fraud by getting other victims involved, you're setting yourself up for investigation by the U.S. Postal Inspection Service, whose penalties for mail order fraud are severe.

Three other consumer scams likely to continue for years are: (1) "You are a guaranteed winner of one of five valuable prizes" (you fork over big bucks for worthless products); (2) "Your humble assistance is highly solicited in transferring millions of dollars—all we need is your bank account number" (a popular Nigerian e-mail con, and a great way to lose all the money in your account); and (3) "You have been selected to receive a fabulous vacation" (a traveler's nightmare). If you receive solicitations like any of those above, turn them over to your local postmaster for forwarding to the Postal Inspection Service.

For more information on the various business and consumer scams, go to the FTC website (**www.FTC.gov**), which has special departments for both consumers and business. If you type "business scams" in the site's search box, you'll turn up a list of nearly 25,000 links to the many scams being run today. Boggles the mind!

See also COD Shipments; Credit/Trade References; Postal Regulations; *and* Internet and E-Mail Scams.

Tip

If you have been targeted by a con artist, that individual has probably hired others to give phony credit references. If you become suspicious, call Information for the telephone number of all companies named as trade references. If different from the numbers you have been given, it's a scam. Be especially wary if the bank reference you have been given gives a glowing report on the company because banks never give out such information to callers.

Schedule C Form

If you are a sole proprietor, you must report your income and expenses from your business or profession on Schedule C (Profit or Loss From Business) and file it with your Form 1040. The amount of net profit (or loss) from Schedule C is reported on the appropriate line on page one of your tax return. If you operate more than one business, you must prepare a separate Schedule C for each business.

See also Business Expenses, Tax Deductible; Employees, Family; Hobby Income; Home Office Deduction; Inventory; *and* Social Security Taxes.

Tip

Look for tax forms in your library and post office, or download the ones you need on the Web at **www.IRS.gov**.

SCORE

The Service Corps of Retired Executives (**www.SCORE.org**) is a nonprofit organization sponsored by the U.S. Small Business Administration (**www. SBA.gov**). It exists solely to provide free business information and advice. SCORE counselors are retired men and women who have had successful business careers as company executives or owners of their own businesses. When you need help, a counselor will be assigned to your case. He or she will offer suggestions, advice, and recommendations for a solution to your problem but will not perform any of the actual work required, such as writing a business or marketing plan. To find a SCORE counselor, check your local telephone directory under SCORE, U.S. Government, or call 1-800-634-0245 to get an information packet and a connection to your nearest SBA or SCORE office. You'll also find a wealth of information on the Web at **www.SCORE.org**. Here, you can find your nearest SCORE office, get a free mentor, and read success stories. You can also download free templates of real business plans and financial and accounting statements, then work with a SCORE business counselor to plug in the numbers. Your taxes help pay for this service, so be sure to use it.

How SCORE Helped One Craft Business

Back in the late 1980s, at a time when Sue Krei was feeling depressed about her business, she called SCORE to arrange for a free counseling session. After just two meetings, she reported this was the smartest move she ever made. Through the years, Sue's Wood Cellar Graphics business has grown to include a large line of originally designed rubber stamps and related paper products such as hang tags and note papers (now on the Web at **www.Wood CellarGraphics.com**). In looking back to her session with SCORE, Sue recalls that the SCORE counselor was impressed with her progress to that point and confirmed she had products with money-making potential.

"This naturally boosted my ego," says Sue. "Some of the things we discussed were the importance of how a mail order business like mine should best be presented, and this led to a discussion of creating a catalog. The counselor talked about the importance of making a commitment to the business and having enough faith in my products to get together whatever funds were necessary to do some healthy advertising. More than anything, my session with SCORE lit a fire under me. The advice and encouragement I received was invaluable, so I can't imagine anyone not taking advantage of this free service."

Tip

> Many fields and professions are represented by SCORE counselors. For best results, ask for someone who is familiar with your particular type of business. If you need help in launching a design business, for example, it won't do you much good to be counseled by a successful grocer.

Self-Mailers

A self-mailer is any mail piece placed in the mail stream without an envelope. Generally, such pieces measure 11 × 22 inches. They are generally folded in half, then in half again to create a mailer that measures 5½ × 8½ inches, but other sizes of paper and types of folds may also be used. The most important consideration here is the weight of the paper. You should strive to keep the weight of a self-mailer to an ounce or less, but if you use anything lighter than sixty- or seventy-pound weight, your mail piece is likely to be chewed up by mail processing machines. Ask your printer for suggestions.

Sewing

If you are building a sewing business, there are a number of listings in this book that you need to read to be on safe legal ground.

See Copyrights in Public Domain; Fabrics (Designer), Commercial Use of; Fabrics, Flammability Standards; Garment Manufacturing; Patterns, Commercial Use of; Maintenance Agreements; *and* Scams, Home Business.

Sheltered Workshops

When you need help in producing craft items but don't want to hire employees, check to see if there is a sheltered workshop in your area such as Veterans Industries, a program of the Veterans Administration (on the Web at **www1.va.gov/Vetind/**). This organization has 108 locations across the country, and if you go to Google.com and search for "sheltered workshops," you'll turn up countless listings of other organizations that hire disabled workers who excel at doing tedious, routine work you may not have the time or patience for. Through the years, several readers have reported their satisfaction with the work done by such organizations. Examples of work that could be done for a reasonable price by a sheltered workshop might include tying on tags or affixing labels, packaging kits or pattern packages, stuffing envelopes, doing routine fabric cutting or hand-painting, and so on.

Shipping and Handling Charges

Q: *How do I figure what to charge customers for shipping and handling of their orders when each order weighs a different amount and cost may vary depending on how they want delivery to be made?*

A note found on the order form of one seller indicates that some crafters don't understand the importance of including "handling charges" to their prices. It read, "I haven't figured out what handling means, but whatever it is, I still don't charge for it." (Not a very professional note, to say the least. Never let your customers think you don't know what you're doing.)

"Handling charges" are your total cost of packing and shipping an order, including the cost of shipping cartons, sealing tape, address labels, packing lists, and something to cover your labor costs in doing this work. You shouldn't charge buyers extra for these costs, but they need to be taken into consideration when you set your retail and wholesale prices.

Shipping costs, however, are to be passed along to customers unless a special offer of free freight has been made. (Sometimes to encourage orders at a trade show, sellers will offer free freight with prepaid orders.) Some sellers charge the actual postage or shipping costs incurred while others work on a certain percentage of the order—usually between 7 and 10 percent—which few buyers will ever question. It's easy enough to figure shipping charges on a wholesale order you are invoicing, but difficult to figure out what to charge when customers are expected to send payment with order. Here's how one craft seller handled this problem in her retail catalog:

Regular ground-service domestic U.S. shipping is included in all the prices. For faster delivery via UPS Second Day Air, add $5 to your order. Canadian and overseas orders, see enclosed chart.

The $5 charge mentioned above is surely higher now, given the way shipping costs have increased through the years. Let this be a reminder that you must always adjust your prices to accommodate increased shipping costs. Don't try to be a nice guy and absorb them.

Most mail order sellers figure out some kind of shipping chart that will work for their products. For example, a pattern seller might set up a shipping chart based on how many patterns have been ordered (i.e., "1 pattern, $2; 2–4 patterns, $2.50; 5 or more, $3") while a product seller might work with dollar amounts. Julie Peterson, who shared her shipping and handling chart for her birch bark products, worked it out like this:

Total price of Items	Add
$ 1.00– $20.00	$4.95
$20.01–$30.00	$5.95
$30.01–$40.00	$6.95
$40.01–$60.00	$7.95
$60.01–$100.00	$8.95
Over $100.00	$9.95

It's difficult to work up a chart like this, and you'll have to do some experimenting to find the right rate structure for your products. Julie said she studied several mail order catalogs and found there was a pattern to what others were charging. "After setting up my shipping and handling chart, I monitored all my shipments for a month to see if I was charging too little or too much," she explained. "I found I had to raise all my prices by a dollar. Sometimes I come out a little ahead, other times I come out losing a bit, but it all works out in the end."

See also Packing Materials *and* Shipping Methods.

Tip

If you're selling only a few items, you might want to build shipping charges into the price of each item. In that case, you would list the price on your order form as $16.95 ppd. ("ppd." means "postage paid.") This is the method I used for years to sell my books, each of which had a different weight. (If you're selling to Canada, you'll need to add an extra dollar or so per item to cover the higher postage rates to that country.)

Shop Failures

Q: *How can I get my merchandise out of a craft shop or mall that has gone out of business but hasn't returned goods to their consignors or renters beforehand?*

This is one reason why you always need to get the name and telephone number of a shop's owner or manager. Sometimes a shady owner will strip a place bare before they leave town; other times, they just sneak away and leave the problem of what to do with all the merchandise to others. If a shop closes and you don't have the name of the owner, call the Better Business Bureau in the city where the shop is located and explain what has happened. One crafter who did this not only got the owner's name and address but a report that an investigation had already been started. In return for this information, she was asked to fill out a legal complaint form.

Problems with shops that close owing you money or the return of your merchandise should also be reported to the Consumer Fraud Division of the district attorney of the county in which the shop was located. Reporting your loss to the proper authorities may make you feel better, but don't expect to get back the money you've lost. The kind of people who close up shop and disappear usually owe not only all the crafters in their store, but state sales tax and other taxes as well. If there is any money to be recovered, you can be sure the government will get its share first.

See also Consignment Laws.

Shopping Cart Systems

If you're planning to sell a line of products on the Web, you must have a "shopping cart program" and merchant status (discussed elsewhere). Most of the companies on the Web that offer merchant status also throw in a shopping cart system, but check around to make sure you're getting a good deal. I regret that I can't give you a step-by-step plan for how to do this, but the options are simply too great, and this is work that Web sellers must do for themselves. I can, however, point you to a couple of websites I've investigated and have also received good reports about:

- Americart (**www.Americart.com**) is a cost-effective shopping-cart system that can be added to any website for a flat annual fee. You can use this system in conjunction with PayPal or your own merchant account system, or mail orders payable by check or money order.

- Mal's E-Commerce is used (and highly praised) by many sellers who have their own merchant account. You use this service to collect orders for later processing. Customers click on a "Buy Now Button" link on your website, and you are notified whenever an order is received. You then go to the administration area of the site to retrieve the secure credit card info stored there and complete the order process. This service is free and is currently being used by PayPal members, but you can upgrade to a premium account later if you want to do online payment processing. At **www.mals-e.com**, you'll find complete information about the shopping cart service as well as an excellent explanation of payment gateways and credit card processors, in case you're still looking for merchant account status. Mal links you to several companies he works with, so you can choose the one that's right for you.

- If you decide to use Mals-E shopping cart, then check out Susan Scheid's excellent OptionCart Catalog, which was especially designed to work with Mals-E shopping cart system. Using this program, you just enter your product information, load your images, and your catalog page will automatically be displayed. "It's the easiest way to create a searchable online ordering catalog to list your products, along with unlimited sizes, colors, and styles," says Susan. "Customers can search for products by category, keyword, catalog number, and/or price range. The deluxe version not only gives you inventory control by item, but also the option to set inventory quantities for the first option (size, color, style, etc.)." Get complete details at **www.optioncart.com**.

- Also check out the personalized shopping cart selection service offered by Michelle Bailey on her site at **www.ShoppingAlaCart .com**. You can get a free, no-obligation quote on your specific needs by completing the questionnaire found on this site.

See also Web Marketing Options.

Show Listings

Q: *I'd like to enter craft fairs and shows outside my area but don't know how to get information about them in advance. Is there a good source for this information?*

Yes, many show listing calendars are available by subscription from publishers in the crafts industry. Depending on the publisher, these publications may be regional or national in scope. Listings include the name and date of each upcoming event and who to contact for entry information. Some publishers also include expected attendance or sales figures from previous shows. All the major show listing publishers now have websites, and here's a list of them with their telephone number in case you don't have Web access:

- **www.ABCCraftEvents.com**; 1-800-678-3566. Serving artists, crafters, entertainers, and food vendors who exhibit, perform, or sell at art and craft events. Some featured events are posted free on the website, but you will need to become a member to access all the national show listings on the Web.
- **www.ArtsCraftsShowBusiness.com**; 1-904-757-3913. A show guide published ten times a year, providing artists, craftspeople, and food vendors with information on arts and crafts shows, fairs, and festivals in Alabama, Florida, Georgia, Mississippi, North Carolina, South Carolina, and Tennessee.
- **www.CraftsFairGuide.com**; 1-800-871-2341. A show listing periodical for the West Coast that includes in-depth reviews and critiques of shows by exhibiting artists and craftspeople.
- **www.CraftMasterNews.com**; 1-562-869-5882. A monthly printed magazine that lists thousands of events throughout the Western states. (You can browse the current month's listings on the website.)
- **www.CraftShowYellowPages.com**; 1-845-790-3413 (info); 1-888-424-1326 (to subscribe). A regional show guide/directory for craftsmen, artists, food vendors, and resellers in Connecticut, Delaware, Maryland, Massachusetts, New Jersey, New York, Pennsylvania, Virginia, Vermont, and more. (Note: This website has a very good archive of craft/home-business articles.)

- **www.events2000.com**; 1-800-337-8329. Your source for the most up-to-date listings and selections of arts and crafts shows, fairs, and festivals across the Southeast. Four *Ronay Guides* serve exhibitors, concessionaires, and festival visitors interested in arts and crafts shows in Georgia, the Carolinas, Virginia, and around the South.
- **www.MidwestArtFairs.com**; 1-800-871-0813. A regional guide to art and craft fairs in the upper Midwest.
- **www.SACNewsmonthly.com**; 1-800-825-3722. A monthly tabloid newspaper with thousands of show listings in every issue. Targeted to sellers at fine art and arts and crafts shows, as well as "pow wow" shows and events across the country.
- **www.SunshineArtist.com**; 1-800-597-2573). A monthly magazine for art festival and craft show exhibitors, promoters, and buyers.

Small Claims Court

Q: *Is it difficult to sue someone in Small Claims Court, and is this a practical way to collect on a bad check or unpaid invoice?*

Small Claims Courts are designed to resolve small monetary disputes, and many small business owners have had success in collecting money owed to them by individuals or companies who gave them bad checks or refused to pay an invoice. Sometimes the mere threat of a suit in Small Claims Court will convince a person to pay up; others may hold out until a judgment has been entered against them and finally pay when they learn that the sheriff can walk into their place of business, make a list of property advertised for sale, and sell enough of it at auction to pay their debt. For the few who ignore a judgment altogether, collection strategies such as garnishing wages, seizing money from a bank account, or filing a lien against real estate may need to be employed.

Generally speaking, however, small claims court procedures are simple, inexpensive, quick, informal, and effective. Filing fees are nominal, and paperwork (generally a one-page form that states your grievance in general terms) is kept to a minimum. Each state has a statute of limitations (usually at least one year) that limits the time you can wait to sue after an event occurs. The amount of the dispute and the maximum amount that can be claimed varies from state to state, but in some states, you can sue for $5,000 or more.

Something you need to check initially is whether you can sue the defendant in your state; that is, do your state courts have jurisdiction over the defendant? If the defendant does not reside in your state or do business there, you might have to sue in the defendant's home state, which might be more trouble than the bad check or unpaid invoice is worth. Also find out if you can file a claim by mail, or whether you must appear in person to present your case. If the defendant fails to show up, you will probably get a judgment by default.

Small claims court offices are listed in your local telephone book under municipal, county, or state government headings. For answers to many questions you may have on how to take a case to small claims court, check the Q&A section of **www.LawGuru.com**. Or see the book *Everybody's Guide to Small Claims Court* by Ralph Warner (Nolo Press; **www.Nolo.com**).

See also Collection Strategies.

Social Security Earnings

Q: *How much can I earn from a part-time business before I begin to lose my Social Security Earnings?*

The amount you can earn changes every year, so you should call your local Social Security office or this toll-free number (1-800-772-1213) to get the figures each year. You may also visit the Social Security Administration on the Web at **www.SSA.gov** and use the calculator on the site to determine the effect of your earnings on your Social Security benefits. The earliest age that you can receive Social Security retirement benefits remains sixty-two even though the full retirement age (FRA) is rising.

If you are under FRA when you start getting your Social Security payments, $1 in benefits will be deducted for each $2 you earn above the annual limit. In the year you reach your FRA, $1 in benefits will be deducted for each $3 you earn above a different limit, but only counting earnings before the month you reach FRA. After you reach FRA, you can earn any amount of income and still receive full benefits.

If you continue to generate income after you begin collecting Social Security income (SSI), you may have to pay income taxes on some of that income. No one pays taxes on more than 85 percent of his or her SSI, however, and some pay on a smaller amount, based on IRS rules explained on the SSA's website.

See also Corporation *and* Social Security Taxes.

Tip

Check your Social Security earnings periodically to make sure your annual payments are being credited to your account. To do this, send a letter to the Department of Health and Human Services, Social Security Administration, Baltimore, MD 21235 and ask for "Summary Statement of Earnings." Include your name as it appears on your card, your address, Social Security Number, and date of birth. (You can also request a statement by visiting the SSA's website and searching for "statement of earnings.")

Social Security Taxes

As a self-employed individual, you must pay into your personal Social Security account by filing a Self-Employment Tax form when the profit on your Schedule C tax report reaches $400 or more. The amount of tax you will pay, and the amount of earnings on which Social Security taxes will be due, continue to increase. (See *Social Security Earnings.*)

If you hire employees—even your spouse—you will have to withhold Social Security and Medicare taxes on wages paid to employees, report to the employees the amount withheld (W-2 Form), remit quarterly tax payments to the IRS (Form 941), and send an annual report to the Social Security Administration (W-3 form and copy of employees' W-2 forms). An accountant can give you details about how to do this.

Sole Proprietorship

A Sole Proprietorship is the easiest kind of business to start and operate. It has no existence apart from the owner and its liabilities are the owner's personal liabilities. Advantages are that the business is controlled by the owner, all profits go directly to the owner, there is little regulation, and earnings are personally taxed.

Although there are no legal formalities involved in ending a sole proprietorship beyond simply stopping the business activity, there are ethical considerations involved, particularly in a mail order or publishing business that is likely to generate orders long after all advertising and promotions have ceased. If you open such mail, and it includes a check or money order, you are obligated to return it. Some people have told me they just tear up the checks, but this is an unethical thing to do because the people who sent these orders won't know what you've done. If you can't afford to answer mail to a dead business, simply order a rubber stamp that reads "Out of business— return to sender." By stamping and returning all mail unopened, it won't cost you anything and you will have fulfilled your ethical obligation to customers. If you've been using a P.O. Box address, mail will automatically be returned to sender if you close the box.

See also Legal Forms of Business.

Sports Logos, Commercial Use of

Q: *I'd like to sell sweatshirts or novelty items that promote local sports organizations. How do I get permission to do this?*

In talking with a business owner who sells merchandise with famous sports logos on them, I learned it is not difficult to get permission to use such logos for commercial purposes. Sports organizations like publicity for their teams, she told me, so their licensing rules and regulations are relatively easy for small business owners to comply with.

For example, if you wanted to make an item that incorporates the logo of your favorite sports team, you might only have to pay a small licensing fee and percentage of your sales for this privilege. The bigger the organization, of course, the higher the licensing fee. For more information, contact a sports organization of interest and ask to speak to its licensing department.

Statement

Statements are generally used when a company regularly ships to customers who have a charge account. They need monthly reminders of their current indebtedness to you and a statement serves this purpose. Small businesses normally send statements on the last or first day of each month.

While an invoice includes details about a customer's purchase, a statement merely recaps the date and total of all invoices still unpaid at the end of the month. Since some accounts are likely to ignore the first statement, you might want to create a standard STATEMENT form as well as a PAST DUE STATEMENT form that includes a note that the account is past due and should be paid immediately to avoid collection costs.

See also Invoice *and* Invoices Not Paid.

Statutory Employees

Q: *What's the difference between an independent contractor and a statutory employee? Are there tax advantages to hiring statutory employees?*

Many people hire help on an independent contractor basis, which, as I have explained elsewhere, is a dangerous thing to do these days. A solution used by many small craft manufacturers is to hire *statutory employees*. Although it costs a business more to hire statutory employees than independent contractors (because you must pay Social Security and Medicare taxes), it is the perfect solution for small manufacturers who want to operate legally. On the other hand, statutory employees are less expensive to hire than employees because there are no unemployment taxes on statutory employees. (Like independent contractors, statutory employees can deduct their trade or business expenses from their W-2 earnings.)

According to IRS's *Tax Guide for Small Businesses,* "If an individual who works for you is not an employee under the common law rules, you do not have to withhold federal income tax from that individual's pay. However, for Social Security and Medicare taxes, the term *employee* includes any individual who works for you for pay in one of the following four categories (two of which are excluded here because they are not applicable to this book's readers):

1. An individual who works at home on materials or goods you supply and that must be returned to you or to a person you name, if you also furnish specifications for the work to be done.

2. A full-time traveling or city salesperson who works on your behalf and turns in orders to you from wholesalers, retailers, contractors (etc.). The goods sold must be merchandise for resale or supplies for use in the buyers' business operations. (You might not think this category is applicable to a small business, but if you were to hire a sales rep who worked only for you and no other companies, that person could be considered a statutory employee for tax purposes but could not legally be called an independent contractor.)

Dodie Eisenhauer, owner of Village Designs (**www.VillageDesigns .com**), uses a combination of regular employees who work in her workshop and statutory employees who work for her out of their own homes. She says it was a big step for her to switch over from independent contractors to employees, but it wasn't as painful a process as she had been led to believe and the benefits have been enormous. "I encourage people who are still using independent contractors to reclassify their workers as soon as possible," says Dodie. "You immediately gain peace of mind from knowing you're operating on a 100 percent legal basis, and you no longer have to worry about the IRS or Department of Labor putting you out of business."

See also Employees, Nonfamily; Sales Representatives; *and article, "How One Manufacturer Solved Her Independent Contractor Problem."*

Tip

Dodie says it used to take hours to do her weekly payroll, figure the monthly tax deposits, and do the quarterly employee tax forms. Now that she has a good computer payroll program, however, she can do this job in about half an hour a week. She uses and recommends *QuickBooks* by Intuit because it is inexpensive and easy to learn.

Stop Payment Order

Q: *It's expensive to stop payment on a check. When is this really necessary?*

A stop payment order makes sense if (1) you have ordered goods or services that prove to be unsatisfactory (which gives you some leverage to get a job done over or merchandise replaced); or (2) a bill payment appears to have been lost in the mail. If you happen to lose your checkbook, notify your bank immediately. (It is their responsibility to verify the signature on a check against the one they have on file for the account holder.) Instead of putting a stop payment on all the checks in your checkbook, it makes more sense to close out the account as quickly as possible. (The bank can tell you which checks haven't yet cleared.) Remember, if one of your checks falls into the hands of a con artist, it will be child's play to modify the name and address information on one of your blank checks and order a new supply of checks from a mail order check-printing company.

See also article, "A Lost-Mail Horror Story."

Supplies, Buying Wholesale

Q: *I would like to buy my supplies and materials at wholesale prices, but many companies won't sell to me, and others have minimum quantities that are too high. What's the solution to this problem?*

If you can't buy supplies at wholesale, it's almost impossible to make a good profit on handcrafts sold at the retail level, and wholesaling them is out of the question. The first thing you need to understand is that there are two types of craft suppliers: those who will sell to homebased business owners and those who won't. For nearly thirty years (that I know of) most wholesalers and manufacturers in the craft supply industry refused to sell to craftspeople who ran businesses out of their homes. In recent years, however, sponsors of the Hobby Industry Association (HIA) shows finally acknowledged that craft designers and "converters of craft materials for the gift market" comprised a legitimate market that had to be recognized. At that point, professional crafters were able to gain entry to HIA

A Lost-Mail Horror Story

"Early in April, after mailing a dozen checks to creditors on March 26, I began to get calls from creditors who had not received my payments yet," one of my readers reported. "They didn't care that the mail might have been lost; they just wanted payment without delay. On April 20, I filed twelve Mail Loss/Riffling Reports (tracer forms) with the post office, and was told that each tracer "would take its own routine length of time."

"As the weeks passed, the creditors continued to call, day and night. I explained again and again the necessity of waiting for notification from the post office. Finally, tired of it all, I told each creditor that I would send a replacement check, but if the post office delivered the first check, they would either have to destroy it or send it back to me. They all agreed to this request. I told each creditor that only one check would clear my bank. At the end of June, I sent each of them a new check. You can guess what happened next. My lost mail finally got delivered and every creditor deposited both checks.

"During the second week of July, I received twelve insufficient funds notices from my bank at fifteen dollars per returned check. And when the March 26th checks didn't clear the bank, several of the creditors sent me an invoice for returned check fees (twenty-five dollars per invoice). With explanations to the creditors (again), they withdrew these invoices. I then called our main branch postmaster, related this situation to her, and requested a reimbursement from their loss of my bills. The postmaster's reply: 'Sorry, we give no reimbursements for lost mail.'"

This story certainly illustrates the importance of putting a stop payment order on any check for more than twenty-five dollars that you believe has been lost in the mail.

trade shows to search for supply sources, but it was still up to individual exhibitors as to whether or not wholesale orders would be accepted from such buyers.

In August 2003, the boards of directors of the Association of Crafts & Creative Industries (ACCI) and the Hobby Industry Association (HIA) agreed to unify the craft and hobby industry under the leadership of a new association called the Craft & Hobby Association (CHA). This association continues to sponsor two trade shows per year. To request buyer information (as well as exhibitor information), visit CHA's website at **www.hobby.org** or call 1-201-794-1133.

Companies interested in selling to homebased craft businesses advertise in periodicals targeted to artists and craftspeople, as well as on the Web (just go to Google.com and search for "wholesale craft supplies" to turn up nearly a million Web pages). In addition to suppliers who serve the arts and crafts community, there are thousands of other manufacturers and wholesalers in this country who welcome your orders. These suppliers advertise in various trade journals, or you can track them down by studying the *Thomas Register of American Manufacturers,* a directory available in most libraries. Its several volumes include a listing of products in alphabetical order with the names and addresses of companies who make them. In some cases, you may be able to buy directly from manufacturers; in others, you will be referred to a nearby distributor or dealer.

See also Discounts *and* Purchase Order.

Tip

Manufacturers and wholesalers are most likely to deal with craft businesses that appear to be professional. In addition to having a resale tax number and the ability to meet supplier minimums, craft sellers should have a business name and telephone number printed on their stationery and cards. One signal that you may be a hobbyist trying to buy at wholesale prices is the way you ask about minimum order requirements. One crafts professional suggests that, instead of using the word "minimum," ask instead about the supplier's *opening* order and recorder minimum.

Surge Suppressor

A typical household receives a hundred power surges of as much as 1,000 volts a month from electrical storms and the usual on-and-off switching of appliances, so don't take this problem lightly. These sudden voltage increases could damage or destroy your computer, fax machine, printer, telephone, or other electronic equipment and appliances in your home or office unless each is protected by a surge suppressor.

A surge suppressor measures the amount of voltage that can pass through after clamping has occurred. The less voltage that gets through, the more effective the protection. Surge protectors are now rated by joules, the higher the better. (For more information on this topic, type "surge protectors" into your browser's search engine and check out the new joule technology circuitry that absorbs and reroutes surge energy to ground, or, in the event of a catastrophic surge, completely disconnects the power.)

Tip

Lightning zaps nearly 100,000 computers a year, and computer losses have increased in recent years because more people now leave their systems on all the time. Since a surge suppressor won't save your computer system in the event of a direct lightning strike, the only sensible thing to do is unplug it during storms.

Tax Audits

Q: *What can I do to keep my chances of being audited as low as possible?*

To reduce your risk of being audited, attach an explanation if you think the IRS might question a large deduction. Make your return as neat as possible, be sure to sign and date it and attach necessary W-2 forms as instructed.

Some people assume they will automatically be audited if they take the Home Office Deduction on their Schedule C, but that is not true. Anything you do to attract undue attention to your return, however, such as filing an amended return, will increase your chances for an audit. If you are ever audited, don't volunteer any information, records, or files. Wait until the IRS tells you what is being questioned and give them only what they specifically request. For detailed guidelines on how to defend yourself in an audit, see the book *Stand Up to the IRS* by tax attorney Frederick W. Daily (Nolo Press).

NOTE: There is a statute of limitations that keeps the IRS from auditing returns after three years have passed. However, there is no time limit to when the IRS can begin an audit if you fail to file a return or file one that is fraudulent.

See also Home Office Deduction *and article, "A Humorous Tax Audit."*

A Humorous Tax Audit

Two years after filing her annual tax return, Beverly Durant was questioned by the IRS about her miscellaneous business deductions, which they said seemed higher than they should be. They said she had to come into their office and bring with her all her tax receipts for that year. At that time, Beverly wasn't very organized about her business, and throughout that particular tax year, she had simply been throwing receipts into a file drawer with no attempt to organize them by category. Naturally irritated that her small homebased business was being audited in the first place, Beverly just pulled all those receipts out of the drawer and dumped them into a big brown box. When she was called into the IRS agent's office, she plunked the box down in the center of his desk and sat down in the chair directly across from his desk.

"With the box between us, I couldn't see him and he couldn't see me," Beverly recalls. "He opened the box, looked in, and asked 'Them's your records?' I said, 'Yep, that's them.' And then he sat back down, filled out a bunch of forms, handed them to me and said, 'sign here.' And that was that. I'll never be afraid of the IRS again," she concluded.

Note: This might not work for everyone. It's possible that Beverly had a little Divine Intervention. Beverly is retired now, but at the time of this incident, she was known in dozens of craft malls as "The Angel Lady."

Tax Deductions

See Business Expenses, Tax-Deductible.

Taxes

President Herbert Hoover was the first president to give his salary back to the government. Now the government would like everybody to do it. "When it comes to taxes," a comic has quipped, "most of us would be willing to pay as we go if we could only catch up on where we've been."

"Some folks feel the government owes them a living," adds another, "but the rest of us would gladly settle for a small tax refund." We may joke about taxes, but we can't afford to ignore them. Here is a brief summary of the various local, state, and federal taxes applicable to small businesses:

- **Local taxes.** Local sales taxes are calculated together with state sales taxes and paid to the state on a regular basis (see *Sales Tax*). In addition, your state or local government may impose an inventory or property tax on business equipment and inventory. Check local officials for more information about this.
- **State taxes.** Most states have an income tax that is calculated on your net income or profit and payable at the time you file your annual federal tax return. Businesses that have employees will also have to pay unemployment tax.
- **Federal Taxes.** These include (1) owner-manager's income tax or corporation income tax; (2) employee income tax and unemployment tax (if you have employees); and (3) estimated tax payments (due from self-employed individuals). Tax forms can be found in your post office, library, or on the Web at **www .IRS.gov.**

For topics related to the filing of tax returns, see also Accountant/CPA; Certified Mail; Financial and Tax Records; Legal Forms of Business; *and* Social Security Taxes.

Tax Exemption Certificate

See Resale Tax Number.

Teaching

Many artists and craftspeople naturally move into teaching after they have perfected their skills and gained experience in the marketplace. If you are teaching any topic related to arts and crafts, several listings in this book are applicable to you.

See Copyright "Fair Use" Doctrine; Copyrights of Others; Health Hazards; Lead Testing; *and* Newsletter/Ezine Publishing.

Telephone Answering Devices and Messages

Whether you prefer an actual answering machine or voice mail, you have a lot of choices and some comparison shopping can be done easily on the Web (just search for "answering machines"). Telephone answering devices may be either digital or tape-based, but digital answering machines offer many timesaving features and may be more durable than microcassette models. Depending on the model you select, total message recording time varies from fifteen to thirty minutes (including your greeting).

Messages for Callers. Poor telephone messages are a pet peeve of mine. If you're still trying to run a business on your personal telephone line, at least answer with your full name (not your business name), and if your spouse is a partner in your business, mention his or her name, too. Often when I try to call a woman who has a home-based business (and has listed her number on her business stationery), I get a message on the machine that goes something like this: "Hi, this is Jim. I can't take your call now, so leave a message at the tone." *Jim WHO?* If I'm trying to reach Susan Jones of SewSmart Services I don't even know whether I've reached the Jones residence or not.

Although I believe all business owners should have a line dedicated to the business, until such time as you can justify the cost of doing this, you might want to modify the message my husband and I used to use when I was still getting business calls on our home phone instead of my business line:

We both cheerfully said *Hello* together, then I said, *This is Barbara Brabec*, and Harry said, *This is Harry Brabec. Please direct your message to either one of us with your name and phone number, and we'll return your call as soon as possible.* Then I said, *If you are calling for information about my books, leave your complete address to receive my free brochure.* Harry then closed with, *Listen for the tone and then start your message,* and we closed together by saying *Thank you!*

Many callers said ours was one of the most charming greetings they had heard, and no one was ever in doubt as to whether they had reached the right number or not.

See also Voice Mail vs. Answering Machine.

Tip

In creating the message you plan to leave for callers, *never* say, "We're not here right now," which is a clue to would-be thieves that no one is home at the moment. Also, if you're a single woman living alone, don't say anything to suggest this. Consider saying, "You've reached the (your last name only) residence; please leave a message," to suggest that others may be living there.

Telephone, Business Use of

Q: *I can't afford a separate line for business. I don't plan to run any ads with my home phone number, but is it okay to list it on my business cards and stationery?*

Legally, you can receive business phone calls on a residential line and make outgoing business calls, but *advertising* your residential phone number on your business card or stationery is likely to be a violation of local telephone company regulations. (Each state has a separate commission that determines the usage of a residential phone, so you need to call your local telephone company for more information.) In some states you could be fined for improper use of a residential phone or simply told that you will have to pay business rates in the future. (I suspect only a few states are as easygoing as Missouri. Once, when I lived in Springfield and called the telephone company to ask what they did when they discovered people who were advertising their home phone for business, a friendly, down-home operator said, "Why, we'd just ask them to stop doing it.")

Telephone companies are savvy about homebased businesses and many now publish newsletters to educate small business owners about the availability of extra lines for business, special phone equipment, toll-free numbers, and so on. An extra line for business may be less expensive than you think. Ask your local telephone company if they offer any "Remote Relay Services" or "phantom phones" that allow calls to your business number to be relayed through your personal phone line and charged separately. Such approved business numbers can then be legally advertised.

See also Fax Machine; Long Distance Carriers; *and* Telephone Answering Devices and Messages.

Tip

If you happen to operate two or more small businesses from your home, you don't have to get two or three different telephone lines. Instead, ask your telephone company about their "custom ringing" options. This service enables one to have three phone numbers ringing on one line, each with a different sound so you'll know how to answer it.

Telephone Number Locators

The result of deregulation of long distance services gave us a mishmash of area codes that no longer reflect any geographic area. Toll-free numbers are easy to obtain by dialing 1-800-555-1212, but only if a company has paid for a listing in toll-free directory assistance. While no charge is made to obtain toll-free numbers, it has now become costly to obtain other telephone numbers from Directory Assistance.

If you are trying to call an old telephone number that has gone bad, it may be only because the area code has changed. If you have Internet access, you can get area codes for any city, state, or country at **www.Americom.com** (click the "Area Decoder" button). If you need someone's telephone number, or their mail or e-mail address, you can locate businesses or individuals through **www.switchboard .com**, **www.Anywho.com**, or **www.Infobel.com/teldir/**.

1099 Form

You must issue a 1099 form any time you pay more than $600 to someone for services rendered. By the same token, you should receive a 1099 form from anyone for whom you have provided services worth $600 or more. For example, writers, teachers, speakers, consultants, and other self-employed individuals would generally receive 1099 forms from publishers, organizations, and businesses with whom they have worked during the year.

Terms of Sale

Q: *I know I will have to invoice my wholesale accounts, but what about large sales to individual buyers? Are there any particular invoicing pitfalls I might avoid?*

When selling at retail, always collect payment from individual buyers at the time of sale, unless that individual buyer happens to represent a business or corporation that must be invoiced (i.e., an order for a hundred items for use as Christmas or employee gifts). Another exception would be taking custom orders for later delivery, in which case you might prefer to ask only for a deposit up front (see *Custom Orders*).

In establishing your terms of sale, decide whether you will offer (1) *Net 30 Days* (full payment within thirty days from date of invoice); (2) *Net 10 Days* (full payment within ten days); or (3) *2% 10 days* or *2/10/30* (2 percent discount if payment is made within ten days). Most sellers request full payment within thirty days, but some do offer the 2 percent discount in an attempt to get their money in hand as quickly as possible. If you do this, however, be aware that some buyers may pay the invoice a month later and still take the discount. If they do, invoice them for the difference and remind them of your terms of sale. Although your terms may be Net 30, you will find that larger buyers who routinely get sixty- to ninety-day terms from others may ignore your thirty-day terms. You'll have to stay on their heels to train them to pay you promptly. In researching this topic, I noticed that one seller in my network was offering Net 15 terms. This was unusual, so I asked her why she worked this way.

"When I offered terms of Net 30, I was lucky to get payment within sixty days," she said, "but when I switched to Net 15, people began to pay me generally between twenty-five to thirty days, which is what I really wanted in the first place. No one has ever given me a hard time about my payment terms."

See also Invoice; Invoices Not Paid; Order Policies; *and* Price List.

Testimonials

Q: *How important are customer testimonials to the sale of my products, and what's the best way to get them?*

Sales are likely to increase when you use testimonials about your products in your brochure or catalog because they build buyer confidence in your offer. If your customers or clients don't send you written comments after purchasing your work, be aggressive in getting them yourself. For example, when a buyer says something great about one of your products, jot down the remark, rewording it to your advantage. Then send the customer a copy and ask if you can use their comments in your brochure, quoting them by name and listing their city and state with the quote.

Try to find something in what your buyer has said that can be translated into a benefit someone else would pick up on. For example, if someone at a crafts fair said at the time of purchase, "I just love your work! This monogrammed pillow will make a wonderful gift for my mother's birthday," jot down the remark right away, rewriting it just a bit so it sounds like a buyer benefit. Your "edited copy" might read: "I was delighted to find that you offer custom-design services. The monogrammed pillow you made for me solved the problem of what to give my mother for her birthday!" Most people will be glad to let you use a remark like this in your printed advertising, even if those weren't the exact words they said. Never quote anyone without getting permission in writing, however, as some people would consider this an invasion of their privacy.

NOTE: If you happen to publish a periodical, the FTC requires reader testimonials used in printed advertising material to be from current (not expired) subscribers.

Tip

> "Don't be sheepish about prompting your customers for testimonials," advises Jeffrey Lant, author of *Money Making Marketing* (**www**
> **.JeffreyLant.com**). "Ask them about particular aspects of your product or service, write down what they say, and then ask for their permission (which you must always have) to use it. The meek do not do well at marketing."

Textile Fiber Products Identification Act

Q: *I've read that textile items are required by law to have some kind of hang tag or label, but what kind of tag is needed, and which craft products are considered "textiles?"*

The Bureau of Consumer Protection (**www.FTC.gov/ftc/consumer .htm**) requires a label or hang tag on all textile wearing apparel and household furnishings, with the exception of textile wall hangings, which, curiously, do not have to be labeled under this act. "Textiles" include any material that is woven, which means all fibers, yarns, and fabrics. "Textile household furnishings" would include such items as quilts, pillows, placemats, stuffed toys, and rugs. To all such items, product makers must attach a tag or label that includes the following information:

1. the name of the manufacturer or other person marketing the textile fiber product
2. the generic names and percentages of all fibers in the product in amounts of 5 percent or more, listed in order of predominance by weight. Examples: "100% combed cotton" or "92% cotton, 8% other fibers." (For other examples of such tags, just open your closet door and check the labels on your various items of clothing.)

All garments must also have care labels to meet the labeling requirements of the FTC, which also requires an additional label on any garment containing fur, any product made from wool, or any textile product that uses imported fibers. Products with concealed stuffing, such as pillows, dolls, or soft sculpture, may require another label under your state's bedding law. (See below for references to information about each of these label laws.) Note that the various tags and labels required by law do not need to be fancy. You can create your own or obtain them at reasonable cost from commercial suppliers named in the listing "Hang Tags and Designer Labels."

See also Bedding and Upholstered Furniture Law; Care Labels; Fur Products; "Made in USA" Labels; *and* Wool and Other Textiles.

Time Management

Q: *I have a hard time meeting deadlines. What can I do to become more efficient in managing my time?*

It's too bad that the time we save on one day can't be placed in storage for use the next day. And just think of all the time we'd save if we stopped showing up in doctors' offices on time. Many books have been written on the topic of time management and organization, and you would probably do well to read one or two of them (check your library or search the Web). In the meantime, here's a trick I've learned from years of experience in pushing myself ever onward: *To get ahead, work backwards.*

For every major job or task I undertake that has any kind of deadline attached to it, I make a written plan that starts at the point where I must be finished and works backwards to the beginning. When there is no automatic deadline, I set one myself to keep me on target. Then I outline all the work involved in the project, estimate the amount of time each phase will take, then plot it to a calendar. This gives me a starting date, which I automatically push back one week more, for good measure. (Although I try to build in extra time for "life's little interruptions," as an eternal optimist I rarely add enough.) As I work, I keep tabs on whether I'm still on schedule or running behind. When I find myself running behind schedule—almost always the case—I begin looking for ways to find the extra time I'll need to finish on time.

I have always related to this popular saying on plaques and sweatshirts, and I'm sure you do, too: "God put me on Earth to accomplish a certain number of things. Right now I'm so far behind I will never die."

See also article, "Deadlines Were Made to Be Broken."

Deadlines Were Made to Be Broken

Brabec's Law is that all home-business deadlines fall (1) before some important holiday you were hoping to have off; (2) the week before you planned to leave on vacation; or (3) the day before company is arriving for the weekend. If you're lucky enough to miss any of the above, you're likely to be delayed by an unanticipated medical emergency, a home maintenance crisis, or a family situation that requires your immediate attention.

This book is a perfect example. When I signed the contract to deliver this edition by a certain date, I had no idea that my husband was going to be hospitalized a week later, and would die six weeks after that. For three months afterwards, as I grieved his loss and tried to get my life back in balance, I simply couldn't work, so I had to ask for an extension of the deadline I had been given.

Once again, I have learned that, no matter how far away a deadline date may be, or how hard I work to do what needs to be done in the interim, something *always* comes along to delay me. In the past thirty-five years, I cannot recall a single instance when I have not found myself wishing for just one more hour, day, week, or month to finish some particular task by the stipulated deadline date. We all need deadlines to spur us onward, but sometimes it's impossible to meet them. When this happens, we must ask for (or give ourselves) an extension of time. If you should ever find yourself unable to meet a deadline, just do the best you can and lower your stress by forgiving yourself. *Sometimes the only way to get it all done without going to pieces is to get it done late.*

Toll-Free Number

Now that toll-free numbers are so affordable, even small home-based businesses are using them to draw prospect inquiries and orders resulting from advertising or publicity. Check your local phone company for information and also search the Web to find a variety of companies that offer toll-free numbers at varying rates.

If you do decide to get a toll-free number for your business, be sure to keep a record of all your incoming calls. If not, you may be losing a tidy sum of money every month. As one of my readers explains: "When you have a toll-free number, you get a list of all incoming calls that shows the date and time of each call, along with the caller's phone number and city. I've found that a lot of people dial the wrong number and then hang up. Although I am always billed for such calls, I don't have to pay for them if I notify the phone company accordingly. The only way to know which calls are invalid is to keep a daily log of everyone who calls. Each month when I get my phone bill, I check each call billed against calls on my log sheet. By being able to identify invalid calls, I have saved as much as $40 a month on my phone bill. Companies that don't keep records like this have no idea how much money they're losing to invalid calls."

Tip

The number of 800 numbers was finite (9,999,999) so when the supply ran out in 1996, it was necessary to introduce a new prefix (888) so another 10 million numbers could be offered. Since then, other new prefixes (877, 866) have been added, and more are likely to be added in the future. In picking a toll-free number, consider that old toll-free numbers have belonged to one or more users in the past, and when you take one of these numbers (especially old 800 numbers), you are automatically assuming the liability for calls coming into the old number that may still be generating calls from one or more companies' earlier advertising. Thus, the newer the number, the better.

Toy and Game Brokers

Q: *I've designed a toy that I think might be of interest to a manufacturer. How can I sell this idea to them?*

I can't help you much here, except to pass on these remarks from an industry insider I once connected with. "Novice inventors don't realize that most companies refuse outside idea submissions, preferring to work with toy and game *brokers* instead," he said. "Milton Bradley alone reportedly receives in excess of 8,500 unsolicited submissions a year that are usually returned without being reviewed. Fraudulent invention-marketing firms charge outrageous fees up to $5,000, but a reputable agent (broker) normally charges between $100 and $200 for a product evaluation. If they agree to market the product, however, they will expect between 40 and 50 percent of all profits."

A search on the Web might turn up the names of some toy brokers you could approach.

Toymaking

Several listings in this book relate specifically to toymakers, who must be especially aware of laws related to the making of children's toys.

See Bedding and Upholstered Furniture Law; Consumer Safety Laws; Fabrics, Flammability Standards; Homework Laws; Labels or Tags Required by Law; Paints, Varnishes, and Other Finishes; Patterns, Commercial Use of; *and* Toy and Game Brokers.

Trade Associations/Publications

Each trade association (or organization) represents a particular industry and generally publishes a magazine or newsletter for its members. Trade publications or magazines are not found on newsstands but are available only by subscription or in libraries. Some associations sponsor trade shows, gift fairs, or expositions, offering members an opportunity to exhibit and sell their wares, but membership is not a requirement if you merely wish to visit a trade show to get the lay of the land or check out the competition. See the *Other Resources* section for a list of selected trade organizations in the fields of art, crafts, and homebased businesses.

See also Home-Business Organizations *and* Trade Shows.

Trademark

Q: *What does a trademark do, and at what point would it be practical to invest in one?*

Much depends on how grand your plans are for the future and how strongly you feel about protecting your creativity. What a registered trademark does is prevent one individual or company from trading on the good name and reputation of another. It may include any word, name, symbol, device, or any combination thereof that a manufacturer or merchant uses to identify his products and distinguish them from the products of others. You cannot trademark generic and descriptive names in the public domain, but you can protect your business logo, your company name, the names of new products, the artistic way you write your name, or even collections of colors and designs.

For example, the inventors of a tool for turning fabric tubes from wrong- to right-side out have named their product FASTURN®, and protected it by trademark. (The *R* in a circle tells us that the trademark has been officially registered.) Designer Patricia Kutza uses the name WHATKNOT™ as the name of her line of fashion accessories. Until this mark is officially trademarked, she can use the initials "TM" to indicate she has laid claim to this descriptive word *(see TIP below)*.

Doing a Trademark Search. Since you cannot adopt any trademark that is so similar to another that it is likely to confuse buyers, you will need to do a trademark search. You can do preliminary research in one of two ways:

1. by using the annual *Trademark Register of the U.S.* Available in large city libraries, this reference book contains every trademark (nearly 800,000) currently registered with the U.S. Patent & Trademark Office.

2. by doing a search on the Web at **www.USPTO.gov**. Although you can check to see if the name you have chosen has been trademarked, this is no guarantee that the name is clear.

An attorney can also order a trademark search for you at reasonable cost. This is a wise thing to do these days because of the thousands upon thousands of new trademarks that have been—and are still being—generated for use on the Web. A simple word you believe to be common or generic may now be claimed by another. (For an amazing example of this, visit the Home-Biz Articles department of my website at **www.BarbaraBrabec.com** for the story of how *Entrepreneur Magazine* has trademarked the word "entrepreneur" and is now able to legally prevent others from using this word in their business name.)

Although the basic fee for a trademark is low, an application can be rejected for a variety of reasons, and the whole process could take as long as two years to complete. If you plan to file an application without an attorney's help, be sure to read a couple of self-help books first to increase your chances for success. Meanwhile, call the Patent and Trademark Office's toll-free number to hear recorded messages on this topic: 1-800-786-9199.

See also Business or Trade Name Registration/Protection; Copyright Categories of Protection; *and article, "Common Law Trademarks."*

Common Law Trademarks

The longer you use any kind of mark in interstate commerce, the stronger your claim to it whether it is ever formally registered or not. This is called a "common law" trademark, and from experience, I have learned it carries considerable power.

It had never occurred to me to trademark the name of my *Homemade Money* book, so I was naturally upset when someone lifted this book's title and attached it to a magazine of questionable quality, thereby suggesting that I was somehow connected to this publication or the company behind it. With the help of an attorney who sent several strongly worded letters for me, I was able to stop a powerful multilevel-marketing company from using the words "Homemade Money" as the title of their magazine or MLM business. The attorney said my case had strength because, by that time, my home-business "bible" had been in print for almost ten years and its title was closely identified with my name and personal reputation.

"In building a trademark case," my attorney said, "much depends on the nature of the two products or publications in question, and whether it is likely that people would confuse one with the other."

Tip

Whether you plan to register your trademark or not, add the letters ™ to the mark. Although this gives you no legal protection and does not obligate you to file a formal trademark application, it does give notice to others that you've claimed a mark and may discourage use by others as a result. If you later decide to register your trademark in Washington, these letters would be replaced with the trademark sign, ®, after every use of the trademark word or symbol. You may also use the words "Registered in U.S. Patent and Trademark Office" or "Reg. U.S. Pat. and Tm. Off.")

Trade Practice Rules

Certain industries must follow established trade practice rules established by the Federal Trade Commission (FTC). If you are wholesaling products that fall into any of the following categories, contact the FTC and request information about rules relating to that industry:

- jewelry making
- leather or ladies' handbags
- feathers and down
- the catalog jewelry and giftware industry
- millinery
- furniture making
- mail order

If you violate an FTC rule and the FTC learns of it, they may order you to cease the illegal practice. Penalties generally occur only if a cease-and-desist order is ignored.

See also Federal Trade Commission.

Trade References

See Credit/Trade References.

Trade Secret

According to the Department of Labor, the legal definition of a trade secret is: "Any confidential formula, pattern, process, device, information, or compilation of information that is used in an employer's business, and that gives the employer an advantage over competitors who do not know or use it." Common trade secrets are colors, flavors, perfumes, and formulas for soft drinks. In the crafts industry, a trade secret might be the glaze formula used for ceramics or the recipe that makes bread dough creations unique. It could also be the way in which a product is constructed. As one product maker told me, "I've put my doll together in such a way the average crafter can't figure out how to copy it and sell it herself."

In summary, trade secrets protect all kinds of business know-how as long as they do not become a matter of public knowledge. Since common law trade secret protection exists, you might have grounds for a lawsuit if someone steals your trade secret.

Trade Shows

Q: *How can I find trade shows through which to market my handcrafts and gifts?*

The type or kind of trade show you will exhibit in depends on what you're selling and the kind of buyer you want to reach. Professional artists, handcraft sellers, and makers of toys, gifts, and decorative accessories can choose from many different shows. Many trade shows are now listed in the subscription-only periodicals published by art/craft show listing publishers listed under *Show Listings*. Here are some additional sources for trade show information:

- The National Craft Association's website includes a national listing of wholesale trade shows for artists and handcraft sellers. Here's the direct page link: **www.craftassoc.com/confer.html**
- The National Needlework Association (TNNA) hosts three trade shows a year. More information is available on the Web at **www.TNNA.org** or by calling 1-800-889-8662.

A search on the Web for "trade shows, art crafts, needlework" will turn up many more listings of specific shows. Small producers who cannot afford the high cost of exhibiting in a trade show may be able to reach this market through sales representatives who regularly exhibit in trade shows or have a presence in one or more gift marts. If you just want to browse a particular trade show to get the lay of the land, be prepared to prove you are in business and not just a hobbyist.

See also Sales Representatives; Trade Associations/Publications; *and* Wholesaling.

Trunk Shows

A trunk show is a marketing strategy used by designers and craft sellers who are trying to interest particular shops or stores into carrying a large inventory of their work. It's similar to what bookstores do when the author of a new book comes in for the day to personally autograph all books sold and answer questions from his or her fans.

Sellers offer to bring a supply of products to the store that they will sell in person over a period of days, giving the store owner an agreed-upon percentage of total sales. Stores will generally send postcards to their customer list about such an event, or run special ads. (It's helpful to give them artwork accordingly.) Stores benefit financially from such a promotion, and the designer or craftsperson also benefits from personal contact with so many new customers who may prompt ideas for new products.

Two-Step Advertising

In one-step advertising, the goal is to get a direct sale. While this can be done in a display advertisement or direct mailing, it is almost impossible to do in a classified advertisement. The two-step method is commonly used here because advertisers understand that people generally need more information to make a buying decision. Generally, a catalog, brochure, or other information is offered (free or at a small fee) in the hope that the more detailed information will generate a sale. Since only a small percentage of people will order in any event, it is always necessary to do follow-up mailings to all prospects who have responded to your two-step ads.

United Parcel Service

Did you know that UPS will pick up packages at your home? You call one day, and they pick up the next. In addition to the shipping charge, you will be charged a modest weekly pickup fee that applies to the first pickup of the week and covers all other packages and pickups in that same week. You will find a toll-free number for UPS in your phone book. When you call for a pickup, the operator will want to know:

1. where the package is going
2. its weight and measurements
3. whether you want it insured for more than the normal amount of $100.

You will be instructed to give the UPS driver a check in the right amount. Although UPS rates are more expensive than shipping by mail, the advantage of using UPS is that packages are rarely lost or damaged and delivery anywhere in the country takes only a few days. If you plan to use UPS regularly, ask for information about their "Ready Customer Pickup Service." Get more information online at **www.UPS.com**, where you can also track UPS shipments.

NOTE: UPS shipments to a remote area may require an additional day or two for delivery. In this case "remote" doesn't mean a rural area but, rather, a residential area. That is, if you're shipping to a business located in someone's home, or are receiving business shipments from suppliers to your home address, UPS delivery may take longer than delivery by the post office (a fact that is upsetting to many craft sellers).

See also Canadian Sales *and* Priority Mail.

Tip

Always check with your Canadian customers before shipping anything by UPS. Such shipments must go through Customs, which causes delays and extra charges to customers who must pick up packages themselves. When possible, ship small packages to Canada by first-class or priority mail. Larger packages can be sent by Standard Mail (formerly called fourth-class mail). This is free from Customs inspection and is delivered right to the customer's door.

Vehicle Used for Business

The IRS allows self-employed individuals to deduct expenses for the part-time business use of a personal vehicle. You are not required by law to keep a travel diary, but you must keep some kind of record to prove your vehicle deductions to IRS. For example, if your daily travel is routine (to places where the mileage doesn't change, such as the bank, post office, printer, etc.), a simple calendar notation should suffice. At month's end it's easy to multiply number of trips times distance to each place to get total business mileage. If you travel to many different locations, it would be wise to log beginning and ending odometer readings to your calendar for each trip. And don't forget to make a note of the odometer reading at the end or beginning of each year.

See also Car Insurance *and* OSHA Regulations.

Tip

The older your vehicle, the more advantageous it may be to figure your vehicle deductions on the basis of total operating costs instead of mileage. How you start figuring deductions in your first year of business is important, says the IRS. If you begin by figuring expenses on total operating costs, you will be locked into using this method forever; however, if you begin by calculating vehicle expenses on the basis of mileage, in following years you may choose whichever method is most tax-advantageous for you. (Since tax laws are always changing, double-check this point with your accountant.)

Voice Mail vs. Answering Machine

Q: *What's the difference between using an answering machine and a voice mail service?*

An answering machine can provide callers with a standard greeting and take only one call at a time while voice mail allows a business to take several calls at once. With voice mail, you can either create a personal greeting or choose the standard greeting. Changing the greeting is just a matter of punching a few buttons to record a new message and listening to it before saving it.

Voice mail records messages when your phone goes unanswered as well as when you're on the phone. Because several calls can be taken simultaneously, voice mail is terrific for those times when you're expecting many customers to call to place orders or when you are simply on the phone a lot. If you sell a product and take credit cards, your voice mail message might say that you'd be happy to return their call, but if they just want to order your product, they should leave the appropriate information. This can be especially handy when you're traveling or on vacation.

Another benefit of voice mail is its ease in retrieving messages when you're away from your home office. You simply call your service, listen to messages, and punch a button to repeat, delete, or save each message for later handling. (My voice mail system allows me to save as many as thirty messages for up to sixteen days.)

See also Telephone Answering Devices and Messages.

Tip

Many people hate voice mail because it sounds cold and indifferent and gives too many instructions on buttons to push, so the shorter and friendlier you can make your voice mail message, the better.

Web Marketing Options

Q: *I know a lot of crafters are selling on the Web, and I can see the advantages of having a presence there, but I really don't have the time, money, or inclination to set up my own website. What other Web marketing options are available to me?*

Not every artist, crafter, or designer needs to be on the Web to have a profitable business, but the public's perception of the Web has changed a lot in the past couple of years to the point where many now think if a business isn't on the Web, it must not be very successful. In the end, whether you need a website of your own or at least a business presence on someone else's will depend largely on whether your particular customers expect you to be on the Web or not.

Before you think about setting up your own domain, consider your other less time-consuming and expensive options for selling products on Web pages others will set up for you at reasonable cost. "There's so much to learn about making websites that it will inevitably pull your time and energy (and creativity) away from what you're really wanting to do," cautions metalworker John Dilbeck, whose website at **http://JohnDilbeck.com** is a good resource for artists and crafters.

If you are primarily interested in selling at art or craft shows, in craft malls or consignment shops, or even selling wholesale to gift shops and other stores, you probably don't need to set up a website of your own. Having a Web page or a sub-site on someone else's site can be very profitable, however. The challenge here will be in deciding which site to get involved with. "The biggest obstacle to Internet marketing for a craftsperson is not a lack of opportunities, but an overabundance of choices," says James Dillehay, author of *The Basic Guide to Selling Crafts on the Internet* (**www.Craftmarketer.com**). "To be profitable, you have to focus your activities in an organized plan that produces online sales and profits while measuring which activities are working and which aren't."

There are literally thousands of virtual shops and galleries on the Web where you might sell your work, but this is research you will have to do on your own. Some of these outlets rent space to sellers or charge an advertising fee to list products or link to one's website. On other sites, products are displayed for free with sellers paying the site owner a commission only when something sells. I have to add, however, that reports from sellers who have had good luck going this route are few and far between, so try to get recommendations from other craft sellers, in person at craft shows, or through discussion lists or chat rooms. I suspect that many of these "virtual shops" have been opened by entrepreneurs who figured they could rake in a lot of money collecting ad revenue, but they may not have the necessary skills to generate lots of traffic and interested buyers.

If you'd like to test the Web waters at low cost and with little need to learn "techie stuff," consider the affordable website services offered by:

• The National Craft Association (NCA), **www.CraftAssoc.com**. Whether you need a single Web page (like having a color brochure online) or several pages (a site of your own), this organization can assist you with a variety of affordable packages priced between $89 and $129 a year. NCA does all the work for you; you just send your photos and text. These prices include both site design and hosting fees, and you get attractive space in one of NCA's Shopping Malls with your page being under NCA's URL. (If you want your own domain name and merchant account, the initial cost will be higher, yet still reasonable and affordable to professional crafters, hundreds of whom now sell through this site.)

• eBay, **www.ebay.com.** Many craft professionals who used to do craft shows or wholesale to shops are now selling full-time on eBay's auction site, getting prices comparable to their usual whole-sale prices and often better than what they would have gotten at shows. Good photos are a must here, so you'll need a good camera and software to make the best Internet presentation.

Instead of auctioning products on eBay, other sellers have opted to open their own eBay store (get details at **http://stores.ebay.com**). Many people have told me how easy it is to learn how to sell this way ("just follow the instructions provided by eBay"). You don't have to have your own website to sell through an eBay store site, but if you do, your sales are likely to increase. As artist Debbie Brown has learned, the cost for an eBay store was significantly less than adding e-commerce options (shopping cart, merchant ac-count, etc.) to her existing website, which promotes her decorative painting shop on Long Island. "In my eBay store, I offer selected painter supplies and materials along with a link to my store's web-site at **www.ExpressionsEast.com**," she explains. "I like how eBay, in conjunction with PayPal, not only offers secure transactions, but keeps track of my inventory of items available on eBay, as well as those previously sold."

For more information on selling on eBay or through a website of your own, read the chapter "Selling on the World Wide Web," in my book *Handmade for Profit* (**www.barbarabrabec.com**). James Dillehay's book *Sell Your Crafts on eBay* (**www.Craftmarketer.com**), may also be helpful to you.

Someone once asked me if I thought the Internet was the wave of the future in crafts marketing, and whether buyers needed that "hands-on visual look-see" where the purchase of handcrafts is concerned. I said I thought both things were true to a large de-gree. There are many crafts that will never sell well on the Web because people cannot touch them. But what makes the Internet so

What the Web Can Do for You

Before you invest in a Web site, make sure you know what you want the Web to do for you. Do you:

- Think you need a website because everyone *says* you need one (or, as a friend of mine puts it, "because everyone and his dog has one")?
- Believe you can sell more of your existing products or services this way, or some new ones you've been thinking about?
- Need to be on the Web because this is where most of your customers or clients can now be found? Or because most of your *competitors* are now on the Web, stealing business from you?
- Want to be able to take orders 24 hours a day, seven days a week all year long?
- Need to make it easy for customers or clients to communicate with you, but don't want to answer common questions personally?
- Want to publish a newsletter and build an e-mail database for marketing purposes?
- Desire to write and publish e-books or sell other products electronically?
- Need an online brochure that will enhance your professional image, or a colorful catalog that will save you printing and postage costs?
- Just *love* technology and a new challenge?

I and many of my home-business acquaintances decided we needed a Web presence not because we loved technology, had the time to learn it, or needed another challenge in our already too-busy lives. Mostly, we ended up on the Web because someone or some circumstance finally convinced us we needed to be there. As your business and personal goals change, you need to constantly rethink how you might use the Internet to your advantage, even if you perceive the transition to be painful. This kind of business move is rather like diving into an icy pool of water—initially shocking to your system but not so bad once you're fully immersed in it.

—An excerpt from *Homemade Money: Bringing in the Bucks* by Barbara Brabec (M. Evans) wonderful is that if you sell at craft fairs and also have a Web page somewhere, you can use the Internet to get follow-up orders and build an e-mail address list so you can periodically communicate with all your prospects and buyers. This gives a seller a lot of power and makes the Web a great diversification tool that will surely increase sales and profits over time. If you ultimately decide that you want your own website, you should read some of the many how-to books (nearly 5,000) that have been published on this topic. Check your bookstore or visit **www.Amazon.com** and search for "website design" noting, in particular, the excellent "Dummies" books that are available.

> *See also* Advertising; Internet and World Wide Web; Merchant Account Providers; Shopping Cart Systems; Wholesaling; *and article,"What the Web Can Do for You."*

Tip

If you do try to market products online, you must be readily accessible by phone or fax, and your chance of capturing orders will increase if you have a toll-free number and can accept credit card payments. If you have a home page, promote it constantly. "Any idiot can get a home page," says web entrepreneur Jeffrey Lant, "but what you need to succeed is constant promotion both inside and outside of the Net."

Wholesaling

Wholesaling is *indirect selling to consumers*. This is impersonal selling, involving sales through retailers, dealers, and other distribution methods. With few exceptions, the same marketing methods are used to sell on both the retail and wholesale levels. The primary difference is that, in wholesaling, the marketer has to shift mental gears because dealers and retailers do not think about merchandise in the same way consumers do.

If you are a small manufacturer, you may think you cannot sell at the wholesale level because of pricing or problems of limited production. Often, this is true. Other times, however, a product can be changed or redesigned in some way to permit increased production at a retail price that's high enough to allow for wholesaling, at least to some markets. By getting your feet wet in wholesaling first to small retail outlets, you will learn whether you are capable of filling larger orders or not. You will have to turn up your own wholesale customers, but a good place to start is by reading ads (or placing one yourself) in *The Crafts Report*. (To subscribe, call 1-800-777-7098 or visit the magazine's website at **www.CraftsReport.com**.)

Wholesaling on the Web. One place I've received several good reports about is WholesaleCrafts.com ("Where Retailers Meet Quality Artists"), which has proven to be a major source of new business for many artists. Note that all sellers here are called "artists," but "craftspeople" are welcome, too, provided they meet the site's special requirements. (All work must be created by artists themselves, must be original in design, and the artist must already be wholesaling to at least two retailers with a storefront location.) Because sellers pay a modest fee to advertise selected products on a Web page of their own, no commission is due when a sale is made, and you can even advertise here if you don't have a computer. Likewise, interested retailers who don't have Web access are also able to connect with artists through Wholesalecrafts.com's printed *Buyer's Guide*, which is distributed quarterly at wholesale shows and mailed to other high-value prospects. For more information, visit **www.WholesaleCrafts.com** or call 1-888-427-2381.

See also Accounts Receivable; Advertising; Bar Codes (UPC); Brochure; Catalog Houses, Selling to; Checking Account; COD Shipments; Collection Strategies; Copyrights of Others; Credit Card Sales; Credit/Trade References; Distributor/Jobber; Fabrics (Designer), Commercial Use of; Fax Machine; Fabrics, Flammability Standards; Invoices Not Paid; Invoicing Policies; Markups; Packing List; Patterns, Commercial Use of; Price List; Pricing Guidelines; Printed Materials; Pro Forma; Insurance, Product Liability; Purchase Order; Sales Representatives; Supplies, Buying Wholesale; *and article, "Pricing Formulas for Handcraft Sellers."*

Wool and Other Textiles

In addition to the textile labeling requirements of the Bureau of Consumer Protection (discussed under *Labels or Tags Required by Law*), the FTC requires certain labels on all textile wearing apparel,

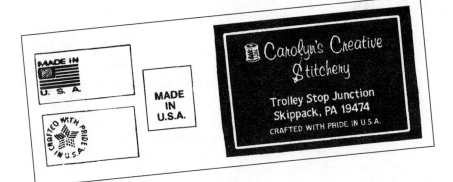

Sample labels provided by Charm Woven Labels. Note how Carolyn's Creative Stitchery has included the "where crafted" information on her regular fabric label

household furnishings, garments containing fur (see discussions elsewhere), and all items made of wool. The FTC's *Wool Products Labeling Act* requires that all wool or textile products bear a label that clearly indicates where the product has been made, and when imported ingredients are used. Thus the label for a shawl woven in the United States from imported fibers would read, "Made in the USA from imported products." Items that originate entirely in this country need only state "Made in the USA," "Crafted in USA," or words to that effect. (These regulations are also applicable to the descriptions of such products in mail order catalogs sent to consumers.)

If you happen to be shearing your own wool for textile products or yarns you sell, your products must also meet certain fabric flammability standards of the Consumer Product Safety Commission (see *Fabrics, Flammability Standards*). The agency will send you more information on request (1-800-638-2772) or you can get it on the Web at **www.CPSC.gov.**

See also Labels or Tags Required by Law *and* "Made in USA" Labels.

Writing

Many craftspeople who have gained experience in a particular field go on to write how-to magazine articles or books about their art or craft. Check my website (**www.BarbaraBrabec.com**) for a collection of articles that will be helpful to would-be authors and self-publishers.

See also Author/Publisher Contract; Book Copyright; Book Publishing; Contracts; Copyright Categories of Protection; Copyrights of Others; Copyrights in Public Domain; First Rights/All Rights Sales *and* Newsletter/ Ezine Publishing.

ZIP Code

ZIP stands for Zone Improvement Plan. Our system of five-digit codes was established in 1963. Large mailers can lower the cost of their mailings by the use of ZIP+4 (additional digits that identify a specific range of delivery addresses). Your postmaster will be happy to provide details on how to do this. To find any ZIP code you may need, go to **www.USPS.com** and click the "Find a ZIP Code" button.

Zoning Laws

Q: *I'm afraid I may be violating local zoning laws. What should I do about this?*

You need to find out where you stand so you can take appropriate action. Either call your city or county clerk or visit the library to get a copy of your community's zoning regulations. Find out what zone you're in and read the section that pertains to home occupations.

To accommodate the large number of home office workers throughout the country, many communities have changed their zoning laws in recent years. Some have eased the restrictions while others have only made them worse by limiting the amount of square footage a homebased business can occupy or the number of employees a business can hire. Some communities still haven't done a thing about badly outdated zoning laws that were written in horse-and-buggy days. If you learn you are currently violating a zoning ordinance, don't panic. Thousands of others who work at home have learned that what zoning officials don't know about a business can often remain a secret that harms no one.

- **General Zoning-Compliance Tips.** The most important thing to do is keep a low profile by not advertising locally, discussing your homebased business with neighbors, or doing anything to annoy them. Zoning officials aren't likely to check on a business or discover a zoning violation unless a business owner has attracted media attention locally or a neighbor has registered a complaint. Things most likely to cause problems in any neighborhood are loud noises, strong odors, obvious customer traffic, or the tying up of parking places, use of a business sign when one is prohibited, or anything else that disturbs the serenity of a quiet residential neighborhood.

- **Home Parties and Other Product Sales.** If you plan to present home parties or sell products of any kind to people who come to your home for a sales demonstration, be aware that zoning regulations in some areas prohibit one from using the home to transfer the sale of merchandise. To avoid breaking the law, accept payment for all orders at the time of the sale but deliver products the next day instead of letting customers walk out the door with them.

- **Holiday Boutiques.** Zoning officials generally view one- and two-day home boutiques in the same light as garage sales, but it's always a good idea to check with authorities before planning such an event. Advertising signs are normally taboo in a residential neighborhood, but temporary boutique or sale signs may be approved by city officials upon request. To make sure your neighbors don't give you problems about the lack of parking spaces during the sale, offer them a sneak preview the night before and perhaps a 10 percent discount on merchandise as well.

Although there have been exceptions, there is usually no financial penalty for violation of U.S. zoning laws beyond immediate cessation of the business activity. Violating the cease-and-desist order, however, would probably trigger a fine.

See also Licenses and Permits *and* P.O. Box Address.

Tip

Some businesses have been successful in obtaining a zoning variance (also called a special-use, conditional use, or special exemption permit) that gives permission to use one's home for any reason that is clearly secondary to its use as a dwelling. Generally, people who apply for a special-use permit must post a sign announcing their application to the local Board of Appeals, then attend a formal meeting to obtain the necessary permission. Having the support of neighbors can make a big difference here.

Other Resources

NOTE: All listings in this chapter appear in alphabetical order by business name within the individual categories. Mailing addresses have been provided only when a business doesn't encourage telephone inquiries.

Business & Marketing Periodicals

This is a selected list of publications in the art, craft, and home-business industries believed to be of special interest to this book's readers. For the names of other periodicals, check library directories such as *The Standard Periodical Directory*, *Ulrich's International Periodicals Directory, Hudson's Subscription Newsletter Directory*, and the *Oxbridge Directory of Newsletters*.

Some of the following publications have been discussed or mentioned in the text. Other publications, such as show listing and home-business periodicals, have been included in the text under the appropriate alphabetical listings. (Check the index for specific page references.)

- *Country Sampler:* **www.CountrySampler.com**. Many crafters advertise in this magazine (available on newsstands) to reach a national consumer audience interested in arts and crafts. Ad rates, call 1-630-377-8000; subscription information, call 1-386-447-6034.
- *Craftrends:* **www.Craftrends.com**; 1-847-763-9612. This trade magazine for craft retailers is available in both print and on-line versions. (The website features news, information, and articles not in the magazine.)

- *The Crafts Report:* **www.CraftsReport.com**; 1-800-777-7098. This business journal for professional artists and craftspeople is available by subscription. Its website features a valuable archive of business articles and resources.
- *Gift Basket Review:* **www.festivities-pub.com**; 1-800-729-6338. Published monthly, this is the leading authority in the gift basket industry.
- *Gifts & Decorative Accessories Magazine* and annual *Gifts & Decorative Accessory Buyer's Guide:* **www.Gifts&Dec.com**; 1-800-309-3332. Includes sources for manufacturing and assembling materials, show and shop display cases, listings of trade shows, and more.
- *The Professional Quilter:* **www.ProfessionalQuilter.com**. A quarterly business journal for quilters, designers, and teachers interested in a career in quilting. Get subscription information on the Web or by writing to 22412 Rolling Hills Lane, Laytonsville, MD 20882.
- *Sew News:* **www.sewnews.com**; 1-800-289-6397. A newsstand magazine for home sewers interested in fashion, fabrics, and home decor. Many informative articles and tips for success will be found on the magazine's website.

Organizations

This is a selected list of art, craft, and home-business organizations likely to be helpful to readers of this book. Check the index to find page number references to organizations mentioned in the text. Some of these organizations sponsor trade shows, and most offer a newsletter or magazine as part of their membership benefits. To find names and addresses of other organizations, check library directories such as the *Encyclopedia of Associations* or National Trade and Professional Associations of the United States.

- American Craft Association: **www.CraftCouncil.org**; 1-800-724-0859. This organization offers insurance plans for art and handcraft sellers who join the organization. Members receive *American Craft* magazine.

- Art & Creative Materials Institute: **www.acminet.org**; 1-781-293-4100. The leading authority on the safety of art and craft materials.
- Craft & Hobby Industry Association (CHA): **www.Hobby.org**; 1-201-794-1133. This international organization serves retailers in the craft and hobby industry.
- Home Business Institute Inc.: **www.HBIweb.com**, 1-888-DIAL HBI. Offers merchant card services and a group health insurance plan. Members receive *Inside Home Business* newsletter.
- National Craft Association: **www.CraftAssoc.com**, 1-800-715-9594. Members have access to insurance programs, discounts on business services and products, merchant card and website design/hosting services, and the *NCA Arts & Crafts Newsletter*.
- National Mail Order Association: **www.NMOA.org**; 1-612-788-1673. For companies involved in direct marketing. Members receive *Mail Order Digest* newsletter.
- The National Needlework Association: **www.TNNA.org**; 1-800-889-8662. This organization hosts three trade shows a year.
- Volunteer Lawyers for the Arts: **www.vlany.org**; 1-212-319-ARTS, ext 1. With branches in many states, this organization is dedicated to providing free legal assistance to artists and arts organizations in all creative fields.

Government Agencies

Your tax money is paying for all the free business information available from government agencies, so be sure to obtain needed information. Check the index to find text references to the following agencies and a reminder of why you need to contact them. A wealth of business information will be found on the websites of each of these agencies.

- Bureau of Consumer Protection: **www.FTC.gov/ftc/consumer.htm**
- Consumer Product Safety Commission: 1-800-638-2772; **www.CPSC.gov**
- The Copyright Office: (202) 707-3000; **www.copyright.gov**

- Department of Commerce: **www.DOC.gov**
- Department of Labor: **www.DOL.gov**
- Environmental Protection Agency: **www.EPA.gov**
- Fish and Wildlife Service: **www.FWS.gov**
- Federal Trade Commission: 1-877-FTC-HELP; **www.FTC.gov**
- Food and Drug Administration: 1-888-INFO-FDA; **www.FDA.gov**
- Internal Revenue Service: 1-800-829-1040; **www.IRS.gov**
- Patent & Trademark Office: (703) 308-9000; **www.USPTO.gov**
- Small Business Association (SBA): 1-800-827-5722; **www.SBA.gov**
- Service Corps of Retired Executives (SCORE): 1-800-634-0245; **www.SCORE.org**
- Social Security Administration: **www.SSA.gov**
- United States Postal Service: **www.USPS.com**
  Postal Inspection Service: **www.USPS.gov/postalinspectors**
  Identity Theft: **www.consumer.gov/idtheft/index.html**

Suppliers and Service Providers

This is a summary checklist of suppliers and service providers mentioned in the text. Check the index for a reminder of their offerings.

- Charm Woven Labels: 1-800-843-1111; **www.CharmWoven.com**
- Checks In The Mail: 1-800-733-4443; **http://secure.checksinthemail.com**
- Discover Network: 1-800-347-7996; **www.Discoverbiz.com**
- Dover Publications *Pictorial Archive Books:* **www.DoverPublications.com**
- E & S Creations/Cranberry Junction: 1-208-356-6812; **www.CranberryJunction.com**
- GraphComm Services: 1-800-488-7436
- Grayarc: 1-800-243-5250; **www.Grayarc.com.**
- Great Papers: 1-800-287-8163; **www.PaperShowcase.com**

- Independent Insurance Agents of America: 1-800-221-7917; **www.iiaa.org**.
- ISBN Agency: 1-877-310-7333; **www.ISBN.org**
- Office Depot: 1-800-685-8800; **www.OfficeDepot.com**.
- OfficeMax: 1-800-788-8080; **www.OfficeMax.com**.
- Paper Direct: 1-800-A-PAPERS; **www.PaperDirect.com.**
- Pitney Bowes: 1-800-672-6937; **www.PitneyWorks.com**
- Quill: 1-800-789-1331; **www.QuillCorp.com**.
- Safeware: The Insurance Agency, Inc.: 1-800-848-3469; **www.Safeware.com**.
- Uniform Code Council, Inc.: **www.UC-Council.org**.
- Viking: 1-800-421-1222; **www.Viking.com**
- Widby Enterprises: 1-888-522-2458; **www.WidbyLabel.com**
- Wood Cellar Graphics: **www.WoodCellarGraphics.com**

Index